Two mainsails, one wingsail, two mizzens

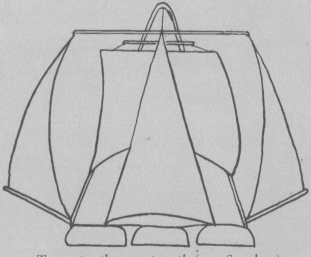

Two mainsails, two wingsails (seen from bow)

SEAWORTHY

Also by T. R. Pearson

SEAWORTHY

Adrift with William Willis
in the Golden Age of Rafting

T. R. Pearson

Crown Publishers

New York

Library of Congress Cataloging-in-Publication Data
Pearson, T. R.
Seaworthy: adrift with William Willis in the golden age of rafting /
T. R. Pearson.—1st ed.   1. Willis, William, 1893–1968.
2. Adventure and adventurers—Biography.   3. Seafaring life.
4. Voyages and travels.   I. Title.
G530.P4135 2006
910.4'5—dc22   2005030083

ISBN-13: 978-0-307-33594-4
ISBN-10: 0-307-33594-1

Printed in the United States of America

DESIGN BY LEONARD HENDERSON
MAPS BY JACKIE AHER

10 9 8 7 6 5 4 3 2 1

First Edition

*This book is dedicated to
Mayor Andy Baxter and to the memory of his beloved wife,
Carley Cunniff, in modest token of my gratitude for
their support, encouragement, and invaluable friendship*

CONTENTS

ILLUSTRATION CAPTIONS

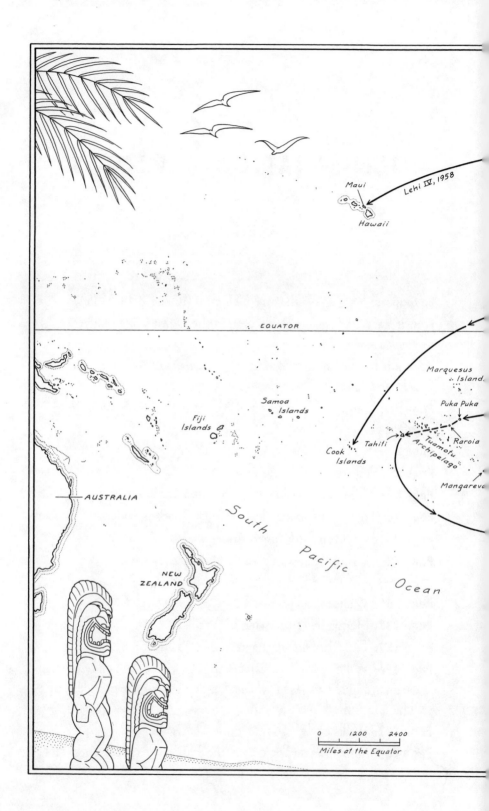

Maui

Hawaii

Lehi IV, 1958

EQUATOR

Marquesus
Island

Puka Puka

Samoa
Islands

Fiji
Islands

Tahiti
Cook
Islands

Tuamotu
Archipelago

Raroia

Mangareva

AUSTRALIA

South

Pacific

NEW
ZEALAND

Ocean

0   1200   2400

Miles at the Equator

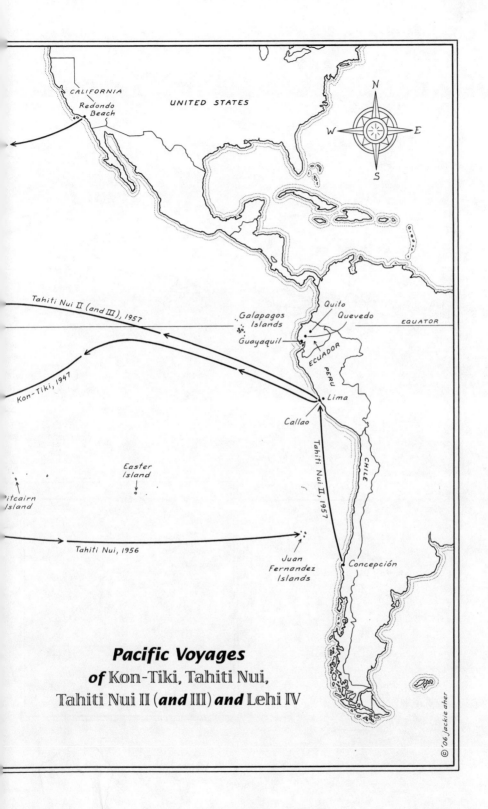

CALIFORNIA

Redondo
Beach

UNITED STATES

N

W   E

S

Tahiti Nui II (and III), 1957

Galapagos
Islands

Quito
Quevedo

EQUATOR

Guayaquil

ECUADOR

Kon-Tiki, 1947

PERU

Lima

Callao

Tahiti Nui II, 1957

Easter
Island

CHILE

itcairn
Island

Tahiti Nui, 1956

Juan
Fernandez
Islands

Concepción

Pacific Voyages
of Kon-Tiki, Tahiti Nui,
Tahiti Nui II (**and** III) **and** Lehi IV

© '06 jackie aher

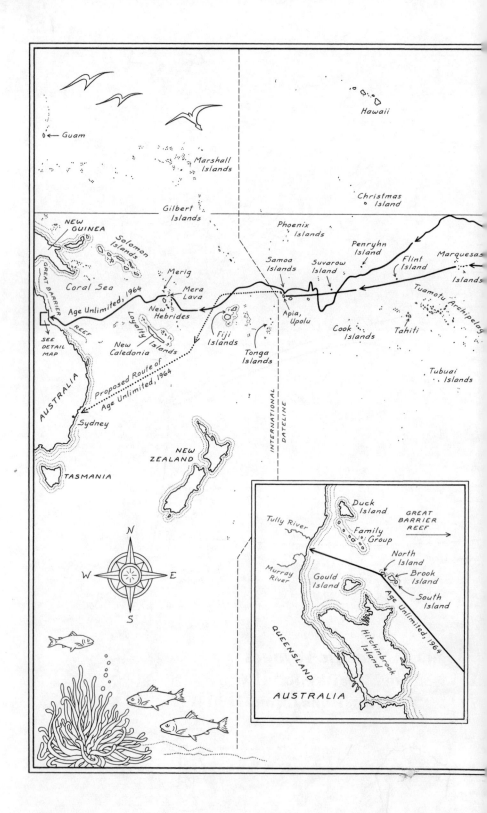

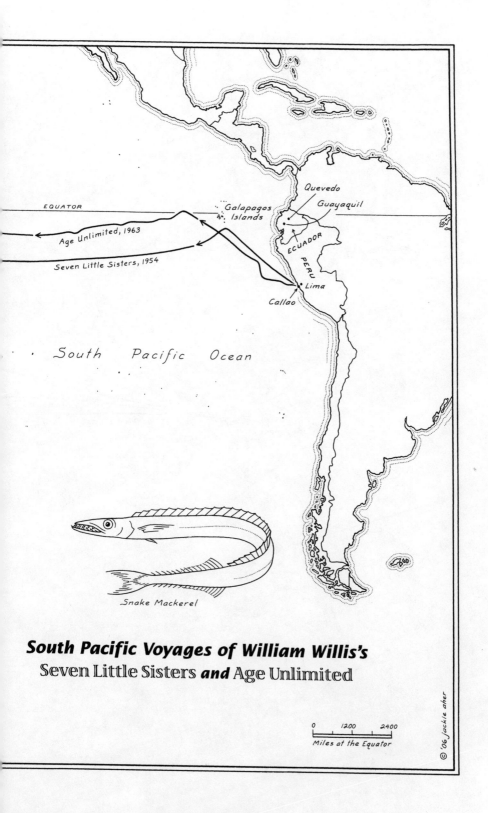

EQUATOR

Quevedo

Guayaquil

Galapagos
Islands

Age Unlimited, 1963

ECUADOR

Seven Little Sisters, 1954

PERU

Lima

Callao

South   Pacific   Ocean

Snake Mackerel

South Pacific Voyages of William Willis's
Seven Little Sisters *and* Age Unlimited

© '06 Jackie aher

0   1200   2400

Miles at the Equator

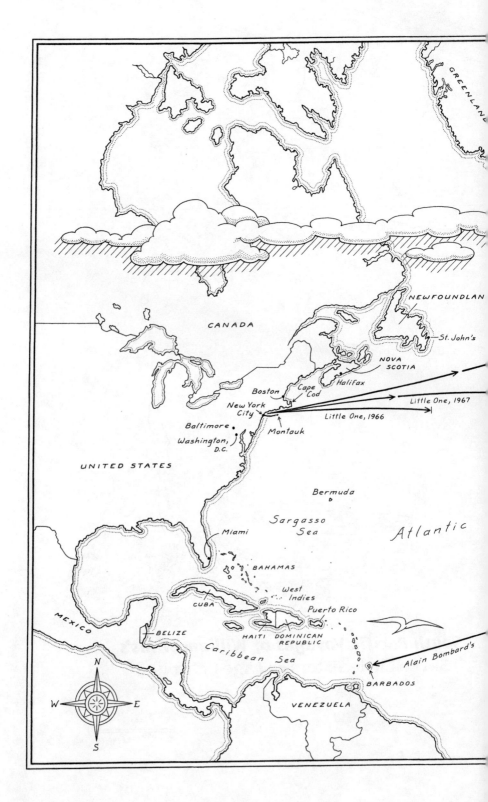

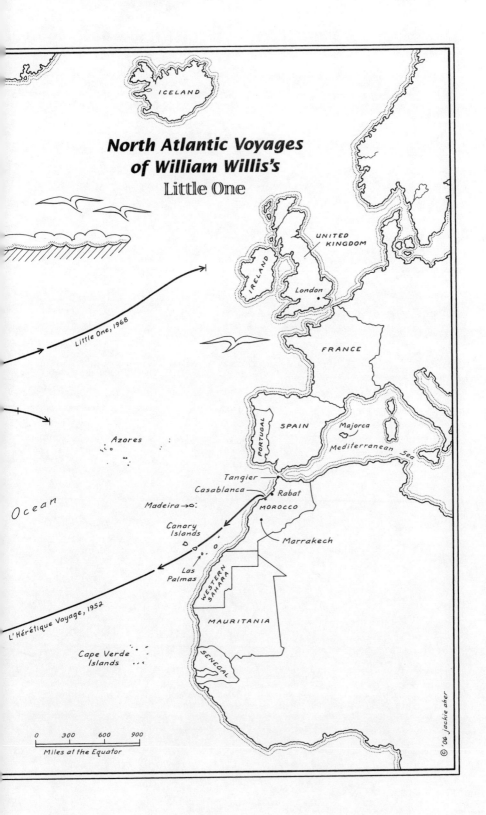

ICELAND

North Atlantic Voyages
of William Willis's
Little One

UNITED
KINGDOM

IRELAND

London

FRANCE

Little One, 1968

Azores

SPAIN

PORTUGAL

Majorca

Mediterranean Sea

Tangier
Casablanca
Rabat
MOROCCO

Madeira

Ocean

Canary
Islands

Marrakech

Las
Palmas

WESTERN
SAHARA

L'Hérétique Voyage, 1952

MAURITANIA

SENEGAL

Cape Verde
Islands

0   300   600   900

Miles at the Equator

© '06 Jackie aher

SEAWORTHY

1

Little One

He carried by way of provisions only olive oil and flour, honey and lemon juice, garlic and evaporated milk. Since he intended to drink from the sea, a personal practice of long standing, he'd dispensed with the bother of stowing so much as the first ounce of fresh water. His radar reflector was a scrap of planking wrapped in aluminum foil, his chronometer a balky pocketwatch, his distress flag a scarlet sweater. He'd shipped no proper radio, had but a sextant for his bearings, sailing directions to guide him into the English Channel past Bishop Rock. Among his papers was a letter of introduction to the mayor of Plymouth, England, from the Honorable John V. Lindsay, the mayor of New York City. It read, in part, "If the bearer delivers this letter to you in person, he will have completed a trans-Atlantic voyage of great merit."

This was his third attempt in as many years at a single-handed crossing of the Atlantic Ocean, all in a craft he'd christened *Little One* in honor of his wife. Hardly more than a glorified dinghy, that boat lived decidedly down to her name. She was eleven and a half feet stem to stern and five feet at the beam. She was sloop-rigged and lone-masted, weighed just over one thousand pounds, had three feet of draft, and was, even in sheltered, benign waters, ungainly.

He'd departed on his maiden voyage directly out of New York Harbor. A tug had taken his boat in tow at the foot of Twenty-third Street and had hauled him down the East River and along the Brooklyn shoreline in a bid to avoid both shipping traffic and bothersome harbor chop. He'd cast himself loose just a couple of miles past the Verrazano Narrows Bridge and had passed his first evening at sea watching the sun set over New Jersey while enjoying for dinner two teaspoons of whole wheat flour moistened with spit.

His first week out, the winds were southerly and the sea fog was persistent. He fell overboard one morning while attempting to set his jib, fairly swamped the boat in the process, and doused everything he'd carried. (He was never entirely dry for the remainder of the trip.) On the open ocean, *Little One* rolled more violently than he'd expected. She bucked and wallowed and generally handled in the manner of a cork, which, when combined with the gloomy weather, rendered his sextant all but useless. He either couldn't see the sun or was too sea-tossed to shoot a useful sight and so had, as a rule, no reliable sense of just where he might be.

Ordinarily, he could have expected to need three months on the water to reach the English Channel from the narrows of Lower New York Bay, but he was plagued by unfavorable weather—a string of gales, and a hurricane—and after five weeks at sea, he found himself off the coast of Nova Scotia, within sight of Sable Island and in some danger from the surf. He was nearly two hundred miles farther north than he'd intended and well west of where he'd reasonably hoped to be.

Steering south, he met with the *Black Swan*, a freighter bound
for Antwerp, and was given a carton of fresh fruit that he welcomed aboard for ballast. He took to riding out storms by
nailing himself in under his canvas decking, which salt and sun
had conspired to spoil the fit of early on. He'd lie with a knife in
hand in case he met cause to slash his way out. He slept little,
was awake for days at a time, and compensated with meditation,
along with a form of rhythmic breathing he'd freely adapted
from Eastern religion. He could be, on occasion, so strict in its
practice and parsimonious with air that he would rhythmically
breathe himself into a faint. He was once unconscious for two
days running, and, having survived somehow adrift, he awoke
to find his chronometer stopped because he'd failed to wind it.

He suffered from heavy nosebleeds and decided, essentially
on a hunch, that they were simply nature's way of staving off
cerebral hemorrhage. He had a bout with a hernia he'd allowed
to go untreated for years and sought to ease his discomfort by
looping the mizzen halyard around his ankles and hoisting himself upside down to the masthead, where he rearranged his guts.
He noted in his log the "pernicious" effects of drinking Atlantic
seawater (he allowed himself a quarter of a cup a day), and he
concluded that the practice "might well lead to madness and
suicide," which, as potential calamities go, proved wholly insufficient to curb him.

His voyage was beset in turn by squalls and windless, fogbound lulls. He met scores of ships and refused all offers to take
him off the water. He sang sea chanteys to lift his spirits. He
measured and recorded his blood pressure daily and performed
each afternoon a simple urinalysis. In testing the transmitter he
had carried in the event of emergency, he discovered that the
contraption didn't work. He drifted east and south in the Gulf

Stream and was convinced he'd make the Azores if the weather cooperated and his hernia gave him some peace. But the wind dropped, and he suffered a series of strangulation attacks, each of which could have led to the rapid, fatal onset of gangrene. He liked to think that his diet of flour, seawater, and condensed milk worked to forestall fever and served (though he couldn't begin to say how) to spare him.

He wasn't persuaded, however, that his luck and health would last, and he settled on the prudent option of cutting short his voyage and attempting another when he was properly mended. But just then sea traffic evaporated, and he saw no ships for a couple of weeks. When he finally spied the stacks of a Boston-bound steamer on the horizon, he inadvertently set his mainsail alight with the flare he'd struck to hail it and managed to go unnoticed nonetheless.

After two months at sea to the day, he crossed paths with the *Sapphire Gladys*, a New York freighter bound for Rotterdam. Again he declined to be taken off, since the *Sapphire Gladys* was eastbound, and instead requested that the captain radio the Coast Guard. The cutter *Ingham* was dispatched and managed to find him the following morning at a point, essentially, due east of Amagansett, Long Island, and due south of St. Lawrence, Newfoundland—a good two thousand nautical miles away from Plymouth, England.

*   *   *

His second attempt, the following summer, was only modestly more successful. In the intervening year, he'd fitted *Little One* with a wooden deck and a cabin that measured all of fifty-two by thirty inches, hardly room enough to sit with any comfort, much less stand. He'd been at sea for three full months when the Polish trawler *Belona* came across him; a crewman saw the scarlet sweater flying from his mast. He was entirely out of food and was in a "cataleptic trance." He came to on the deck of the ship and asked to be put back onto the water, insisting he was capable of finishing the voyage, but the trawler captain sensibly refused.

Overall, *Little One* had traveled thirty-five hundred nautical miles, but only about two thousand of it was easting. Gales and squalls were largely to blame, though in a statement to a reporter, the skipper confessed that he'd known "some trouble navigating."

Refitted and freshly resolved, he set out again the following spring. He'd arranged for a tow to the sea buoy twelve miles off Montauk Point, where he dropped his line and set his sails and struck out again for Plymouth. It was Wednesday, May 1, 1968. His name was William Willis, and he was seventy-four years old.

2

Beginnings

WILLIAM WILLIS'S ATTEMPT to cross an ocean in his twilight years was, as much as anything, an act of symmetry. He'd fairly started life a blue-water sailor and was determined to finish as one. Born in Hamburg, Germany, in 1893, Willis signed on as a deck boy on the *Henriette* at the age of fifteen in a bid to help support his family, lately abandoned by his father. She was a square-rigger, the *Henriette*, a five-masted bark bound for Santa Rosalía in the Gulf of California with a cargo of coke for a copper smelter.

The *Henriette* carried a crew of thirty-four all told, only one of them a holdover from the previous voyage, which had seen the captain, a soundly detested martinet, die under sail of an infected boil. Once his body had been unceremoniously pitched overboard, command was assumed by the first mate, who proved equally harsh and appreciably less sane. He took to wearing the late captain's sumptuous dress uniform—many sizes too large for him—and touring the deck with a brace of pistols he would discharge whimsically at seamen in the rigging.

The crew mutinied, after a fashion. They barricaded themselves belowdecks, sending a lone man to the wheel each watch until the *Henriette* was brought safely into the port of Iquique in northern Chile, where the first mate was overpowered and hustled off the ship.

On Willis's maiden voyage, the new captain was very little in evidence as the *Henriette* sailed south through the English Channel and into the North Atlantic on a course for the Drake Passage around Cape Horn. The crew was the typical mongrel lot of the times—Germans, Poles, Danes, Russians—and the shipboard conditions were all but medieval. Although illness and injury were commonplace on such voyages, there was no medicine on the *Henriette* but for a "cathartic" that was suspected of being "strong enough to put a leak in the ship if poured into the bilges." Broken limbs were rudely splinted, amputations performed with the carpenter's saw. Most lapses in decorum and failures of sound sense were met with a belaying pin to the cranium and a stint in irons in the sunless hole beneath the poop deck.

Rations consisted primarily of bean soup and salted beef, along with a weekly half cup of brown sugar. The sea biscuits were maggoty, and the hold was overrun with roaches, no few of which found their way into the stewpot. The barrel of gin intended for the crew, supplied by the ship's owners, was never dispensed, because it—along with a fair bit of crew rations—had been lowered to a boat in the Elbe and sent to the captain's house, a brand of thievery widely sanctioned as a custom of the sea.

At first Willis's duties were largely custodial in nature. He swept the decks, chipped rust in the dank, airless chain locker, and repainted the lifeboats, while the more experienced seamen were occupied overhauling the rigging of the ship. Starting at the mastheads, they worked their way down, replacing every gear and brace and block and line while the sailmakers, on the deck below, patched and mended the acres of canvas one of the largest four-masters on the seas carried when fully under way. At night, between watches, Willis would climb recreationally into the rigging, making treacherous progress up the masts and back down to get a feel for the ratlines beneath his feet, the rolling pitch of the ship, the wind in the shrouds.

Willis and his fellow deck boys spent part of each watch learning the ropes with the help of the first mate. A beast of a man, he would shout out, "Main topgallant staysail downhaul" or "Foretopmast staysail halyard!" and the deck boys would run to the rope he'd named, with the mate hot behind them. Mistakes were punished with lashes from a length of tarred hemp. All quivering complaints from the victims were met with the same suggestion: Jump overboard anytime you please.

At thirty-eight degrees south, just below Buenos Aires, the crew bent on the storm sails intended to carry the *Henriette* around Cape Horn. The weather worsened. The seas steepened. The ship ran before gales at as much as ten knots while the temperature dropped and the crew broke out oilskins and sea boots. Willis was soon cured of his fascination with the rigging. He was ordered into the shrouds in sleet and hailstorms to take in sail high above the rolling ship on squally, frigid, pitch-black nights. When a breaking sea washed through the galley and injured the cook, the crew had no hot food for days, living on cereal and hardtack softened in cold coffee. Their clothes were either wet or frozen. There were no gloves on board, just mittens for the helmsmen. The men's mattresses and blankets were soaked through. No fire burned on the ship at all.

Close upon the Horn, the *Henriette* met a Finnish bark sailing north under little more than rags on splintered masts. She lay deep in the seas with her bowsprit and bulwarks torn away. Her crew was pumping furiously, hoping to make Port Stanley in the Falklands. She raised no signal of distress but plunged on, half buried in the combers, just another victim of the roaring forties and fit warning of what lay ahead.

Gales and even hurricanes blown up from the Antarctic were unremitting as the *Henriette* cleared the Scotia Sea and entered the longest uninterrupted fetch of water on the planet. When, after weeks of storms, the sun finally peeked through for mere seconds, the captain took a sight and discovered that the *Henriette* had been driven dangerously close to the cape. He ordered a change in tack in a tremendous rolling swell that was accomplished with two lifeboats smashed to bits and the galley half destroyed from a breaking sea. But the maneuver succeeded, and the ship drifted south, away from the land and into the grip of the Southern Ocean.

The sails, the stays, the yardarms, all were soon sheathed in ice. Storm-plagued, fighting the currents and prevailing winds, the *Henriette* ventured so far south as to meet with bergs broken off the Antarctic pack. Watches were suspended, and the crew did duty for days on end, alternately setting sail and taking it in as the *Henriette* threaded her way through and around the danger. Even a glancing collision could readily have breached her hull and sent the ship to the bottom, and as the ice thickened around the *Henriette* and the threat became all but constant, the nervous crew sent a delegation to the captain.

Three seamen sought out the man in his quarters to suggest he set an easterly course to escape from the ice. Two of the party were immediately clapped in irons and confined for insubordination. The third was sent back to the crew with a message from the captain: "Tell them forward that I am setting the course on this ship."

Crowded with canvas but for upper gallants and royals, the *Henriette* drove west by north before gales in a sea littered with ice. The true position of the ship remained a mystery for days on end as the sun stayed hidden from view and no proper sights could be taken, but the *Henriette* held together and plunged on, finally rounding Cape Horn and heading north into the Pacific, where she shed her storm sails and the crew reworked the rigging and scrubbed the fouled pine decking with sand and stones until it shone white.

It was along about this time that William Willis was exposed to a practice of the sea that would inform the balance of his seagoing life. The ship's cook, battered by the destruction of the galley and a little out of his mind, had become so severely constipated that the mates feared for his survival. The man's abdomen had hardened, and he was incapable of standing up, so he was dragged naked onto the deck for treatment, with Willis and his crewmates looking on.

A chunk of soap was shoved into the cook's rectum "to get things started," Willis reported. While crewmen poured hot water on his belly, the second mate massaged it with his bare feet until the cook gave a groan, shouted out, "*Ja, ja, ja—ich muss!*" and was dragged to the rail, where he evacuated memorably, at least for Willis, who was instructed by an old salt in the vicinity, "Drink a cupful of seawater every day, and you will never have any trouble like that." This advice would effectively save Willis's life in the same waters some forty years later.

The *Henriette* dropped anchor in the roads off Santa Rosalía 168 days out of Hamburg. The following morning she was towed to the wharf, where the crew set about unloading the five thousand tons of coke she carried. The cargo was removed by hand, shoveled into baskets, and winched onto the dock from six in the morning until seven in the evening. The work continued for nearly two months, until the hold was scoured clean, whereupon the process was reversed and ballast was taken on in the form of slag from the local smelter.

Evenings the sailors were free to venture ashore into the small port town, which owed its existence to a French copper mine. The ships in the harbor, two dozen or so, had all come around Cape Horn on voyages lasting five months or more, so the crews were ripe to let off steam. Long-simmering resentments, tamped down by strict shipboard discipline, were frequently acted upon ashore, keeping Santa Rosalía's jail and hospital full to overflowing. Willis's brief stay saw several murders (one a decapitation), numerous stabbings, and countless brawls. Desertions were commonplace, and many of the crews were soon depleted, which made for a booming shanghai business in town. Sailors senseless from drink all too often awoke to find themselves on strange ships miles from shore, sold into service by the local police for a few pesos.

With her ballast nearly loaded, the *Henriette* was due to sail for Vancouver, where she would take on timber for Australia and return north with coal to the Chilean port of Valparaíso to load nitrate for the voyage back to Hamburg. The entire trip promised to take more than two years, and when the first mate informed Willis he would pass the voyage as a deck boy with no hope of promotion to ordinary seaman, Willis could see no fit reason to stay and decided to jump ship. He took what little he could carry, leaving his sea chest behind, and slipped off the *Henriette* the night before she was due to sail. He found a British ship at anchor in the roads, the *Bermuda* out of Glasgow, and he signed on to her crew as an able-bodied seaman earning four pounds a month, sixteen times his pay on the *Henriette*.

She was a flush-deck bark, the *Bermuda*, with but a solitary deckhouse forward and all quarters below. To Willis she looked a bit like a yacht, with her steamer rail instead of bulwarks and her clean sweep of decking. She was just under sail and standing out of the bay when Willis met with occasion to learn his first scrap of English, the word "bucket," which was followed straight-away by the prevailing modifier on board: "bloody."

The crew of the *Bermuda* was even more of a mixed lot than Willis had known on the *Henriette*—Germans and Brits and Danes and Finns and Swedes and Scots, Americans and a soli-tary Australian. The atmosphere shipboard was less grim than Willis had met with on his maiden voyage, and the food was far more palatable and varied. The only breach in discipline was slight and brief: For the first two weeks at sea, the captain per-mitted the second mate to lie drunk in his cabin. The man was summoned each morning and would answer, "I'll be right up," but never stirred until he was finally dragged on deck at the captain's orders and his supply of liquor was confiscated. (Or rather it was shifted to the captain's cabin.)

Upon leaving the Gulf of California, the *Bermuda* swung on a broad westerly arc into the Pacific, south across the equator, and then back east to the Chilean port of Mejillones to load nitrate. Shorthanded, she then called a few miles to the south at Antofagasta in search of supplemental crew. The captain turned up but a lone sailor, a drunk sixty-five-year-old Briton who'd been living for a year and a half on the beach. So the *Bermuda* approached Cape Horn with only half the hands she normally carried, which meant all but endless watches for the month it took to clear the cape and drive north into the Atlantic.

The *Bermuda* was bound for Hamburg to unload, and she reached the Elba River 128 days out of Antofagasta with no casualties other than Willis's Australian shipmate, who'd broken his leg in a fall.

Willis was paid out with the crew, and he carried his twenty gold pieces home to his mother and two brothers, who were scraping by on the meager income Willis's mother managed as a seamstress. In the course of his voyages, Willis had grown to doubt that the seaman's life was for him. The financial rewards were modest, and he found shipboard existence "deadening to the mind." Worse still, sail was yielding to steam at the time, and Willis could hardly picture himself in a lower hold firing a boiler by way of a career. Homeward bound on the *Bermuda*, Willis had pumped his watchmates for news of countries where they'd jumped ship and taken employment on shore. The wages, he learned, were highest in the United States, and Willis settled on America as the land of his future.

He planned to sign on to a westbound ship and abandon it in the States, and when he visited the British shipping office at the Hamburg waterfront, he learned that the Leyland Line's *Inkula*—due to sail the following day from Bremerhaven, bound for Galveston—needed an able-bodied seaman. Willis signed the articles, bade his family good-bye, and shipped out on a crossing of thirty days that brought him to Texas and the Galveston docks, where strapping black stevedores swarmed on board the *Inkula* and immediately set about loading cotton into her hold for the return trip. If Willis were to jump ship, he'd need to do it in short order.

Willis wandered the town of Galveston with a dollar draw from his pay in his pocket. He found broad, leisurely Texas English easy to understand, and he was assured by a longshore-man he quizzed on the matter that there was no end of work in Galveston for a man willing to do it. Local stevedores, or cotton jammers, earned the highest pay in the state of Texas—six dollars a day for stowing ninety bales of cotton. (The going rate for common labor at the time was no more than a dollar and a quarter a day. A skilled tradesman could expect two dollars.)

The trick for Willis was to find a way to jump ship and avoid arrest by local authorities, who'd be sure to put him on the next ship that needed men, no matter where it was headed. A Galveston barman allowed Willis to stow his gear—slipped off the *Inkula* one piece at a time—in the attic of his saloon. On the night before the ship's scheduled departure, Willis climbed over her rail and shimmied down her hawser to the dock. He caught a train to Houston and took a room in a boardinghouse. It was the summer of 1910, and he was all of seventeen years old.

After six days of lying low in his hired room, Willis paid the last of his money (a fee of two dollars) to secure a job cutting timber in the Brazos River bottom, but he soon found he missed the sight of the far horizon and the smell of the sea and returned to Galveston, where he took work on a dredge in Galveston Bay for forty dollars a month. Subsequently he would hire on as a coal passer on an army transport, a stevedore on the Galveston docks, and a cotton jammer in Texas City, until the summer of 1915, when work on the Texas waterfront became so scarce that Willis took to the rails, riding freight trains and following the wheat harvest north through Oklahoma and into Kansas. In Erie, Pennsylvania, Willis unloaded freighters hauling flour from Duluth, Minnesota. He joined a construction crew in Cleveland, worked briefly as a riveter in a San Francisco shipyard and a plumber's helper in a Kansas City packing plant before hiring on to build timber derricks in the boom fields of west Texas.

Later Willis passed a season constructing salmon traps in

Alaska before returning to California, where he lived for a year and a half in Monterey in what had been a mule stable. He worked at odd jobs one day a week to supply his needs and spent the balance of his time composing an epic poem on the life of Christ. Twenty-seven hundred polished lines later, Willis moved to San Francisco, where he attended a series of lectures on health and nutrition and became acquainted with the discipline of yoga.

Instinctively, Willis had long subscribed to the manner of diet followed routinely by yogis. Both his tight finances and his native gastric disposition ensured that Willis ate unrefined foods, many of them grown under natural conditions. He had long preferred whole wheat and could afford fruits and vegetables only when they were plentifully in season. During the lecture sessions he attended, Willis was particularly struck by the combined yogic discipline of chewing and rhythmic breathing. He learned that it was common practice for a yogi to chew his food while holding his breath, so that each morsel would become sufficiently mixed with saliva to effectively release its vitamins. Accordingly, studied control over respiration was given out as key to the health and well-being of the body.

By coincidence Willis had been practicing a brand of rhythmic breathing since the age of fourteen. He'd come across a passage in a book promoting the salubrious effects of strict respirational discipline, but apparently Willis's method had long been a little askew. At one of the last yoga lectures he attended in San Francisco, Willis suffered himself to be sized up by the speaker:

> You are a seeker. You are very slow developing on the intellectual side which you must overcome before you find your path on account of your excessive physical energies which demand an outlet first. . . . You breathe too

deep now, meaning too much towards the sides of the chest which keeps you a dreamer. You must try to fill the upper lobes of the lungs which alone develop the intellectual faculties of the brain. That must be your breath before you can advance.

Willis decided he'd be best served by doing the bulk of his seeking and breathing in the main branch of the New York Public Library. Some years before, he'd been enchanted by the facility on a visit to the city, and he felt certain the time was ripe for him to "get away from the frontiers with their untrammeled ways and big wages." He intended to give himself over, to the extent he could afford to, to "literary work."

In 1926, Willis took a room in a brownstone on West Sixty-third Street and, as good as his word, fairly haunted the main branch of the public library on Fifth Avenue. He read extensively, biographies mostly, wandered through Central Park by way of recreation, and wrote each night into the small hours. By his own calculation, Willis held over fifty jobs in the course of his first few years in New York. His budget was grievously tight, and he tended to be frugal nearly to the point of starvation, but still he managed to work feverishly at his writing.

He cranked out novels and poems and cartoon sketches in absurd profusion, suffered every submission to be rejected, and presently began to harbor second thoughts about those untrammeled ways and big wages. Willis bought a secondhand steamer trunk, loaded it with his manuscripts, and sent it off to a warehouse for storage. He joined the New York branch of the National Maritime Union, and after twenty-four years, William Willis returned to the sea.

3

Devil's Island

EARLY IN 1938, Willis was recovering from a spill he'd taken on the SS *Western World,* a liner traveling between New York and Buenos Aires. He was hobbling around on crutches and living at the seamen's YMCA on Manhattan's West Street at Seventeenth while drawing his meager eighteen-dollar-a-week sick benefits from the union when he ran into an old shipmate who offered to set him up with cheaper accommodations. Willis's buddy took him to a rooming house on West Twenty-second Street between Eighth and Ninth Avenues, an establishment operated by a Madame Carnot, who let rooms upstairs for two dollars a week and lived in the basement with her daughter, Jeanne.

The pair had immigrated from France nearly ten years before, but Madame Carnot's English was still sufficiently spotty to allow Willis ample opportunity to brush up on his passable French. He spent many evening hours chatting with Madame Carnot and her daughter in their basement kitchen and eventually learned of Madame Carnot's son, Bernard, who was imprisoned in the South American country of French Guiana, convicted of murder.

The family had owned a small hotel on the Toulouse high-way where Bernard had been party to a brawl in the hotel bar room in which a man had died, having fallen in the scuffle and struck his head on a chair. Though there was scant evidence Bernard was directly responsible, the court's judgment had gone against him, and he'd been condemned to eight years in the penal colony commonly known as Devil's Island, a sentence which effectively meant banishment for life. By the time Willis first learned of Madame Carnot's son, Bernard had been in French Guiana for sixteen years, eight of them spent in the prison in St. Laurent on the mainland and the balance passed in the surrounding equatorial forest as a *libéré*, or freed prisoner. Due to the gravity of his crime and the length of his sentence, Bernard was ineligible for repatriation, which meant he could only hope to leave Guiana by escape or death.

Though unbidden by Madame Carnot, Willis immediately began to contemplate a rescue, spending hours in the library reading up on Devil's Island. The grim history of the penal colony dates from 1852, when French prisoners were first transported to the *Iles du Salut*, the Islands of Salvation, a few miles off the mainland near the city of Kourou. Devil's Island itself was saved for political prisoners, most conspicuous among them Alfred Dreyfus, the French army captain accused of spying for Germany and later cleared of the charge, but only after fourteen years of confinement.

St. Joseph Island, some two hundred yards removed from Devil's Island across a shark-infested channel, was the destination for those prisoners considered incorrigible. It boasted a compound the inmates referred to as *mangeuse d'hommes*, devourer of men. The worst of the worst were isolated within it by way of additional punishment. Absolute silence was demanded of the inmates. Guards walked their watches on the barred ceilings over the prisoners' heads. Punitive confinement in the mute isolation of the devourer of men could last upwards of six years.

Royal Island, the largest of the three, served as the weigh station and clearing house. Here the prisoners were sorted and dispatched either to one of the other islands or to the facility at St. Laurent on the eastern shore of the Maroni River, which divides French Guiana from what was then Dutch Guiana, now Suriname. Bernard Carnot had served his sentence at St. Laurent and had been released into the forest of what was, at the time, a nationwide penal colony. Barred by law from leaving the country, he was effectively a prisoner for life.

So in 1938, in the main branch of the public library on New York's Fifth Avenue, William Willis, an able-bodied seaman by profession and a "seeker" by yogi diagnosis, sifted through what information he could find on Devil's Island and quite seriously entertained the notion of traveling by boat to South America in search of an inmate he knew only by name, a *libéré* buried alive in a country the size of Indiana.

The chances for success, by any objective measure, were minuscule. Willis would have to locate Bernard Carnot, secure the means for and assist in the man's escape from French Guiana, and leave the country himself without being arrested and subjected to the local hospitality. Most men would surely have sought some other means of consoling a landlord, but William Willis wasn't remotely most men.

It seems the yogi who had encouraged Willis to fill his upper lobes with air had also informed him, "The impossible attracts you," which Willis saw fit to embrace as an article of faith. He was forty-five years old in 1938 and claimed to have already decided that there would be "no real aging for me, neither physically nor mentally." He credited his "vital parents," his rhythmic breathing, and his diet, along with what he termed his "philosophy," a blend of gauzy mysticism and wishfulness that, for practical purposes, might best be distilled into the sentiment "What the hell."

Once he'd determined to rescue Bernard Carnot, in spite of the odds, Willis accounted for his decision this way: "Deep in my heart I knew that my venture was a natural one for me—I had always followed the Don Quixote trail."

Willis told Madame Carnot he was simply working a ship to South America and would nose around for her son if he got the chance. The truth was a trifle more complicated. Willis secured a Dutch visa, giving himself out as a miner, a profession common to the territory. He intended to land at Paramaribo, the provincial capital of Dutch Guiana, work his way south and east into the jungle, and cross the piranha-rich Maroni River to the French side in the vicinity of St. Laurent. From there he would make inquiries—this the profoundly "philosophical" portion of the venture—leading him to Bernard Carnot, and they would together improvise some means of escape.

Willis had determined to work part of his passage to economize, and he signed on to the crew of the SS *Ponce*, bound for Puerto Rico. Willis stood the first wheel watch and so literally brought the ship out of New York Harbor, through the narrows between Brooklyn and Staten Island and into the open Atlantic, embarking upon a mission that had about it the look of dire folly.

At San Juan, Willis was paid off and booked passage on the *Santa Katarina*, bound for St. Thomas, a port of call for bauxite ships traveling south to Dutch Guiana. Following a wait of a few days in the Virgin Islands, a Norwegian vessel, the *Ingrid*, made port. She was headed for Georgetown, British Guiana, present-day Guyana, where Willis was assured he could catch a Norwegian freighter for the hop to Paramaribo. The *Ingrid* carried seven passengers, among them a young woman from New York who went by the name Teddy. She worked in Manhattan at a talent agency and was the sort of creature who could readily construe a voyage on a bauxite freighter to obscure malarial ports in the West Indies a vacation. She and William Willis seemed all but manufactured for each other.

They were soon inseparable shipboard, and Teddy even petitioned Willis to take her into the jungle with him so that she might see his mining operation. He put her off but promised to be in touch when he returned to New York. They parted company in Georgetown, British Guiana, where Willis boarded the *Thyra*, Paramaribo bound, and Teddy continued inland, up the Demerara River, where the *Ingrid* was to load for her return voyage.

In Paramaribo, Willis sought out the American consul, who both arranged for Willis to work the placer mine of a local acquaintance and advised him to buy a gun to carry with him at all times. The consul informed Willis that the *libérés*, freed not just from confinement but from shelter and meals as well, were slowly starving in the jungle and customarily traveled in gangs, robbing and often killing whomever they came upon. Those who ventured across the Maroni River to the Dutch side, classified as *évadés*, or escapees, were more desperate still, and no unarmed civilian was likely to survive an encounter with them.

Willis responded with a spot of belated introspection: "I did not feel hopeful about what I had come to do. I was not depressed, but I felt no drive, no urge to go into action. Perhaps the enervating climate had something to do with it." Perhaps.

Willis took a boat up the Commewijne River from Paramaribo to Moengo, a shabby little settlement organized around a bauxite mine operated by Alcoa. Having spent the night there, next day he headed overland for Albina, one of two passengers in an old Ford sedan making a mail run through the jungle. The car was driven by a half-mad Chinese immigrant who barreled along at full speed, undeterred by the fact that the foliage kept him from seeing more than a foot or two ahead. In just under three hours, they made Albina, a bedraggled mining outpost that owed its existence to the Inini gold boom at the Brazilian border, long ended. Downriver a scant mile on the opposite bank lay Willis's destination—the town of St. Laurent, in French Guiana.

A launch made regular crossings from Albina to St. Laurent, and Willis was on it the following day with a complement of Chinese shopkeepers from Albina who had commercial interests in St. Laurent as well. They advised Willis (in futility, as it turned out) to keep to the main street, to avoid the local rum houses, and to resist the temptation to so much as speak to the starving *libérés* who were a pestilential and cadaverous presence in the town. Willis arrived in time to watch as crews of inmates were marched out of the jungle and in through the notorious Black Gate of the penitentiary for their midday meal. They made for an appalling sight, many of them fever-ridden and ashen.

Willis, shaken by the grim spectacle of hundreds of doomed, wasted men, walked to settle himself and clear his head. Straightaway he ventured off the main street and back among the shacks where the *libérés* lived. He found a few of the men in the shady corner of a market square and attempted without success to strike up a conversation. They were occupied watching a trio of vultures separate a snake from its intestines and appeared to Willis completely spent, "beyond thought and speech." He left them to visit a nearby rum house, a bar and dance hall called Au Petit Coin de Paris (A Little Corner of Paris), where he drank cognac and entertained overtures from the lone waitress, who invited him to buy her a drink and retire with her to an adjacent bedroom. Willis declined and passed his time instead watching the two small daughters of the proprietor playing in the middle of the dance-hall floor. They were naked and looked to Willis "like cherubs" until one of them squatted among her toys, a smile on her face, and indulged in an uncherubic bowel movement.

Willis took the afternoon launch back to Albina and passed his evening in the company of the soldiers guarding the launch dock. One was a Dutchman named Franz, the other a young native. Both spoke passable English, and Willis teased from them what information he could about the *libéré* population on the French side of the river. The soldiers boasted of *évadés* they had captured, for which they were paid one guilder a man. They told of countless failed escapes by *libérés* on rafts, in rude local canoes, drifting on logs. If they survived the piranha in the river, they invariably met with the sharks in the sea.

The persistent barking of a dog drew Franz out of the guardhouse and into the streets of Albina, where he captured two *évadés* on the Moengo road. He confined them to the barracks, would escort them back come morning, collect his guilders, and have his rum. All *évadés*, Franz explained to Willis, were returned to St. Laurent, except for Germans. Most of the German nationals had been convicted of crimes while serving in Africa in the French Foreign Legion. An agreement between the Dutch and Hitler provided that captured German *évadés* would be returned to Germany. It was mid-1938, and Hitler anticipated need of them.

Willis accompanied Franz and his two prisoners across the river to St. Laurent the following morning. Out of sympathy, Willis offered the convicts French banknotes but was instructed by Franz to give them coins instead. The men took the silver and swallowed it, planning to keep passing and swallowing it until they had fit use for it. Once Franz had turned over his charges, accepted his guilders and his shot of rum—a prison courtesy—he joined Willis in a St. Laurent bar, where they soaked up entirely too much *tafia*, a potent native concoction made from sugarcane, and came stumbling out into the street to catch the last launch of the afternoon back to Albina.

By then Willis was convinced he had no hope of finding Bernard Carnot without help, specifically without the assistance of a *libéré* he could trust, and he sought out a Chinese shopkeeper in Albina with whom he'd become friendly and asked if the man could recommend a guide, a *libéré* who might be willing, for a fee, to show Willis around St. Laurent. The shopkeeper professed to know just the man, and he sent his son with Willis to make the introduction.

Willis hired a bushman to carry them to St. Laurent in his dugout, and the boy found the man they were after along the riverbank at the far end of town, on a strip of beach littered with *libérés* gazing idly out over the water. The candidate's name was Jules. He wore the uniform common to *libérés*, a thin undershirt and dungarees rolled up the knees. He looked to Willis to be in his mid-fifties and had been in the colony for nearly thirty years, having been convicted of aiding in a robbery. He proved willing enough to show Willis about town, the first duty requested of him, but he was quite sure they would exhaust the sights in no more than an hour's time. They had walked hardly more than a block when Jules pointed out a storefront. "Here is a little place, monsieur," he told Willis. "It is quiet, and the wine is not bad."

The establishment was run by a *libéré*, a hulking Italian in a torn undershirt, his torso and arms covered with self-inflicted tattoos, most of them obscene. Another *libéré* entered shortly after Willis and Jules and sat near them just as Willis had begun to probe Jules on the disposition of the prisoners in the colony.

Jules put a finger to his lips to silence Willis. Once they'd finished their wine and returned to the street, Jules explained that the man at the adjacent table, though dressed like an inmate, was actually with the French security force, the Sûreté, yet another lurking hazard Willis had not anticipated. Grateful that Jules had shut him up and spared him, Willis chose to take Jules's finger-to-his-lips gesture as an endorsement of Jules's character, a sign of his utter trustworthiness. Willis liked to think he could sniff out decency unerringly, and once he'd deemed a man honorable, little shy of a monstrous betrayal could shake Willis in his view.

As they walked along a slummy back street in St. Laurent, Willis quizzed Jules on the particulars of escape from the colony. How was such a thing managed—overland or by river and sea? If by water, what sort of craft was required, what manner of provisions? How much would such a vessel cost, and where could one be had? Jules informed Willis that, with money enough, every detail could be seen to readily. He calculated that Willis could mount a respectable escape for around two thousand francs, the equivalent of about fifty dollars at the time.

Inevitably, such talk led to mention of the prospective escapee. Jules had no knowledge of a Bernard Carnot, but he professed himself willing to hire out to Willis and accompany him upriver and into the jungle to search for the man. Willis sealed the agreement with a handshake. "I liked his voice," Willis wrote of Jules. "I liked his face and his eyes—I had confidence in him."

Jules, a bit more savvy in the ways of human frailty, chose at first to withhold his confidence in Willis, or his faith anyway in Willis's sanity. They traveled up the Maroni River toward Willis's mine, Willis in a hired native dugout and Jules following a day behind in a canoe. They spent their first night together sleeping in the boat, or rather Willis slept while Jules stood over him with his machete, mindful of Willis's gold teeth, of the money he carried, of the pistol he'd brought—riches enough to see Jules into a new life in a new land. Willis awoke to find Jules glaring down at him.

"With one stroke of my saber, I could cut off your head," Jules informed him. Willis, in typical fashion, reaffirmed his trust in Jules and invited the man to put his machete away and lie down beside him. When Jules lay quivering on the canoe bottom, Willis assumed he was enduring spasms of gratitude over the faith Willis had demonstrated in his character. (It seems more likely Jules was quaking from having to sleep next to a madman.)

Before traveling upriver to meet Willis, Jules had made inquiries in St. Laurent about Bernard Carnot. He had learned that there was such a person somewhere in French Guiana, though no one could say precisely where. Furthermore, there existed the real possibility that Carnot had died in the jungle, since *libérés* robbed and slaughtered one another with fairly ghastly abandon. It was possible as well that he had contracted leprosy and was confined to the leper colony on an island in the Maroni. Bernard Carnot was a very small needle in an altogether perilous haystack.

Jules and Willis's search for Carnot was halting and rather aimless by necessity. Willis was passing for a *libéré*, wearing the same shabby clothes Jules wore. Taking the lead, Jules instructed him to pass himself off as a mute French convict and thereby avoid having to open his mouth and expose his gold fillings.

After some weeks Willis managed to tease from Jules the story of his existence in the colony. Jules had attempted several escapes through the years but had always been caught and returned to custody. He was routinely punished with solitary confinement on the island of St. Joseph.

Once back in the general population, Jules would work on crews in the jungle, chopping wood, and he grew convinced in time that malaria would surely kill him if he didn't succeed in an escape. Word eventually reached the colony of the gold strike in

Inini, a jungle outpost well south of St. Laurent near the border with Brazil. Jules reasoned that a man with a little luck and no fear of work could become rich quickly in Inini, rich enough to pay his way out of Guiana and start fresh elsewhere. Since the alternative was slow, fevered death, Jules set about planning his next escape.

Jules had come across a child's dugout drifting down the Maroni and had hidden it against the day when he might need it. Determined to find his fortune and his path to freedom in Inini, Jules failed to return to the penitentiary with his work crew one evening, slipped instead into the jungle, recovered his small boat, and took it across the river to a native village upstream from Albina, where the chief of the village hid him until a trio of escapees on their way to Inini agreed to take Jules with them.

Jules and his companions traveled for a month, first up the Maroni and then east through the jungle to the mining camp, where Jules was given a shovel and told to dig. This felt like freedom to him, and he worked day and night in a race for riches and against malaria. The ground might have been full of gold, but the jungle was rife with fever, and the miners (mostly escapees) worked like madmen, collecting ore until their bodies could no longer sustain them. The king of Inini, as Jules described it, was quinine. It was sold at a premium and in such a diluted form—mixed with baking soda—that it was effectively useless, so fever raged among the miners.

Word of the riches to be had in Inini traveled widely, bringing in more men to work the mine and rogues to prey on them. Along the length of the Maroni River, clear down to Albina and St. Laurent, thieves waited for the miners to come out of the jungle and killed them for their ore. There was so much carnage, in fact, that the mining company was forced to hire a plane to fly all the gold to the coast. The miners turned in their ore for receipts redeemable in Cayenne, if they could ever reach the place.

Jules stayed on at the mine—digging for the company during the day, for himself at night—until malaria weakened him to the point that he could no longer hold a shovel. In the company of an equally ailing Dutchman, Jules traveled downriver in a canoe. They moved by night, avoiding gangs of *évadés* out to plunder any loose ore they might carry, and they were only three days above St. Laurent when they were captured on the shoreline in Dutch Guiana by bounty hunters. Jules was returned to the prison in St. Laurent, where he was tried for his escape and sentenced to a year in solitary confinement on St. Joseph Island. He'd made no escape attempts since and professed to be resigned to his fate.

"This is my home," he told Willis. "Where could I go?"

And how could he get there? Escape from the colony was, as a rule, a desperate undertaking, attempted primarily by sea in native dugouts fashioned for river travel. In the course of their search for Bernard Carnot, Jules and Willis assisted a trio of inmates in their escape attempt. The undertaking was difficult enough under ordinary circumstances, but this group was encumbered with a woman and a baby. She'd been a maid in the house of a guard where one of the convicts occasionally worked. The child was his, and she was determined to accompany him out of French Guiana and into his new life.

Jules helped the five escapees gather provisions and bartered for a native canoe large enough to hold them. He scavenged civilian clothes for the three men, and he and Willis towed their loaded boat to the spot where they hid along the riverbank. The night was squally, with the promise of foul weather at sea. The men poured down Jules and Willis's *tafia* for courage, settled the woman and child into their canoe, and loaded in after. They had but four inches of freeboard and demonstrated among them no instinct for seamanship. They could hardly manage the boat's paddles.

With the tide flowing, they took their leave of Jules and Willis and entered the current that would carry them, with luck, past the shoaly mouth of the Maroni and into the Atlantic, where they would follow the coastline west to the relative anonymity of Paramaribo or, more likely, breach and drown. Either was thought preferable to life in the colony.

By this time the search for Bernard Carnot was fairly stymied. Jules's inquiries had come to nothing, and the only potential source yet untapped was a convict of Jules's acquaintance who'd worked for years in the prison's administration office. By way of complication—there was always a complication—the man had contracted leprosy and had been confined to the leper colony on St. Joseph Island in the Maroni River. Jules couldn't be sure his source was still alive, he had no way of knowing if he could provide the merest scrap of information about Bernard Carnot, and anyone visiting the leper colony without proper authority ran the risk of being summarily shot by the guards who patrolled the island. Add to that the possibility of infection from contact with lepers and you have just the sort of mission (a blend of futility and peril) that William Willis evermore seemed helpless against.

He volunteered immediately. Willis insisted on going to the island, over Jules's objections that any information gained wouldn't likely be worth the risk of gaining it. Once Jules had ferried him over in the dark of night, Willis hid in scrub at the water's edge until morning, when he ventured out to speak to a lone convict who'd wandered down to the shore.

The man was startled by the sight of Willis but raised no alarm. Willis showed him the camera he'd brought along and told the man he'd come to take pictures of the lepers for the wife of an official in St. Laurent. Sensibly, the gentleman—a former college professor with a face disfigured by the disease—hoped the lady was paying Willis extravagantly well, given the real possibility Willis might be gunned down or infected, and he agreed to gather discreetly those of his fellow inmates who'd be willing to have their pictures taken. Willis had carried with him a sack of tobacco he was prepared to dole out for payment.

Before they could part company, a guard approached from the hillside above them. There was nowhere for Willis to hide, and the inmate instructed him to strip out of his *libéré* clothing, certain to give him away. The leper shed his soiled shirt and trousers and offered them to Willis. As the inmate was known to the guard, he planned to carry Willis's clothes into the river with him and make out to be enjoying a morning dip. Willis, in leper's clothing, would likely go unquestioned and, more significantly, unshot.

With the convict naked before him, Willis got an appalling look at the man's ravaged body and debated risking contamination by putting on the leper's clothes or taking his chances by diving into the river and swimming for the far shore. In typical Willis fashion, his choice was more an act of compassion than a rational decision: "The pleading eye of the old man decided me and I took off my clothes and put on his."

Willis walked, as instructed, slowly up the bank away from the river and into a grove of breadfruit trees. The guard took him for an inmate and allowed him to pass unchallenged. By then Willis was less worried about being gunned down than about being infected. The leper's clothes were warm and clammy from the man's sweat and felt, Willis noted, like they were "melting into me and flooding me with disease." After the guard had moved out of sight, Willis stripped naked, plunged into the river, and scoured himself with sand.

Once the danger had passed, true to his word, Willis's professorial leper brought to the riverbank throughout the day assorted inmates for Willis to photograph. Among them was the administrator Jules had spoken of—he professed to remember the name Bernard Carnot and thought the man lived between St. Laurent and the town of St. Jean, though he could hardly be sure of that and remembered nothing else of Carnot. Such was the feeble morsel Willis had risked his life to collect.

Worse still, as Willis was readying his dugout to leave the island, he was set upon by an enormous inmate carrying a club. The man slipped up behind Willis and prefaced his attack by blurting out, "You have a lot of gold in your mouth." Willis's pistol was out of reach in the dugout, and he'd dropped his saber into the water and was searching madly for it with his foot as the man attacked. The brute flailed at Willis, tried to brain him with his club, gouge Willis's eyes with his fingers. Willis fought back, clawing at any of the inmate's rotted flesh he could reach. His fingers found the man's mouth, and Willis pulled until his "whole cheek came out in a gory mess."

The leper wailed in pain and staggered back, his blood spurting all over Willis, who shoved his dugout away from the shore and tumbled into it. Eventually, the current carried him downstream to an eddy, where he rolled out of the boat and rinsed himself of the infected blood. Willis was covered in scratches and had genuine reason to fear contracting leprosy, but, in typical Willis fashion, he also located a benefit from the tussle. His lower back, sore for weeks, was quite suddenly pain-free.

Once Willis had returned to his jungle camp, Jules dressed his wounds with potash, and Willis inspected himself throughout the following week for signs of a telltale rash until he was put off the enterprise by a devastating dose of malaria that reduced him to a feverish stupor. The concentrated quinine Jules gave him had no effect, and when Willis began raving, Jules decided to take him for treatment—not to the hospital in St. Laurent but several days upriver to a native village, where the chief was also a sort of bush witch doctor.

After sizing up Willis's condition, the chief dispatched a few bushmen into the jungle with their bows and arrows. They returned with assorted wounded Amazonian parrots. The chief split one in half from head to tail and applied the bloody pieces of parrot to the soles of Willis's feet. Leaves were layered on, and the poultice was strapped in place with twine and left untouched for three hours. When it was removed, the delicate pink flesh of the bird had changed to "poisonous-looking black."

The process was then repeated, and repeated, and repeated. The treatment went on for days, with bushmen fetching back parrots and the chief hacking them in half and binding them to Willis's feet. Willis was fed regular rations of monkey broth, too, until the parrot flesh, in a hopeful development, blackened hardly at all. The chief then dispensed with the birds and set leeches upon Willis. He laid open one of the bloated creatures and dripped Willis's blood into a bowl of water, where it floated on the surface in a thin coating.

"Your friend," the chief informed Jules, "will not die." Apparently, sinking blood would have indicated that Willis, quite beyond dissected parrots and primate consommé, was altogether doomed.

Jules loaded Willis into their dugout and carried him to their jungle camp, where Willis lay in his hammock for the better part of a week while Jules nursed him fully back to health. In his lassitude and in the lonely hours when Jules was upriver in St. Laurent gathering supplies, Willis knew the leisure to consider his circumstances in depth and frankly contemplate the driving motives behind his "crazy quest," as he called it:

> Why had I come to the Penal Colony? Don't kid yourself, Bill, a voice said, you did this for yourself, not for Madame Carnot or anybody else. Devil's Island was a challenge and you took it up. . . . It was another experience needed to round you out and see your fellow man in his agonies, for you always identified yourself with suffering and were chastened by it. That's how you were born.

In addition to the debilitating effects of malaria, Willis was soon stricken with a nasty rash, a form of jungle rot he chose to think leprous, along with chiggers under his toenails that he was obliged to dig out with a knife blade. He began to look for all the world like a genuine *libéré* as he hobbled around the jungle with his ruptured skin and his bloody feet, in his nasty, ragged clothing. In passing moments Willis could even believe himself condemned, while Jules preferred to think him simply innocent and naive, perhaps even hopelessly so. Willis had come all this way and endured these hardships to find a stranger. Even in the wake of his more unsavory experiences with the *libérés* who infested the jungle, Willis still seemed to Jules overly trusting by nature and insufficiently suspicious of the motives of the convicts they met, most of whom (in Jules's view) would have quite happily removed Willis's head in order to get at his bridgework.

"Monsieur, you are like a priest," Jules told Willis, "who has never been outside his church and mingled with the people." He found Willis's faith in the virtues of human nature incomprehensible and more than a little appalling, and so assumed the role of Willis's protector. Even after he'd recovered from his fever, Willis was routinely left in camp while Jules traveled to St. Laurent and sought out *libérés* in the surrounding jungle who could possibly know something of Bernard Carnot.

His efforts finally paid off when Jules learned of a *libéré* with a name something like "Carnot" who had recently returned from a long stint upriver and was said to live in a shack in the vicinity of St. Laurent. Jules tracked the man down, met with him, and established that he was, in fact, Bernard Carnot. Jules told him nothing of Willis's quest, leaving that for Willis to do himself the following day once they had trekked to Carnot's hovel in the jungle a few miles above St. Laurent.

Willis put into Bernard Carnot's hands a photograph of his mother, and the man wept as Willis supplied him with news of his family in New York. Willis then went on to describe his plans for Bernard Carnot: He would obtain for the man a persuasive if counterfeit passport of a sort readily available in the colony and a berth on a smuggling sloop bound for Brazil. (Jules had been attending to the details throughout his visits to St. Laurent.) While most *libéré* escape attempts were, by necessity, rash and improvised on the cheap, Willis had enough cash at his disposal to guarantee Bernard Carnot far better odds of success than enjoyed by the usual *évadé*.

Jules and Willis carried Bernard Carnot downstream to the mouth of the Maroni in their dugout. They found the sloop they had hired hidden, as promised, in the lee of one of the Dutch islands where the Maroni met the sea. She was a ship of twenty tons, trafficking in all manner of contraband between Cayenne and Brazil. She carried anything that would pay, including convicts.

For his part, Willis was a trifle disappointed that a sloop was available to whisk Carnot out of the colony. "I had intended," Willis confessed, "to buy a canoe from the Indian turtle-fishers on the coast, rig it and sail Carnot to Brazil myself. That, of course, would have been to my liking." Instead Willis and Jules helped load Carnot and his meager possessions onto the ship and watched from their dugout in the river as she raised anchor and nosed out to sea. The price of Carnot's passage, of his freedom, was all of twenty-five dollars.

On their way back upriver to their jungle camp, Jules and Willis were approached by a patrol boat with a crew of prison guards in search of four escaped convicts. As the boat's spotlight found their dugout, Willis slipped into the water, preferring the risk of piranhas to the threat posed by the guards. The men searched the dugout and inspected Jules's passbook as Willis looked on from the darkness. "Suddenly it came over me that

I had had enough of French Guiana," he wrote. "More than I could take."

Once the patrol boat had moved on downriver, Willis climbed back into the dugout and confessed to Jules that he'd had all of the colony he could endure. "Let's go to the Dutch side."

They tied up in the bushes on the west bank of the Maroni. Come morning, after Willis's clothes had dried in the sun, he walked into Albina.

Willis departed Guiana two days later on a coastal steamer carrying balata to Paramaribo. Jules saw him off with an embrace and a gift, a box of morphos, brilliant blue Amazonian butterflies Jules had collected with his makeshift net. As Willis's ship steamed across the Tiger Banks at the mouth of the Maroni and into the open sea, his last view of French Guiana made for a wholly suitable tableau—vultures circling low over the headland jungle.

As if to confirm what he suspected of his underlying motives and his appetite for selfish, quixotic adventure, Willis provided but a brief, cursory epilogue to his Devil's Island caper. While Madame Carnot and her daughter heard directly from Willis that their son and brother had found his freedom, there was never a reunion. Bernard Carnot remained in Brazil, working as a gardener in Recife until the outbreak of World War II, when he joined the French army and returned to his homeland, only to die in battle before Strasbourg.

In 1943, Willis would receive a letter from Albina informing him that Jules had been taken by fever. Three years later a rising tide of scathing French public opinion signaled the end of Devil's Island as a penal colony. By 1952 the final boatload of inmates had departed for repatriation to France.

4

Seven Little Sisters

WILLIS RETURNED FROM French Guiana to New York City in the summer of 1938, and the moment he cleared customs, he phoned Teddy, the young woman he'd met on the *Ingrid* while outward bound. They made a date for that evening, rekindled their attachment, and were married on November 21 at City Hall in lower Manhattan. Willis was so strapped for cash that Teddy had bought her own wedding band and returned to her office in Radio City immediately after the ceremony.

Teddy worked at a theatrical agency operated by her brother-in-law, Charles V. Yates, who counted among his clients Bob Hope and Gypsy Rose Lee. Willis, for his part, took the occasional job on merchant ships plying the eastern seaboard but was chiefly content to allow Teddy to be the breadwinner while he indulged in a second artistic spasm and pursued his intellectual and literary interests. "I was as unsuccessful as ever with my writing," Willis confessed, "but always appeared to be near a break-through. This kept me hopeful and on my toes."

The couple had taken an apartment on Seventieth Street just off Central Park West, and Willis had been quick to inflict his brand of austerity on his wife. He prepared all of their food, which he described as "plain." They ate meat occasionally, but chiefly vegetables and whole grains, without the benefit of terribly much seasoning, not even salt. Teddy had been in the custom of riding the subway to work, but Willis prevailed upon her to walk through the park and down Sixth Avenue to her office. He would escort her, morning and evening, and would march the poor woman on weekends over the Hudson River to Palisades Park, where they routinely covered upwards of twenty miles. Willis allowed that Teddy had been "doubtful" at first of his general program of diet and exercise but warmed to it over time.

Willis was a regular visitor to a gym on West Forty-second Street operated by the retired welterweight champion George Bothner. There Willis kept himself in shape by wrestling all comers, and he was a devoted student as well of the novelty acts his wife booked into venues around the country. They were jugglers and contortionists, acrobats and clowns, men and women in remarkable physical condition who shared with Willis their insights into diet and exercise, which Willis, ever adaptable, frequently embraced as his own.

Willis and Teddy had managed between them to scrounge up the price of a sailboat, a thirty-one-foot sloop on which they vacationed in the waters off Florida when schedules and finances allowed. Occasional Caribbean cruises kept Willis's navigational skills passably sharp and his sailing sense a little keener than his paying work allowed. Though Willis shipped out on the odd merchant vessel and worked passage for weeks at a time, his duties as an able-bodied seaman were generally more in the way of janitorial than nautical, and he construed the physical demands of shipboard work as welcome exertion "necessary to keep a man from degenerating mentally and spiritually."

What Willis missed, however, what he longed for, was adventure of the sort he'd known in French Guiana and on the deck of the *Henriette* in ice-plagued waters off Cape Horn. Willis's appetite for trial, for hardship, even suffering, was going largely unsatisfied by an existence that struck him as all too safe and steady. So while he worked his voyages, honed his physique, ate his bland whole grains, wrote his epic poetry and unpublishable novels, William Willis itched for an authentic challenge and only eventually landed on his true calling—what would become the signal events of his life—as he approached his sixtieth birthday.

*   *   *

The year was 1951, and Willis had signed on to the SS *Charleston*, a collier plying the waters between New York and Norfolk, Virginia. At the time his wife was recovering from thyroid surgery in a Manhattan hospital, and she had insisted Willis work a passage to take his mind off her condition. On the New York–to–Norfolk run, he was chatting in the mess room with his crewmates when talk turned to castaways, to "lifeboats and life rafts and emergency rations and what a man had to go through when he was adrift at sea."

The crew of the *Charleston* had been driven to the topic by one of their mates who was thought to suffer from raft fever. He'd been set adrift from his torpedoed ship in World War II and had become a bit unhinged before his rescue. Willis's interest, however, was more in the general challenge of deprivation, and he began to entertain thoughts of a raft trip across the

Pacific in order to find out "how much I really can go through in the way of hardships—I mean living on starvation rations and working around the clock—working day after day without sleep and exposing myself to everything the sea and sky have in the way of bad weather." The allure for Willis lay firmly in the prospect of "slow death staring over the gunwale."

When, back in New York, he revealed to Teddy that he was thinking of building a raft and sailing it single-handed across the Pacific Ocean, she proved immediately and emphatically opposed to the scheme. "You're not going on any raft," she assured him, "not alone and not with me."

By this time Willis had done little blue-water sailing in almost twenty years, and the last coasting excursion he'd made with his wife in 1948 had nearly ended in disaster when their sloop began taking on water in squally weather, and a ship from the navy station in Key West had to tow them to safety. So Teddy had fit reason to object to her husband's plans, but Willis continued to nurse them in secret, and he would broach the topic every half year or so to test his wife's resolve. Frequently, Teddy would remind Willis that the *Kon-Tiki* of Thor Heyerdahl's celebrated 1947 expedition carried a crew of six and knew trouble enough to keep them all occupied. Willis would reliably respond by framing his voyage as "an endurance test—endurance of body and mind." So it was imperative, as he saw it, that he make the trip alone.

Willis seemed to consider himself the anti-Heyerdahl. The *Kon-Tiki* had been constructed and launched in an attempt to mimic a voyage of migration from the coast of South America to the islands of the western Pacific. It was a route, Heyerdahl proposed, that had likely brought fair-skinned continentals to the shores of Polynesia as early as the sixth century A.D. Willis, for his part, didn't intend to "prove any scientific theory, or discover and set up any new course of any kind for others to follow." Willis's voyage was to be something else altogether. "It was a pilgrimage," he insisted, "to the shrine of my philosophy."

This would be the same philosophy, shrineless at the time, that had sent Willis into the jungles of French Guiana. He suspected that a Pacific crossing would serve as a similar test of his mettle. Willis anticipated "endless labor and sleeplessness on primitive, scanty food." He welcomed exposure to the elements and "the terrors of loneliness, like a soldier in battle, living under continual threat of death." By way of afterthought, Willis also proposed he "would perhaps contribute some knowledge about survival at sea."

Willis was nothing if not determined, and once Teddy realized that her husband's enthusiasm for the voyage had hardly flagged in the face of her misgivings and prohibitions, she relented and gave her permission for Willis to go on his fool trip if he wished. "But don't blame me," she told him. "I don't see how you can make it."

Willis kicked off his preparations as he had with his Devil's Island adventure. He visited the main branch of the New York Public Library in the summer of 1953, where he studied charts and maps of the Pacific Ocean in a bid to acquaint himself with the prevailing winds and currents he would likely encounter on his voyage. Willis devoted little time and energy to the fundamentals of raft construction, since he "intended to follow no ancient design, evolved and proven by the masters of past centuries." His plan was simply to build "a raft one man could sail and that would not come apart," if such can be called a plan.

A wealthy friend of Willis's, Werner Woehlk, an industrial-
ist from Milford, Connecticut, agreed to back the expedition.
Teddy, for her part, laid down a few conditions for Willis to
meet in order to gain her full blessing for the trip: She requested that he carry a transmitter on his raft and take a course
of study in the International Code, a modification of the
Morse code in common use at sea. And she insisted he ship a
rubber lifeboat just in case his raft that "would not come apart"
came apart.

Willis made a halfhearted bid to accommodate her. He signed
up for a course in the International Code at the local YMCA
and even stuck with it for two weeks before he dropped out. He
informed Teddy that he'd decided to take a receiver rather than
a transmitter, so that he could get time signals to check against
his chronometer. Teddy, understandably shaken by the news,
asked her husband, "How will I know where you are or if something happened to you?"

Willis responded that men had been crossing oceans for thousands of years without radios and that, to his way of thinking,
carrying one would be a sign of weakness. "If I have to depend on a transmitter to give me courage," he told his wife, "I
have no business going." More to the point, Willis felt he
hadn't the time or energy to learn to operate a radio properly
and suspected that the conditions on a seagoing raft would put
one out of commission pretty quickly.

Teddy shifted her attention to the lifeboat, demanding that
Willis carry the sort of inflatable raft preferred by the navy.
Again Willis resisted. "Being more primitive," he allowed, "I
decided to take along a canoe, an Indian-built dugout. That
would be my lifeboat. It should be a seagoing canoe of the kind

used by Indian fishermen off the coasts of northern South America." If this sounds like a familiar sort of vessel, it should: Willis had hoped to spirit Bernard Carnot away from French Guiana in such a boat but was thwarted by the unfortunate availability of a seagoing smuggling sloop.

Willis arranged for Orlon sails to be made on City Island in the Bronx. He had the sextant and compass from his pleasure craft calibrated and purchased charts of the Pacific Ocean at the U.S. Hydrographic office in lower Manhattan. To economize, Willis bought the smallest scale available, which meant three plats to cover the entire area from the coast of South America to Australia, over ten thousand miles. Finally, he ordered one-and-one-half-inch manila rope, enough for lashing his raft together, and had it shipped directly to Ecuador. He followed on a snowy January day in 1954, flying out of Idlewild Airport (now JFK) bound for Guayaquil, where he would build his raft and from where he intended to embark on an open-ocean voyage of six to ten thousand miles.

Willis anticipated that, with any luck, his route would carry him from the Gulf of Guayaquil west on the South Equatorial Current and before the southeast trade winds to a landing on either the Samoa Islands or, missing landfall there, Australia. He anticipated a trip of four to six months that held the promise of ample hardship, particularly for a man Willis's age. He had turned sixty in August of 1953.

*   *   *

Willis's search in Ecuador for logs of a suitable size to build his raft was arduous and, for a good while, frustratingly unproductive. He was after balsa in the jungles and had originally hoped to find standing trees of three feet in diameter, but balsas of such girth are rare to begin with—thirty inches is the norm— and the big ones are all too commonly afflicted with what is known in Ecuador as *corazón de agua*, or "water heart." The larger trees tend to go soft at their cores, growing spongy and rotting from the inside out.

Worse still, balsa trees aren't cultivated in any organized way. They grow scattered throughout the jungle rather than in groves or on plantations and often in stands of a half dozen specimens or fewer. Willis was obliged to hunt them from the air in small planes he hired. He identified candidates by their massive leaves—up to four feet across—plotted the trees on a map, and then trekked in on foot for closer inspection. Most were too spindly for his purposes or were properly sized but diseased.

Willis also made his search a bit more difficult than it needed to be by insisting that male, or *macho*, trees were the only ones suitable to his task. One of his Indian guides had told him that the sap-laden *macho* balsas were far preferable to the lighter *hembras*, or females, for oceangoing purposes. Debatable, as it turned out, since the female balsa logs are appreciably more buoyant to begin with, a key consideration given that a raft begins to sink as soon as it's put in the water. The logs are guaranteed to become saturated over time and gradually lose flotation, so a voyage on a balsa raft is fundamentally a race between arriving at a destination or suffering the craft to become too water-bound to float above the waves.

Willis took the view that the male trees would be stronger if slightly less buoyant, and he had reason to be focused on strength. He'd been at his search for over two months, was hard approaching the end of March, and was mindful of the fact that the western Pacific typhoon season began on July 1. The trees for his raft would have to be located, cut, and transported to Guayaquil, where Willis, with little help, would need to construct his raft and provision it before setting out on a voyage that, to judge by Heyerdahl's expedition, would call for at least one hundred days at sea and possibly very much more than that. It appeared almost certain that Willis would be on the water when the threat of typhoons was greatest.

Willis had succeeded at locating a number of serviceable trees near the Clementina River in northwest Ecuador and was preparing to have them felled and floated down to Guayaquil when an American businessman with whom Willis had become acquainted in the capital advised him to hold off until he could visit the area around Quevedo in the Andean uplands, a region storied for its massive balsa trees.

So Willis flew north from Guayaquil and searched for several weeks in the jungle near Quevedo before he located specimens that were both massive enough to suit his purposes and not so deep in the jungle as to be unextractable. He marked seven towering balsas in the space of several acres near the Guayaquil-Quito highway, along with an eighth, slightly smaller, that he decided to take for insurance. As the native woodsmen prepared to chop down the first tree, a white cockatoo shrieked from its upper branches and flew away. A bad sign, they informed Willis.

Taking an ax from one of the men, Willis assured them, "All signs are good," and sank the blade into the trunk with such energy and skill—he'd cleared many an acre along the Brazos bottom in Texas—that the natives soon relented in their misgivings and joined Willis in the work. A swath was cleared through the

jungle, and oxen in yoked teams of six dragged the balsa trunks
to a proper roadway, where the trees were hauled singly to
Quevedo on a logging truck and rolled down the bank into
the Palenque River. There the trunks were lashed together,
weighted with banana stalks to keep them low in the water, saturated so they wouldn't dry and check in the sun, and floated by
a trio of river men down the Palenque on the two-hundred-mile
trip to Guayaquil. Delivered, the logs would end up costing
Willis eight thousand sucres, roughly twenty dollars each.

(The progress of Willis's balsa logs from standing trees to
raft flotation mirrored almost precisely that of the *Kon-Tiki*'s.
Thor Heyerdahl and his crew had enlisted the services of Don
Gustavo von Buchwald, a gentleman Heyerdahl referred to as
"the balsa king of Ecuador." Buchwald had a brother, Don Fed-
erico, with a plantation near Quevedo, and he had arranged for
Heyerdahl and his men to visit the area and harvest twelve of
Don Federico's giant balsas, which they then floated down to
Guayaquil, riding the makeshift raft in the company of two na-
tive oarsmen. Their logs were then shipped on a steamer to
Callao, Peru, the port of Lima, where the *Kon-Tiki* was con-
structed.)

Willis hoped to build his raft at the mouth of the Palenque
River, since he still intended to embark upon his voyage directly from the Gulf of Guayaquil. To that end, Willis had secured the assistance of a Mr. Henri Kohn, identified by Willis
as "the balsa king of Ecuador," suggesting that either the crown
had passed since Heyerdahl's visit in 1947 or the Ecuadoran
balsa business was filthy with royalty. Mr. Henri Kohn owned a
sawmill on the water at Guayaquil, and he agreed to provide
Willis free use of the facilities and a place to build.

It was already early April when construction got under way. Willis had for assistance four Ecuadorans and a Swiss, all on loan from the sawmill. Two were handymen, two carpenters, and one a mechanic by trade, with not so much as a recreational sailor among them. Things got off to a balky start when the Ecuadorans noticed that Willis's logs had been stained with blood from a nearby slaughterhouse—vultures feasting on a fallen steer had spent a night in overhanging tree limbs dripping gore onto the logs. A very bad sign, the natives told Willis, who responded with his usual plucky obliviousness: "All signs are good. . . . Let us begin, amigos."

Willis had no blueprint, not even a sketch to work by—the design, inasmuch as there was one, existed only in his head. He decided, chiefly due to time constraints, to cut no channels in the trunks for the lashings as Heyerdahl had but simply to bind the logs together, each to the next. He left the logs to lie just as they had on their trip down the Palenque from Quevedo in an attempt to keep himself "on the best of terms" with his logs and as a way of "making them feel at ease on the voyage." It probably didn't hurt that, just as with the chiseled grooves, repositioning the logs in the water was something easier left undone.

As the logs were of varying lengths, the raft wasn't built on the square, but rather the longest of the logs, at thirty-three feet, lay in the center of the pack and the others lay in diminishing lengths to the left and right of it. The raft was therefore longest at its center point, from stem to stern, and measured but twenty-eight feet on either side. Due to the natural tapering of the logs, the craft was twenty feet wide aft and eighteen feet wide forward. To keep the platform from racking as it rolled in the sea, Willis lashed three stout mangrove beams across the logs from port to starboard, spacing them out evenly from end to end. He filled in the gaps between the beams with more balsa logs, six of them, and then constructed a deck of split bamboo that could be lifted in sections to reveal storage cavities between the cross braces.

With two additional lengths of mangrove, Willis constructed a bowsprit that extended eight feet beyond the center log. It was to serve two purposes: first, as a jib boom for the foresail Willis intended to carry in heavy weather when winds were too treacherous to allow him to fly his large square mainsail, and second, as a forward support for the forestay of the mainmast, a stepped affair of balsa and mangrove thirty feet tall. The forestay was routed over the tip of the bowsprit and anchored to the balsa below. Such an arrangement would permit Willis to set his mainmast far enough forward on the raft to make ample room for the smaller aftmast he intended to mount as well. Willis hoped to carry as much canvas (Orlon, in his case) as possible, both for speed and as a hedge against the equatorial doldrums, when every square inch of sail would matter most.

Willis employed planks as centerboards, what are called *guaras*, a rafter's traditional substitute for a keel, but he decided against the native style of tiller, or sweep, that Heyerdahl had used on *Kon-Tiki*. These were, effectively, oversize oars and had to be manned virtually without interruption for the duration of a voyage. Since Willis intended to sail alone and was unencumbered, by ready admission, with a theory to prove or an anthropological ax to grind, he was hardly bound by rafting tradition and so opted for a more modern steering system that he intended to strap into place when he was sleeping or otherwise occupied. Willis bought a standard ship's wheel that he connected by steel chain to a wooden rudder. The rudder, in turn, was attached to a triangular mangrove support that pivoted on pins.

Popular opinion around the Guayaquil waterfront held that the whole steering rig would be smashed to bits by following seas in fairly short order.

For shelter, Willis erected a hut with a footprint of six by eight feet and a height of four and a half feet. Its framework was constructed of five-inch-thick bamboo rounds lashed together, and it was lined on the inside with balsa boards and sheathed without in a double layer of split bamboo. The roof was fashioned from galvanized iron topped with more split bamboo and an outer layer of palm leaves (strictly for cosmetic effect). The structure was situated amidships but left of center to allow more deck space on what would be the leeward side as Willis sailed west across the Pacific before the southeast trade winds. Windward of his hut, Willis positioned a seagoing canoe, a dugout produced in a nearby village. It had been formed from a red cedar log and was twenty-six feet in length and three feet at the beam.

Willis's stated intent was to depart from the Gulf of Guayaquil and beat to the west against both a north-flowing current and southerly prevailing winds in a bid to clear the Galápagos Islands, eight hundred miles offshore. Willis was sufficiently acquainted with nautical charts of the area to suspect that holding a westerly course from the Gulf of Guayaquil on a balsa raft (with no proper keel, mind you, just *guaras*) would be an almost monumental challenge. But he hewed to his plan in the face of unanimous skepticism from local seamen and fishermen who were well acquainted with the coastal waters and knew that, even in the favorable summer months, Willis's proposed route would be difficult to manage. For what was looking increasingly like a June departure—midwinter in the Southern Hemisphere—informed opinion held that Willis's intentions were sheer folly.

In summer the Humboldt Current, flowing north from Antarctica and parallel to the western coast of South America, is deflected to the northwest at Punta Negra, where the Chilean coastline juts decisively into the sea. For sailing purposes this means that a raft leaving the Gulf of Guayaquil, some two hundred miles to the north of Punta Negra, could conceivably beat westward to find the deflected current and ride it up and under the Galápagos Islands into the westerly equatorial drift. A difficult proposition at best in the summer; in winter, however, the Humboldt Current is much more forceful and the deflection at Punta Negra far less emphatic. So a rafter or even a proper boatman intending to bear due west from Guayaquil is all but certain to get caught in the northerly drift and far more likely to end up in the Gulf of Panama than in the vicinity of the Galápagos Islands.

Willis acknowledged that holding to the course he'd set himself would make for a "formidable task" and was "perhaps impossible," but as his Devil's Island adventure had illustrated, Willis was afflicted with an abiding affection for forbidding enterprises, and he declared that the overwhelming chances of failure "fit in well with the spirit of my voyage, to test myself in endless labor against almost hopeless odds." Willis professed to be at least half convinced that he could hold a westerly course with what he described as his "new type of raft."

With the craft nearing completion, Ecuadoran seamen redoubled their efforts to dissuade Willis from a Guayaquil departure, even enlisting a local gentleman who owned one of the Galápagos Islands and who assured Willis that a Gulf of Guayaquil departure would be disastrous for him. Tellingly, it was a European, a Swiss archaeologist/fisherman (odd combination, that) who finally succeeded at convincing Willis to change his plans. He'd recently returned from the Galápagos and, by sheer happenstance, ran across Willis in a restaurant one evening.

The Swiss was keenly interested in Willis's voyage, listened to a full accounting of his intentions, and then flatly informed him, "You can't make it." He assured Willis that the winter current would take hold of his raft as soon as it cleared coastal waters and carry Willis north to the counterequatorial current, which would route him east to Panama. Willis wondered if he might have his raft towed to Punta Negra and start from there, but he was told that the season was too far along for such half measures and that his only chance of success was to depart from Callao, the port of Lima, Peru. Willis was well aware that the *Kon-Tiki* had left out from Callao, seven hundred miles south of Guayaquil, but he'd persuaded himself he'd constructed a raft with sufficient innovations of sail and maneuverability to allow him to embark from wherever he wished and beat to his destination if need be.

But Willis's Swiss acquaintance remained unpersuaded. "It can't be done," he said.

Willis wrote to share the news with his wife in New York, who tried to convince him to put off the trip or, better still, drop it altogether. "It's too much for one man," she responded. "Everybody can see that. Better give it up, and we'll take our loss." But Willis wasn't about to give it up, or even postpone the voyage for that matter, since he feared that in a year's time his raft would have either rotted in the estuarial mud at the mouth of the Palenque River or dried and split in the sun. Willis couldn't give up now. He had far too much invested— "all the work and all the dreaming."

Willis cabled Teddy with the approximate weight and precise dimensions of the raft and instructed her to find a ship to carry the vessel to Callao. (This she was to do from her Rockefeller Center office in midtown Manhattan.) Teddy contacted Grace Line, which operated both passenger and cargo-passenger ships sailing between eastern U.S. and South American ports, but the company's New York operation was hobbled at that moment by a labor strike and their shipping schedule was very much up in the air. Teddy cabled back that there was no Grace Line ship with a hoist capable of handling a ten-ton raft booked for Puná (the port of call, thirty miles below Guayaquil) in the foreseeable future.

Once Willis had quizzed local shipping agents and had learned that no boat with heavy cargo gear was due in the area for at least two months, he cabled back to Teddy encouraging her to enlist the help of the Peruvian ambassador to Washington, Fernando Berckemeyer. Teddy made an appointment with the gentleman and visited him in his Washington office. While he was a bit flabbergasted that Willis intended to raft alone across the Pacific and pronounced the voyage "foolish, very foolish," Ambassador Berckemeyer added that "brave men must be helped, even to the utmost." He told Teddy, "Go back to New York and do not worry—you will hear from me."

And she did. A hasty settlement of the New York labor dispute meant that the Grace Line ship *Santa Cecilia* would soon be available to call in Puná to pick up Willis's raft and carry it to Callao. Fernando Berckemeyer also was pleased to pass along to Teddy the news that the government of Peru would grant free entry to Willis's raft and equipment and that Willis would be afforded full use of the Peruvian naval base at Callao for the completion of construction on, and the provisioning of, his raft.

Willis immediately sent for his wife to join him in Guayaquil, and she wept upon seeing her husband, who was worn and drawn, far thinner than she'd ever known him to be. When he escorted her to the waterfront for a look at the craft he'd christened the *Seven Little Sisters* in honor of the seven balsa trees that made for her foundation, Teddy fixated on the want of a railing. She could readily imagine her husband pitching overboard in the rolling Pacific and insisted, "You can't go without a railing."

Willis assured her he'd "rig up something," but he never quite got around to it.

A Grace Line launch towed Willis's raft to the port of Puná, located on an island in the Gulf of Guayaquil, where Willis tied up to wait for the *Santa Cecilia*. In what should have been the uneventful few hours before the ship's arrival, Willis was idling on his raft when a motor-driven barge, a tanker nearly seventy feet long and loaded with gasoline, warped away from the dock it shared with the *Seven Little Sisters* and was driven by a flowing tide in Willis's direction.

Willis signaled to and shouted at the captain, but to no effect, and when he saw that a collision was unavoidable, Willis positioned himself at the stern of his raft in hopes of making do as a sort of human bumper. He knew he had a few feet of slack in his

moorings, so Willis pushed against the steel hull of the oncom-
ing barge in a bid to absorb the force himself and ride the ten-
ton raft back out of danger before any damage could be done.
He succeeded in sparing the raft, but he had reason to suspect
he'd been ruptured by the strain of staving off the collision.
Willis retired into his small shelter and examined himself, confirming a tear in his abdominal wall, which he immediately
decided to reveal to no one. "I'll wrap myself up in rope if it
comes to the worst—out on the ocean," he wrote. "Nobody
is going to know about this.... Nothing is going to stop
me now."

Once the *Santa Cecilia* arrived, its crewmen prepared Willis's
raft for hoisting by lashing two mangrove timbers beneath her.
The cables of the winch harness were looped around the timber
ends, and the hoist operator (a man far more capable than
Willis had feared) lifted the *Seven Little Sisters* gently out of the
water and brought her onto the deck of the *Santa Cecilia*, where
she was settled onto a hatch cover and strapped into place for
the three-day trip to Callao in what was, commonly, a heavy
coastal swell.

On the trip south, Willis's fellow passengers plagued him
with questions and requests for photographs. Willis professed
to being "a little bewildered by this attention which almost
seemed homage." He feared that it was possibly "deference to a
man they thought insane."

The *Santa Cecilia* arrived at the port of Callao on May 10,
where she was met by a swarming contingent of photographers
and reporters. Fernando Berckemeyer had spread word of
Willis's voyage, and Willis and Teddy arrived in Peru celebrities. They were whisked through customs, Willis's raft having

been designated "accompanied baggage," and they were carried directly to the Peruvian naval base, where Willis was introduced to one of the commanding officers, who confirmed that the facilities of the base were entirely at Willis's disposal. A naval tug was then dispatched to the *Santa Cecilia* to tow the *Seven Little Sisters* into the security of the navy shipyard.

The following morning Willis went to work on his raft. The sails had to be attached, the running gear reeved, the radio receiver installed along with its generator, and Willis had to gather and stow his provisions, which, consistent with his nature, were not to be standard seagoing fare. Willis had intended from the first to "take only primitive food along to keep in spirit with my venture," but he'd been slow to settle on which primitive foods precisely. "This was," he wrote, "in true keeping with my usual philosophy that at the right time the right idea will come."

While in Ecuador, Willis had remarked on the strength and stamina of the local Indians, who, though relatively small of stature, were capable of carrying loads of three to five hundred pounds on their backs. An Ecuadoran acquaintance had informed Willis that it wasn't unusual for these men to exist exclusively on a diet of Andean rye flour, called *máchica*, mixed into a paste with a little water. This impressed Willis as the right idea at the right time, and he decided on the spot that *máchica* would be the principal food on his voyage, along with an Andean cereal called *cañihua*, which, according to Willis, "was supposed to have exceptional power to promote strength." He shipped fifty pounds of each.

Willis settled as well on the need for an Ecuadoran raw sugar, *raspadura*, along with forty cans of lemon juice as an antiscorbutic, a gallon of lime juice for variety, a store of instant coffee, a case of evaporated milk, twenty pounds of shelled corn and rice, and 120 gallons of fresh water stored in 5-gallon tins beneath the deck *(see photo page 72)*. Willis hoped to supplement his diet with what fish he could catch.

Each morning when Willis showed up to work on his raft, a naval officer would ask him what he would require that day in the way of labor and materials, and whatever Willis wished for, the Peruvian navy supplied. So Willis's work was far less of a chore than it might have been, and it was touched as well by the brand of serendipity that always seemed to hang about a William Willis enterprise. One afternoon as Willis worked on his raft, he was approached by a trio of businessmen. A Peruvian naval officer made the introductions, and Willis learned that one of the gentlemen was Sir George Nelson, a descendant of Lord Nelson of Trafalgar fame and the owner of both the Marconi Radio Company and the English Electric Company.

Sir George, on a tour of the South American continent, had gotten wind of Willis's voyage and had decided to come down to the harbor and see the raft and its captain for himself. He wandered around the *Seven Little Sisters*, took a few snapshots, and asked Willis what sort of transmitter he intended to carry on his trip. Sir George was shocked to learn that Willis had decided to go without one. "Without a transmitter in this day and age? What if something should happen to you?" he asked Willis, who confessed he'd failed to complete his code course and had concluded he'd rather not carry a transmitter he couldn't operate.

Sir George departed, saying nothing further on the matter, but he arranged for a Marconi emergency transmitter, the

Salvita III, to be shipped to Callao from London within the week. It was presented to Willis in a ceremony attended by local notables, which made it all but impossible for Willis to decline to accept it and mount it on his raft.

The Salvita III was a lifeboat transceiver with a hand-cranked generator, broadcasting on the 500-kilohertz mediumwave and 8364-kilohertz shortwave, both international distress frequencies. This particular model had been designed for use by two men: One man supplied power by turning a pair of generator arms while the other keyed in messages and listened through headphones for response. Although the radio would be difficult for Willis to operate alone and hardly compensated for his deficiencies in International Code, it would allow him to send brief, regular "all's well" transmissions, along with coordinates, and would serve to console Teddy with hope that her husband could raise a ship if he met with trouble at sea.

At the request of the Peruvian navy, Willis agreed to broadcast his position twice a day, at 11:00 A.M. and 6:00 P.M. eastern standard time. The naval radio operator was to respond with a simple "okay" as confirmation the coordinates had been received. News of contact from Willis would then be passed to the U.S. Naval Office in Washington, D.C., which would in turn inform Teddy that her husband was in communication and presumably safe.

Willis dutifully installed the radio on board the *Seven Little Sisters* and mounted its antenna atop his mainmast, though he secretly suspected that the aerial might not be tall enough to broadcast or receive a signal with any useful range.

What Willis had intended to be a week or two of final preparations turned into more than a month, and only on June 18 was he ready for a trial run, which lasted hardly more than two hours. The raft carried Willis and his wife, a couple of their acquaintance from Lima, and three Peruvian sailors. There was little wind, but Willis publicly professed to be delighted with the way the raft handled. (Later he confessed to Teddy that he would probably be a month or more at sea before he'd truly know how best to sail the thing.)

Willis set his departure for four days later, June 22, 1954. He couldn't be certain how long the voyage might take, as he still wasn't entirely sure just where he might be going, and he continued to entertain thoughts of sailing clear to Australia, almost eleven thousand miles away. Willis was dissuaded from the last, however, by Teddy, who made him promise he'd travel only as far as Samoa.

Nearing departure, Willis attempted to insure his life with Lloyd's of London, but the firm declined the opportunity, for much the same reason that private promoters and insurance companies had resisted Thor Heyerdahl's overtures: A trip on a raft across the Pacific was widely thought a suicide voyage. During final preparations on the *Kon-Tiki*, a contingent of diplomats had dropped by for a look, and Heyerdahl was informed rather famously by an "ambassador of one of the Great Powers" that "your mother and father will be very grieved when they hear of your death." The fact that the crew of the *Kon-Tiki* survived the trip and a collision with the Raroia Reef in the Tuamotus was still considered a bit of a fluke seven years later, as Willis prepared to embark on his journey.

In the hours before departure, Willis admitted, if only to himself, that his decision to carry but one set of sails was a potentially fatal mistake that could "bring about my downfall, condemning me to a drift that might never end." His fears were well founded. If Willis were to find himself on a raft with its sails blown to tatters, a vessel at the mercy of Pacific currents, it was readily conceivable that he could circulate, handed off from current to current, for as long as his vessel stayed afloat, without so much as seeing land, much less reaching it. That prospect must have been on Teddy's mind when she responded to Willis's assurances that he'd be on his raft when it came ashore by telling him, "Perhaps dead."

On the morning of June 22, Willis visited the harbormaster of Callao and requested official clearance for Samoa. While this sort of authorization was ordinarily reserved for ships, the harbormaster performed the courtesy of providing Willis with a document identifying Samoa as the destination for his raft. This was, by all indications, the only token of license and permission Willis sought or received for his voyage, and it was more a matter of vanity than anything else. Heyerdahl and his crew, by comparison, were so burdened with correspondence and paperwork in advance of their expedition that they were inspired to weigh the welter of documents they'd felt duty-bound to collect. Their folder tipped the scales at ten pounds.

Near noon Willis embraced his wife on the dock in Callao Harbor and climbed down to the deck of the *Seven Little Sisters* before a crowd of thousands who had come to see him off. Three Peruvian sailors attached a towline between Willis's bow and the *San Martín*, a naval minesweeper. The sailors were to remain on the raft for the sixty-mile tow, but even once they'd departed, Willis wouldn't be alone. He'd be accompanied on his voyage by a parrot and a cat.

The parrot is easy enough to account for. Given Willis's

experience in French Guiana, his salvation by parrots hacked in half and applied to the soles of his feet, Willis could well have cultivated an uncommon affection for parrots, which, conveniently, were widely considered lucky by Peruvians. It probably didn't hurt that Heyerdahl and his crew had carried a parrot along on the *Kon-Tiki*. Their bird had been thrust upon them by a well-meaning resident of Lima. Willis advertised for his. He put out word through a local newspaper that he was hoping to take a parrot with him, which immediately earned him candidates from all over Peru. The creature he eventually selected came to him from the company supplying the drinking water for his trip. The bird was bright green with a spot of red on his tail and a bit of vivid blue on his wings, and he was given to giggling and laughing and singing as if he'd been raised, Willis suspected, in a girls' school. Willis named him Ickey in honor of one of the characters in a comic strip Willis had labored over unavailingly years before. In the mouths of Peruvians, the name came out "Eekie," which Willis decided to go with instead.

The cat is a bit more of a puzzlement, particularly given the fact that Willis initially hoped to carry with him one of the feral cats that roamed the naval base. He'd identified a couple of likely candidates and had taken to feeding them in hopes they might grow to trust him sufficiently to allow him to get close enough to snatch one or the other up. (A man who would intentionally confine himself on a thirty-by-twenty-foot raft in the open Pacific with a feral cat could well be said to know absolutely nothing of felines.) A Peruvian submarine commander who learned of Willis's scheme and who was doubtless a cat fancier supplied him with a tame and lethargic kitten, a solid black adolescent Willis characterized as "sort of unresponsive," saying it as if this were a bad thing. He called the creature Mickey, the name of the other character in his comic strip, which soon became Meekie.

So in the company of three sailors, a cat, and a parrot, Willis waved a last farewell to his wife, loosed his moorings, and was towed by the *San Martín* across the harbor toward the breakwater. Yachts, launches, and trawlers blasted their horns and sounded their sirens as the *Seven Little Sisters* left the calm of sheltered waters for the wind-whipped chop of the Pacific. It was noon on Thursday, June 22, 1954.

The *San Martín* followed a westerly course through the afternoon and through the night, and with the coming of dawn the captain ordered his men on the raft to let go the towline. They had reached their mark—sixty miles offshore. Initially the captain hoped to take his men off the *Seven Little Sisters* by bringing *San Martín* alongside, but the swell was too violent, so he decided to lower a lifeboat for them instead. Willis wrote a last message to Teddy, confirming that all was well and that he would be broadcasting twice a day as promised. He gave it to one of the sailors, asked generally, "Do you think I will make it?" and earned by it no response from any of the three.

At 7:50 A.M. on June 23, the crew of the *San Martín* saluted Willis with a blast from their siren as the ship swung about heading east for Callao. Willis was finally and irrevocably under way. "Now," he wrote, "I had to learn raft sailing."

* * *

At first Willis steered west-northwest in order to put as much distance between himself and the continent as quickly as possible and head off the chance that a westerly gale might drive him back to land. Once he felt at a safe remove, he would bear more truly to the northwest, sailing with the Humboldt Current and before the wind. Willis experimented with the set of his sails and made lashings for the wheel to see how the raft would hold its course unmanned. The results were discouraging. The *Seven Little Sisters* tended to wallow, veering back and forth across a given heading as much as ten degrees either way, and threatening with some regularity to run up into the wind. This meant Willis would have to man the helm more assiduously than he'd hoped or intended.

As a half remedy, Willis wound white surgical tape around the midship spoke of his wheel, the spoke that would be at twelve o'clock when the rudder was parallel to the keel (the centerboards, in Willis's case). That way he could keep track of his heading from anywhere on the deck and more quickly make adjustments when the raft strayed from her course.

At 6:00 P.M. precisely, Willis cranked the generator on his transmitter and sent out his first message, knowing that his wife would be awaiting word from him. He thought little of the fact that he failed to receive the agreed-upon reply. He then wrapped Eekie's cage in oilskin and secured it in the cabin for the night. He located Meekie sleeping among coiled ropes near the mainmast and settled in for a dinner of *máchica* mixed in a cup with a bit of water and supplemented by a few spoonfuls of raw Ecuadoran sugar for energy.

His first night at sea, Willis was awake at the helm. The sugar helped, but nerves alone would probably have been sufficient to drive away sleep. He fretted over the construction of his raft, worried about the strength of the lashings and the soundness of the design. He feared that the masts wouldn't hold, the sails would tear. Hardly a quarter hour passed without Willis playing his flashlight beam on the rigging, alarmed by one spot of racket or another. Worse still, his general misery was compounded by the damp, chill weather; Willis wore both of his sweaters and his pea coat in a futile bid to stay warm.

The Humboldt Current, flowing north from Antarctica, is effectively a river of frigid, deep-sea water. When combined with the heat and humidity of the tropics, the result is a persistent haze, a dogged, bone-chilling fog on the surface of the sea and an overcast above that rarely allows for unadulterated sunshine. So there was gloom within and gloom without, and Willis had to struggle his first hours, his first days under way, to locate his customary strain of enthusiasm for the brand of adventure he'd embarked upon and renew his taste for "the Don Quixote trail."

It didn't help that he was beset by equipment trouble early on. His twice-daily transmissions of his coordinates continued to prompt no reply, and his new chronometer, tested for him by the Peruvian navy and confirmed to be a "perfect instrument," stopped working almost immediately, with Willis forced to resort to his pocketwatch for navigational purposes. The radio he'd shipped exclusively for time signals had yet to receive one, and he was obliged to pass the bulk of his first week at sea darting between the helm and the mainmast, where he worked makeshift improvements on the tackle and the rigging. "Everything was turning toward the primitive with me," Willis wrote. "A surprising lot of things had gone wrong since I left Callao."

Add to his woes the fact that he'd almost lost Eekie the parrot on his second day at sea. Willis's bird had very nearly imitated the feathered mascot of the *Kon-Tiki* right into extinction.

Two months out from Callao, the *Kon-Tiki*'s parrot had been knocked off a mast stay by a rogue wave and washed overboard. The men failed to notice that the bird was missing until it was far too late to save it, "far too late" being a relative term in this context, since almost anything that went overboard was straightaway beyond saving.

Heyerdahl and his men were well aware that they had no chance of stopping their raft. Even if they brought it up into the wind, the current would continue to carry it away from a bird, in this instance, or even a man. Accordingly, the crew of the *Kon-Tiki* had early on settled on a mantra, an unavoidable seagoing truth of open-ocean rafting: "Once overboard, always overboard."

Eekie was more fortunate. Willis had let him out of his cage to roam the raft, and the threat of a lurking cat had driven the parrot on its clipped wings up into the rigging. "Suddenly," Willis wrote, "he gave a squawk and flew out beyond the raft." Eekie dropped into the water and immediately started swimming back toward the stern, flapping his stumpy wings for propulsion. Willis held a stick out to the bird, who grasped it with his beak and held on until he was safely on the deck, where he became immediately and violently seasick. He was "a spectacle of utmost misery" and vomited heroically.

But apparently the company of a seasick parrot and occasional attention from what turned out to be a flea-ridden cat couldn't entirely dispel Willis's nagging sense of loneliness and desolation. He blamed his mood, in part at least, on what he called "my Stone Age 'disaster diet' of cereals and sugar," which Willis believed responsible for an ongoing bout of "merciless introspection." He traded off between sullen apathy and brief, fiery rages and found but partial consolation in the fact that the trepidation he'd known at the outset had largely dissipated. He was no longer afraid the raft he'd built would come to pieces at sea but instead seemed vaguely disappointed that it wouldn't, that his ongoing confinement was all but guaranteed.

Oddly, Willis's troubling sense of solitude was finally put to rout by the appearance of a brown shark. A slim, nine-foot specimen with fins tipped in white, the creature assumed a position at the starboard stern corner of the raft and swam along in the same spot, day and night, near enough for Willis to have reached out and touched him from the helm. Willis named the shark Long Tom and welcomed his companionship, though he was well aware of the brand of treachery Long Tom represented. "If I were to fall overboard," Willis mused, "he probably would have his teeth in me before I was fully in the water."

One might be forgiven for assuming that the constant sight of a nine-foot shark would have finally prompted Willis to tie a knotted float line to his stern in keeping with a promise he'd made to his wife. But even while puzzling over his possible motives, Willis failed to do any such thing.

* * *

After a little more than two weeks at sea, though he was prevented by the incessant haze from taking a proper sight, Willis calculated by dead reckoning that he was 150 miles or so due south of the Galápagos Islands. His mood had improved to the extent that the "nervous tension caused by many months of preparation" had largely dissipated, replaced by a brand of placid resignation. "I was sailing into the hurricane season but felt calm about it," Willis wrote, "more so every day." He claimed to have made his peace with the fact that the destruction of his rigging and his sails in a storm could put him on an open-ended drift. "I was mentally prepared for it," he insisted, "and the prospect was not frightening."

Nothing, in fact, was frightening to him any longer. Willis had noticed a creeping sense of detachment taking hold, a numbness, a "happy oblivion." Doubtless, lack of sleep had something to do with it, since he rarely dozed for more than fifteen or twenty minutes at a time. But whatever the cause, his logy state of mind could only serve to heighten his peril in a situation fraught with potential disaster. The weather was heavy, the seas were steep, the deck of the raft was invariably wet and slippery, and yet Willis confessed that his mind was "adrift in space with no shore in sight." With the passing of each day, he grew increasingly insensible of the lurking dangers until, finally and inevitably, catastrophe struck.

On the morning of July 12, after twenty days at sea and roughly one thousand miles west of Callao, Willis baited a hook with a flying fish that had found the deck in the night and cast his line off the stern of the raft. He'd made fast the end to a cross log and played out the full two hundred feet. Willis was hoping to land a dorado (more commonly known in the western Pacific as mahimahi) and had a bite in less than a minute. His catch sounded, and Willis struggled to bring it up to the raft, which was sailing at a good clip before a strong wind. The creature surfaced eight feet off the stern. But this was no dorado—it was a shark, a six-footer that Willis hauled onto the deck. He had no use for the thing but was anxious to get his hook back.

Willis gaffed the shark in the lower jaw and held firm to the handle with his left hand while, with his right, he reached into the shark's mouth to free the hook. The animal tolerated the procedure without flinching until, just as Willis worked the hook loose, the shark thrashed so violently that the gaff handle was wrenched from Willis's hand, jerking him off balance. He lost his footing on the slick deck and pitched headfirst into the sea. Instinctively, Willis reached back with his right hand for something to hold on to as he fell. He found the inside of the shark's mouth and was gashed bloody, nicking an artery in the process.

Weighed down by his clothes, Willis struggled to the surface already well astern of the *Seven Little Sisters*. "In one strange, all-seeing moment," he wrote, "I took in its beauty as it rose on the blue sea, white sails spread out in the wind—my golden raft, mingling with the clouds and receding with them, sailing away."

The six-foot shark, still thrashing and writhing, succeeded at last in rolling off the deck and followed Willis into the water.

5

Colleagues

WILLIAM WILLIS WOULDN'T HAVE been on the Pacific atop his primitive balsa raft (or bobbing forlornly behind it) in July of 1954 if Thor Heyerdahl hadn't mounted a similar expedition that embarked seven years earlier. Heyerdahl's letter of invitation to his prospective crewmates laid out the general thrust of the voyage with characteristic economy: "Am going to cross the Pacific on a wooden raft to support a theory that the South Sea islands were peopled from Peru," Heyerdahl wrote. "Will you come?"

A zoologist by training, Thor Heyerdahl was collecting specimens on tiny Fatu Hiva in the Marquesas when he first entertained suspicions that human and cultural migration in the Pacific may not have occurred in anything like the fashion leading ethnologists and anthropologists of the day preferred to believe. It was commonly thought that any movement of ancient South American Indians into the western Pacific was prohibited by the fact that the Indians had no seagoing boats. The archaeological record confirmed rafts and small coastal craft exclusively, and prevailing opinion held that an extended open-ocean excursion in either sort of vessel would have been impossible. Heyerdahl disagreed. Not necessarily because he was persuaded of the inherent seaworthiness of balsa rafts, but due instead to cultural vagaries among the western islands that suggested to Heyerdahl early influence from the east.

During his work on Fatu Hiva in the late 1930s, Heyerdahl had become acquainted with the local tribal legend of Tiki. Thought to have been both a god and a chief, Tiki was said by the natives to have brought their ancestors to the island from a country beyond the sea. Heyerdahl had already noticed that stone carvings on Fatu Hiva, on Easter and Pitcairn islands, and ziggurats on Tahiti and Samoa were remarkably similar in style and iconography to artifacts left by long-extinct tribes in South America, peoples predating the Incas. Legend held them out to be tall and bearded, white-skinned and not unlike many of the natives Europeans came across on their voyages of discovery to the South Sea Islands. Startlingly distinct from brown-skinned Polynesians, these fairer people called themselves *urukehu* and claimed to be descended from the first chiefs on the islands.

Heyerdahl's research led him to the Inca legend of the sun-king Virakocha, whose more common name in ancient Peru was Kon-Tiki, or Sun-Tiki. He was said to be the leader and high priest of the tribe of white men who'd left ruins of their settlements on the shores of Lake Titicaca. According to legend, Kon-Tiki's tribe was attacked by Indians from the lowlands and was largely massacred, but for the chief and several of his closest companions, who escaped to the coast and took to the sea.

Heyerdahl was convinced that Kon-Tiki and the remnants of his tribe had abandoned their home in ancient Peru in the sixth or seventh century A.D. and had sailed west on rafts to the Pacific islands, bringing with them their fair skin, their craftsmanship and artistry, their tribal legends, and their agriculture in the form most significantly of *Ipomoea batatas* and *Lagenaria vulgaris*—the sweet potato and the bottle gourd. Both have long been found on South Sea Islands, well before the arrival of Europeans, and both have traditionally been called by the names given them in ancient Peru, from where we now know they originated.

Heyerdahl set down his revolutionary theory of South Sea island migration in a book-length manuscript entitled *Polynesia and America: A Study of Prehistoric Relations*, and he suffered his argument to be met with ridicule by every proper anthropologist who came within sniffing distance. It was settled and accepted, for academic purposes, that migrations had occurred from west to east in or around the twelfth century, not from east to west six hundred years earlier, as Heyerdahl suggested. The reason was simple and implacable: no proper boats. Heyerdahl was told time and again that South American Indians could not have migrated to distant Pacific islands, given that they had nothing to migrate on. His protestations that balsa rafts could well have carried the ancestors of the *urukehu* across the Pacific generally earned the same response: Would you, sir, cross an ocean on a raft?

Once Heyerdahl had decided he just might, the *Kon-Tiki* expedition was born.

Heyerdahl's explicit and stated intention was to "test the performance and quality of the Inca raft, its seaworthiness and loading capacity, and to ascertain whether the elements would really propel it across the sea to Polynesia with its crew still on board." Heyerdahl had been assured that a balsa raft lashed together in the ancient method either wouldn't survive the violence of the open ocean or would lose buoyancy and sink in a matter of weeks.

For a nautical model and template, Heyerdahl and his men had little to go on beyond rudimentary sketches of native rafts made by early European explorers. Their balsa, twelve massive trunks, was felled in Ecuador, floated down the Palenque River to Guayaquil, and then shipped to the naval yard in Callao, where the *Kon-Tiki* was constructed. The nine largest logs were selected for the body of the raft, and each was meticulously grooved with channels in which the lashings would lie. Both the deck and cabin were built from bamboo. The forward stepped masts were of mangrove. A steering oar was attached by pivot to the cross log at the raft's stern, and the *guaras* or centerboards were fixed into place along the keel line. This setup was a departure from ancient practice. Traditionally, the *guaras* were maneuverable and were raised and lowered as a means of steering the raft, which made an oar or sweep all but unnecessary.

So Heyerdahl was largely correct in claiming that the *Kon-Tiki* was "a faithful copy of old vessels in Peru and Ecuador," and it was certainly a sufficiently arresting sight among the warships in Callao Harbor to rattle the Peruvian naval brass. The minister of marine, upon seeing the nearly completed raft, summoned Heyerdahl to his office to sign a document absolving the Peruvian navy of any responsibility for the fate of the *Kon-Tiki* and her crew.

Beyond the design and construction of the raft, however, Heyerdahl's expedition was to be a modern enterprise. While

Heyerdahl hoped to demonstrate that raftsmen on the open ocean could collect rainwater and catch sufficient fish to provision themselves en route, he would put his crew under no real constraint to do so. The *Kon-Tiki* would carry a full supply of military field rations donated by the Pentagon, along with the latest in survival gear from the quartermaster general's experimental laboratory—waterproof sleeping bags, Primus stoves, floating kitchen utensils, shark repellent, sunburn ointment, water kegs, rubber boots—most anything in need of testing at sea. The Naval Hydrographic Institute supplied Heyerdahl with its most recent charts of the Pacific, specifically the four-thousand-mile expanse Heyerdahl intended to travel, which was well removed from all established shipping lanes.

A corner of the *Kon-Tiki*'s cabin was given over to a six-watt shortwave radio that proved as useless as Willis's more modern incarnation until the raft was two weeks at sea and had cleared what Heyerdahl suspected was a "dead zone of the Andes." The radioman's signal, unanswered for fourteen days, finally raised a response from a ham operator in Los Angeles, a movie projectionist named Harold Kempel. He was to become a regular contact throughout the course of the expedition, a conduit for news passed between the crewmen and their families and for weather data forwarded from the crew to the U.S. Weather Bureau.

Unlike with Willis on the *Seven Little Sisters*, nagging, uninterrupted solitude was hardly a consideration for Heyerdahl and his crew. If anything, they had far too little of it, what with almost daily radio chatter from the world beyond and, raftboard, six grown men confined to a vessel no larger than the average living room. The phlegmatic Nordic disposition common to the crew (five Norsemen and a Swede) must have been a virtue, and it couldn't have hurt that the *Kon-Tiki* performed, even on gale-tossed seas, more capably than Heyerdahl likely feared.

Heyerdahl had worked out calculations predicting the potential loss in buoyancy of the balsa logs, and they performed essentially as anticipated, with their incremental saturation more than offset by the ongoing depletion of weighty supplies as the men worked their way through their water and rations and radio batteries. Only halfway through the voyage did the crew discover, virtually by accident, that it was far easier to steer the raft simply by maneuvering the *guaras* up and down rather than manning the tiller in two-hour shifts, so their watches became less demanding as the voyage proceeded.

Fish had turned out to be much more plentiful in midocean than seagoing lore suggested, and the crew of the *Kon-Tiki* dined regularly on tuna and dorado, most caught with flying fish for bait. Ever accommodating, those creatures would fling themselves onto the deck in the night, usually a half dozen or so, but twenty-six on a record evening. And they were joined on one occasion by a fish so rarely seen that it was thought in some quarters extinct. Skeletons of the *Gempylus*, or snake mackerel, had been found along the South American coast and in the Galápagos Islands through the years, but no one had come across a live specimen until Torstein Raaby, Heyerdahl's radio-man, discovered one lodged in his sleeping bag.

The elusive snake mackerel became almost laughably common thereafter, and there are very few accounts of raft and open-boat excursions following Heyerdahl's that fail to include an encounter with a snake mackerel or two (or ten). (William Willis, a credit to consistency, was about as interested in ichthyology as he was in anthropology. His snake mackerel, identified as a "rare mackerel shark," is lumped in with a bunch of flying fish in a Willis photograph that features, far more prominently, Eekie the parrot on a tour of inspection.)

Heyerdahl's expedition confirmed the general seaworthiness of a tautly constructed balsa raft on the open ocean and proved beyond doubt that ancient South Americans could well have negotiated the considerable distance from the continent to the South Sea Islands. The *Kon-Tiki* averaged a little over forty-two miles a day with a twenty-four-hour record of seventy-two miles. Food proved plentiful, and the crew discovered that a brackish mixture of sea and rainwater was singularly refreshing.

By late July the *Kon-Tiki* had endured quite enough squally weather and violent seas to have suffered for it at her lashings. The ropes had stretched noticeably, so the slick balsa logs now had sufficient play between them to present a fresh peril to the crew. As there was no decking to speak of fore or aft, a man losing his footing in a pitching sea could well have been crushed between the massive logs as they clapped together. Fortunately for Heyerdahl and his men, they were approaching land and so wouldn't require the raft to hold up for terribly much longer.

By the last week in July, the *Kon-Tiki* was almost equidistant from the Marquesas to the north and the Tuamotu group to the south, each about three hundred miles away. At first the steering winds and currents seemed intent on taking the *Kon-Tiki* directly between the two island chains and forcing her west toward Samoa, but with foul weather came a blow from the northeast, and the raft was pushed south toward the Tuamotus, an archipelago of low atolls and dangerous submerged reefs.

Bringing a primitive balsa raft to shore promised to be a testy bit of business, given the craft's modest maneuverability and its all-but-helpless drift before the wind and with the current. There was little or no close steering to be done in any meaningful sense. Heyerdahl and his crew would essentially have to wait until a chunk of solid ground was put in their way. On the evening of July 30, after ninety-two days at sea, the *Kon-Tiki's* lookout spied the low, dark outline of an island on the horizon. Consulting their *Sailing Directions for Pacific Islands*, the crew identified tiny Puka Puka at the northeastern extremity of the Tuamotus. Well to leeward, however, the island was already out of reach.

Two days later the men found themselves on a favorable course for Angatau, and for three days and nights they steered with that island's wispy cloud cover as their guide. Upon closing on the atoll, they could locate no opening in the surrounding coral reef that would permit them safe passage. They were close enough to smell the smoke from the natives' fires, the fragrance of the island's flowers. This was their ninety-seventh day at sea, which had been Heyerdahl's original estimate for the "absolute minimum time in which, in theoretically ideal conditions, we could reach the nearest islands of Polynesia."

Once the raft had been spied by natives on the shore, a greeting party was dispatched, two men in an outrigger canoe whose grasp of English began and ended with the words "good night." In leaving the lagoon for the sea, the natives revealed to Heyerdahl a gap in the reef that would accommodate the *Kon-Tiki*. Unfortunately, the wind was blowing from an unfavorable quarter, so the crew dropped all sail and attempted to paddle the raft ashore. Heyerdahl tried to enlist the help of the natives, but they preferred to stand idly on the raft's deck and smoke cadged cigarettes. Finally one of the natives, in dumb-show, encouraged Heyerdahl to start his outboard engine and was mystified when the crew finally convinced him they didn't have one.

A host of additional native craft was soon on the scene, and lines were attached from the raft to several of the canoes in hopes that the *Kon-Tiki* might be towed into the lagoon, but an ebbing tide defeated the effort, and the raft drifted west into the open ocean. A full three days passed without further hint of land. With Angatau as a plotting reference, Heyerdahl could now be certain of the *Kon-Tiki*'s course, which showed her drifting toward the Raroia and Takume reefs that served effec-tively as a barricade of almost fifty miles of sea. The raft was all but certain to crash and snag on one or the other, so the men planned for a shipwreck, provisioning their rubber life raft and establishing procedures they would follow once the *Kon-Tiki* had met with the coral.

The onset of a persistent northbound current drove the raft toward the Raroia Reef on her 101st day at sea. For some hours she drifted sideways, carried in by the swell breaking vio-lently on the exposed coral, which, tellingly, was host already to the wrecked hull of a sailboat dead on the *Kon-Tiki*'s course. By ten in the morning, the raft was but a hundred yards from the breakers. A last radio message was sent to communicate the *Kon-Tiki*'s coordinates and predicament before the men gath-ered on the deck, held to stays and guy wires for support, and rode their already weakened balsa raft into the towering surf. Waves broke over her, submerging the raft and driving her at last onto the reef proper, where the *Kon-Tiki* hung up on the spiny coral and took a battering from the surf.

One by one, the men escaped onto the reef. The tide was receding, exposing increasingly more of the coral, and the crew was able to hike across the outcroppings to the lagoon and then wade an additional seven hundred yards to the safety of a sheltered island. Their raft was visible from the shore, dismasted and abused by the waves but with her nine balsa logs holding doggedly together. The island proved uninhabited, and for a week the men lived on fish and coconut milk before natives from across the lagoon on larger Raroia Island spied their campfire and came to investigate. The tribal chief, educated in Tahiti, arrived to inquire of Heyerdahl if he was personally acquainted with Bing Crosby.

The crew was fetched away by the *Tamara*, a Tahitian government schooner, and the men were carried to the harbor of Papeete with the *Kon-Tiki* in tow, where throngs of Tahitians had gathered to see the *pae-pae*, the raft that had come from America.

In the appendix to his account of the voyage, Heyerdahl acknowledges that his theory of South Sea Island migration was "not necessarily proved by the successful outcome of the *Kon-Tiki* expedition." What the raft and her crew did demonstrate, Heyerdahl goes on to write, was that "the Pacific Islands are located well inside the range of prehistoric craft from Peru." Provided, of course, that the given craft is well constructed—the channels chiseled in the logs were key to the survival of the *Kon-Tiki* at Raroia—and the raft makes landfall before the logs soak in sufficient seawater to lose their buoyancy. Four months at the outside, to judge by Heyerdahl's calculations.

By this standard, William Willis's expedition was wanting on both fronts. Given his shortcuts during construction and his lone set of sails, Willis had run from the beginning the genuine risk of finding himself still at sea in six months' time. Or, more likely, finding himself beneath it. As a further complication, Willis was traveling alone, which all but guaranteed the sort of psychological stresses that Heyerdahl and his men had avoided by sheer numbers.

Theirs was a shipboard society of six. They read and discussed books. They traded off duties. They took meals together. They reassured each other. And even still, Heyerdahl had remarked a maddening sense of stasis on the open ocean, as if the *Kon-Tiki*, slow and lumbering on its best days, weren't moving at all but was instead just sitting in the middle of an "endless, all-dominating sea." The raft seemed a platform on which the crew was confined while they waited for land to come to them. The company, fortunately, made the confinement readily tolerable. Willis's term on the *Seven Little Sisters*, being solitary, promised more demons than Heyerdahl and his men had been obliged to endure. Worse still, Willis was traveling under what he readily acknowledged to be "shipwreck conditions." Since his Primus stove was unreliable, the fish he ate were chiefly taken raw, and early on he'd noticed a brand of despondency settling in that he chose to attribute to what was largely a grain and raw-sugar diet but that surely had its roots in his isolation as well.

Consequently, the voyage of the *Seven Little Sisters* functioned both as a practical confirmation of Heyerdahl's theory that a balsa raft in the Inca style could stand up to the open ocean and as potential occasion to bear out conclusions drawn by another sailor on another sea.

* * *

Two years before Willis's voyage, in August of 1952, a French physician named Alain Bombard had set out from Casablanca in a rubber raft, one of the early Zodiacs, in hopes of demonstrating that a man could survive adrift in an open boat by living on plankton and raw fish and judicious amounts of seawater.

Bombard's interest in the fate of castaways had originated with a shipwreck the previous spring. The surgeon on call at a hospital in the port town of Boulogne-sur-Mer, Bombard had been summoned in the night when a trawler struck a harbor breakwater in the fog. Though the weather was seasonably cold, a calm sea and the fact of ladders every twenty yards or so along the face of the jetty left Bombard feeling more irritated over his spoiled night's sleep than anxious about the threat to the ship's crew, who stood to be exposed to the chill water only an hour or two at most and were in little danger, given the conditions, of perishing from exposure. Then a fire truck arrived at the hospital bearing forty-three dead sailors in their life jackets, stacked one upon another like cordwood. "I think it was at that moment," Bombard wrote, "that the full measure of tragedy conjured up by the word 'shipwreck' was brought home to me."

Bombard had already been making an active study of the effects of privation on humans. He'd focused chiefly on the case histories of prisoners and undernourished populations in famine-ravaged lands, but he was quick to recognize that the plight of castaways made for a unique strain of privation in starkly concentrated form. As a scientist, Bombard was well aware that the human body can exist for ten days without water and thirty days without food, which left him surprised and puzzled by his initial inquiry into the general history of castaways, many of whom died within hours or a scant few days of being set adrift, yielding well shy of physiological limits.

Bombard's research revealed that at the time fifty thousand people perished annually in lifeboats, many seized by a strain of demoralizing despair that quite frequently devolved into madness and almost invariably led to death. Bombard surveyed the available case histories of castaways, acquainting himself most particularly with the notorious details of the wreck of the French frigate *Medusa*, which stands as both a monstrous example of what has come to be known as "raft fever" and a scurrilous indictment of human frailty.

The *Medusa* had sailed from France in the late spring of 1816 bound for Senegal. She carried a crew of 160 men and passengers numbering 240, including women and children, along with the new provincial governor. The ship was to travel in convoy with four other vessels, but the *Medusa*, the swiftest of the lot, had soon separated from the pack, and her inexperienced captain followed a senselessly treacherous route south toward the African continent.

Commonly, Senegal-bound vessels would bear well west into the Atlantic, continue south to the estimated latitude of their destination—St. Louis or Dakar—and swing due east to come to harbor. Such a route served to compensate for the uncertain quality of early-nineteenth-century charts and took into account that the greatest danger to ships of the day, all under sail, was inadvertent landfall, not storms at sea. The *Medusa*'s captain pursued a more coastal heading, which demanded he negotiate passage between Madeira and Porto Santo, through the Canary Islands, and approach the Senegalese coast from the north rather than the east, putting his ship in perilous proximity to the Arguin Banks off the western Sahara.

Sandy shallows extending upwards of forty miles to sea, the Arguin Banks remain a notorious danger to shipping, and vessels routinely steer a wide arc around them, but navigational miscalculations by the captain and his pilot brought the *Medusa* on a southeastern heading directly into the shoaly water. On July 2, 1816, the ship ran aground and stuck fast. Once all efforts to play out her anchors and winch her free had failed, it was decided that the *Medusa* should be abandoned. Land lay but twelve leagues to the east, roughly thirty-five miles, but the frigate carried only six lifeboats. They were sizable craft—two barges, a longboat, a pinnace, a port launch, and a yawl, all between twenty and thirty feet— but there was not among them anything close to room enough for 400 people.

Proposals to ferry passengers ashore held no sway with the captain, who decided instead to construct a raft that would carry everyone who couldn't fit into the boats and would be towed ashore by them. The ship's masts were taken down and employed as the raft's foundation, with planks nailed haphazardly upon them to serve for decking. When completed, the thing inspired little confidence. The raft was approximately sixty by twenty feet and only passably buoyant even unloaded. When freighted with 150 people, the deck sank well below the surface, and the raft's passengers found themselves waist-deep in the Atlantic.

Effectively a sea anchor, the raft resisted what proved to be halfhearted efforts to tow her, and the lifeboats soon dropped their lines so that the passengers among them might save themselves. The raft was left to drift, its half-submerged occupants left to die.

Initially, the raft's passengers were far too stunned by their plight to make any concerted effort to save themselves, but despair and disbelief were soon supplanted by a galvanizing appetite for revenge against the shipmates who had left them behind, a group including virtually the entire hierarchy of the *Medusa*, from the captain and provincial governor down. Enlivened by bloodlust, the passengers organized themselves sufficiently to mount a mast, fly a sail, and attach a makeshift railing to the submerged raft in what proved a futile bid to prevent the occupants from washing off in increasingly turbulent seas. A violent gale blew up in the night, and the dawning revealed a raft lighter by nearly forty passengers, carried away and drowned in the storm.

The raft had been provisioned with casks of wine and water, barrels of flour, and sacks of ship's biscuits, which were rationed out among the survivors. Only twenty-four hours into their ordeal, some among the group were already despairing of rescue, and no few of them voluntarily left the raft for open water. Come evening, a band of soldiers broke into and emptied a wine cask, and one of the drunken, deranged men took an ax to the raft's lashings, which earned him a quick, mortal saber blow from an officer on board. His besotted comrades mutinied on the spot, some taking their knives to the raft's bindings and others battling the modest band of officers with whatever came to hand. The fighting was fierce, with the underequipped mutineers, many of them conscripted from prisons, charging upon the officers, who were badly outnumbered but far better armed.

Survivors' accounts acknowledge a dementia among the mutineers, a strain of collective insanity that seemed to ebb and flow. They would abandon the battle, beg forgiveness from the officers, and then rejoin it, spitting and clawing like madmen. The fight continued through the night, depraved and grim beyond belief. The morning sun rose on sixty survivors, many of them hacked and wounded. This after only forty-eight hours adrift.

The water casks had gone overboard in the night; a little wine remained. All other provisions were exhausted, and the survivors began to complain of nagging hunger following, on average, a day and a half without food. A few of them attempted to catch a shark lurking nearby, but the venture failed. Others chewed their belts and gnawed their clothing, while a significant number of survivors began, on but their third day at sea, to eat of the dead. By the following morning, cannibalism was the rule aboard the raft. Those who had died in the night were pitched into the water, save one carcass for feeding. Human flesh was mixed with that of flying fish to make it more palatable.

On day four the black sailors among the castaways, in league with a few Spaniards and Italians, launched an insurrection against the remaining officers. A spasm of close fighting and butchery ensued, in which the officers again prevailed. The cost was twenty dead. Ten of the thirty survivors were grievously wounded, and the rest were afflicted with what was identified as a "malaise"—a strain of emotional lethargy that was touched with paranoia and enlivened by hallucinations. The prevailing view among those castaways still sane enough to care was that the *Medusa*'s lifeboats had never reached the African shore, had foundered or broken up in the surf, so there would be no rescue, and all on the raft were doomed.

The truth was somewhat different. Four of the boats, their passengers desperate from thirst, had chanced the breakers, and the castaways had been carried rudely but safely to shore. They were confronted, however, with two hundred miles of inhospitable desert between themselves and any trace of civilization. The heat was punishing. Water was scarce and brackish, and the survivors feared that the Arabs in the region would likely slaughter them on sight. The two barges, the most seaworthy of the craft, had continued south toward St. Louis and had arrived in the shipping roads before the town on what would have been the raft's fourth night adrift.

The barges came upon the *Echo* and the *Argus*, a corvette and a brig that had been among the *Medusa*'s original convoy. A rescue attempt wasn't organized until the following morning, when the provincial governor issued his orders. The *Argus* was to proceed along the coast to search for those castaways who had reached land and then locate the *Medusa* (the *Argus*'s draft was far shallower) so as to collect three barrels of gold francs hidden in her storeroom. Implicit in the governor's instructions was the assumption that the occupants of the raft were already dead.

And they were very nearly that, down to twenty-five after two sailors caught siphoning wine from the last of the casks were pitched overboard and two of the more severely injured castaways were executed so that their meager rations might be divided among the others. In the ensuing four days, ten more died, slipping away with no encouragement from their raft-mates. By the dawning of July 17, the wine was exhausted and the human flesh left to the survivors had spoiled in the sun.

That same morning the *Argus*, unable to locate any cast-aways on shore, was driven out to sea by a southwesterly wind, and the captain decided to take advantage by searching for the *Medusa*. He set a course to the north, and after a few hours' sail-ing, the ship's lookout spied some manner of makeshift craft riding low in the water. Fifteen men would be plucked from the raft and carried to the hospital in St. Louis. Of them, five would die in weeks, leaving ten survivors of the original 150 set adrift. The raft of the *Medusa* had been twelve days at sea.

For Alain Bombard the story of the castaways of the *Medusa* and their alarming descent into madness and depravity served as an acute manifestation of what he'd discovered to be a com-mon problem for shipwreck survivors adrift at sea. The uncer-tainty of their circumstances, the merciless sun, paltry rations (if any) of food and water tended to coalesce into a despair suf-ficiently morbid and headlong to make death seem welcome and all but guarantee it in short order. And yet the sea teemed with provisions and the stars overhead provided a nightly navi-gational aid to a castaway equipped to use them. Accordingly, Bombard couldn't help but wonder if a man supplied with only the rudimentary tools of survival could sustain himself on an extended drift in the open ocean.

Bombard approached the matter scientifically. He studied plankton, analyzing its nutritional value and confirming the rel-ative ease with which it could be gathered through the use of a small conical net that might double as a sea anchor. He then turned his attention to the fish most likely to be caught by a castaway equipped with a proper hook and line and discovered that they were comprised, on average, of nearly 70 percent water (the fresh, unsalted variety), with the balance going to protein and fat. But by Bombard's calculations a man would need to ingest almost seven pounds of raw fish a day to satisfy his body's need for liquid.

Consequently, Bombard contemplated seawater as a ready supplement. A physician, he was well aware that consumption of seawater in volume was sure to lead to nephritis—inflammation of the kidneys—and ultimately to death. If fish were scarce, however, a castaway might have little choice but to drink from the ocean, so Bombard acquainted himself with the chemical makeup of Atlantic water and discovered that a gallon of the stuff—while consisting in small measure of magnesium chloride, magnesium sulfate, calcium sulfate, potassium chloride, and calcium carbonate—was over a quarter sodium chloride (forty-five ounces, to be precise). This meant that a castaway could safely ingest but a pint and a half a day, and then only if the seawater were his sole source of salt.

In advance of his voyage, Bombard tested his findings by removing all salt from his diet but for that which he swallowed as seawater, a practice unnatural to Bombard but long observed by William Willis, who had survived for years on bland, unseasoned food, which had rendered him exceptionally tolerant of salt on those occasions he couldn't avoid it. (Adrift with limited supplies on a balsa raft in the Pacific comes to mind.)

More significant to the castaway than food and water was what Bombard identified as the "whole question of morale." Bombard feared that once he was adrift in the Atlantic in his open boat, he might prove weak against offers of help from

passing ships and thereby bring his experiment to an untimely
and unsatisfactory conclusion. He hoped to head off the problem by settling on a westerly route across the Atlantic, well out
of shipping lanes, and he calculated that between the Canary
Islands and the West Indies he stood a reasonable chance of
enjoying two uninterrupted months at sea. In the event that
"enjoying" proved an appreciable overstatement, Bombard decided to carry emergency supplies under seal, since he hardly
intended to mimic the castaway experience to the potentially
baleful end.

The craft Bombard settled on was "a sort of horse-shoe
shaped inflatable rubber sausage, some fifteen feet long and six
feet wide." The stern end was closed off with a wooden tran-
som, and a latticework of light boards covered the membrane
decking. The vessel carried a lone mast in the bow. We would
recognize the boat today as a primitive precursor of the ubiqui-
tous Zodiac, and Bombard's specimen was sizable enough to accommodate two passengers in relative comfort. Consequently,
Bombard had room for a fellow sufferer, and he found a volun-
teer in Jack Palmer, a recreational sailor who was short of both
cash and viable seagoing options. Participation in Bombard's
expedition held out the possibility of making a man like Jack
Palmer famous, if it failed to make him dead instead.

Bombard dubbed his boat L'Hérétique in acknowledgment of
the heresies fundamental to his expedition. He intended to
reach a predetermined destination in a craft commonly thought
incapable of navigation and was persuaded that he and his companion could survive exclusively on what the sea provided.
Worse still, Bombard's boat was a "ridiculous cockleshell" by
his own admission and was generally expected to stand up

poorly to foul weather. The unofficial consensus among French seamen was that Bombard and his mate would likely perish, and sooner rather than later.

L'Hérétique was towed from the harbor of Fonvielle in the early-morning hours of May 25, 1952, for a Mediterranean shakedown cruise in advance of the proposed Atlantic crossing. Her sea anchor, a sort of miniparachute that doubled as a plankton net, supplied Bombard and Palmer with their first bit of foraged food—a couple of tablespoons of copepods, which tasted to Bombard like lobster pudding and was pronounced by him "really quite a feast." (The stuff had met with appreciably less enthusiasm on the *Kon-Tiki*, where the flavor was described as something like a mixture of "stewed crab and wet paper.") It was the only food Bombard and Palmer would know for their first three days under way. Bombard supplemented his plankton with a daily dose of seawater, but Palmer refused initially to drink the stuff and made do with the condensation that ran down the sail and gathered in the boat bottom at night.

Both men suffered cramps from want of food and were comprehensively constipated, which served in Bombard's case to dispel the myth of the laxative effect of seawater. Though they'd trailed a fishing line almost from the moment of departure, they'd not known so much as a bite until the afternoon of the twenty-seventh, when Bombard landed a grouper, which was gutted and sliced into servings the men took raw. The carcass was then put into the fruit press Bombard had shipped specifically for this purpose, and Palmer and Bombard drank the liquid they managed to extract.

As the Mediterranean was rather cluttered with ships, Bombard and Palmer spent a fair bit of their watches avoiding collisions by attempting to make their low, tiny craft visible in the water. The prevailing wind and current carried them on a south-southwesterly heading toward the Balearic Islands, as Bombard had anticipated, but the fishing along the way wasn't nearly as productive as he had hoped. After their first catch, the men went so long without even a nibble on their line that Bombard began to think of the surrounding sea as a "watery desert."

Bombard soon noticed that even slight cuts and scratches he and Palmer suffered failed to heal and usually went septic—a consequence of their poor diet, he concluded. By then the two men had been living on plankton for a full five days, and the cramping they'd known early on had been supplanted by a strain of lethargy. "Neither of us," Bombard wrote, "wanted to do anything but sleep." They grew indifferent to the dangers of their enterprise, and Bombard recorded the onset of a pitch of lassitude similar to that remarked by William Willis after his grain-and-raw-sugar diet had taken hold. Bombard sensed that both he and Palmer had surpassed hunger and were bordering on starvation. "We were starting to use up our own store of proteins," he wrote, "feeding on our last physical reserves."

Worse still, a shifting wind was hampering *L'Hérétique*'s progress toward Majorca, the largest of the Balearics, and the men had yet to raise a response on their radio (all attempts to lift their antenna with a kite had been laughable failures), so they feared that their worried families might press officials for a search and thereby bring their experiment to an ignominious end. Accordingly, they decided to hail a ship, both as a means of testing their signaling devices and as an opportunity to pass along their coordinates to friends and family. In talking through the matter, Palmer and Bombard ultimately agreed that they had proved quite enough in the Mediterranean, had met their shakedown objectives, and would be best served by getting to Tangier or Gibraltar as quickly as possible so that they might embark on their true test in the Atlantic.

Upon reflection on solid ground, however, Jack Palmer decided he'd had quite enough of the castaway experience, and he left Bombard to continue on the Atlantic leg alone. *L'Hérétique* was transported to Tangier Harbor, and Bombard was obliged to fight his way against the prevailing current around Cape Spartel and into the Atlantic proper on the morning of Friday, August 15.

Like William Willis, who confessed only once under way that the time was probably ripe for him to learn to sail his raft, Bombard conceded as he entered the open ocean that he could stand to bone up on his navigational skills. Taking sextant readings, performing the attendant calculations, and plotting the course of *L'Hérétique* had fallen to Jack Palmer on the shakedown voyage, so Bombard was obliged to pass his first full days alone at sea learning to use the Cras ruler (a nautical plotting device), acquainting himself with the charts he carried and the declination tables, shooting sights with his sextant, plotting his position.

After a stopover in Casablanca, where he was greeted by the headline L'HÉRÉTIQUE LOST IN THE GULF OF CADIZ, Bombard set a course for the Canary Islands. He found conditions in the Atlantic far preferable to those in the Mediterranean. Bombard boasted of catching mackerel daily and growing to savor the taste of raw fish, and he pronounced Atlantic seawater "absolutely delicious," noticeably less saline than the Mediterranean variety and utterly refreshing. Bombard's plan was to call at Las Palmas on Grand Canary as an offer of proof that he could in fact go precisely where he wished in his rubber raft, "essential for the castaway who . . . must be able to reach the point he has selected." And on the early evening of September 3, Bombard succeeded at beaching *L'Hérétique* ten miles south of Las Palmas after a crossing of eleven uneventful days.

In preparation for the more ambitious leg of his voyage—the two-thousand-mile crossing to the West Indies that constituted the genuine test of the expedition—Bombard had the Puerto de la Luz harbormaster recalibrate his sextant, and he was pleased to accept the donation of a wireless radio receiver for daily time checks. Bombard settled on Sunday, October 19, as the day of departure, and he was towed from the harbor among a flotilla of well-wishers until he was released at last to raise sail before a favorable north-northeast wind.

As he had in the Mediterranean, Bombard carried emergency rations under seal, along with proper fishing gear that he was determined to make use of only in extremity. He was keen to endure the genuine castaway experience and soon found conditions in the Atlantic congenial to that end. Bombard was hardly out of sight of land before a following sea all but swamped his boat, soaking everything he carried, and then the sail that had seen him safely through from the coast of France to the Canary Islands ripped in gale-force winds. Unlike Willis, Bombard carried a spare, but he rigged the new sail imperfectly and had only just raised it when a gust carried it away—halyards, mainsheet, and all.

Bombard's only option was to stitch his old sail together as best he could with the darning needles and common household thread he carried, and from that point forward he couldn't eye the mend without a pang of fear. It looked to him "rather like a piece of scar tissue that threatens to burst." Like Willis, Bombard was threatened thereafter with the very real prospect of a sail blown to tatters and a helpless drift on the current.

One pleasant surprise for Bombard was the wealth of sea life that shadowed his boat, an "absolute shoal of fish that never abandoned me." Initially, Bombard rigged up a harpoon with a bent knife blade lashed to an oar handle, and he managed to land a dorado with the thing, a fish that provided him a natural hook in the form of a bone behind its gill cover. Bombard attached the bone to a strand of rope removed from the pontoons of his boat and employed for bait the flying fish that collided nightly with *L'Hérétique*'s sail. From that point forward, he could dine whenever he wished. Bombard noted in his log, "Before I left, I was convinced that my chief anxiety would be to obtain food and drink, but it transpires that worry about equipment and the no less problem of humidity, are worse."

By "humidity" Bombard meant his wet, clammy clothing, which he was obliged to wear to conserve body heat. After his full baptism his second day out, his bare skin against wet fabric made for ongoing misery, but Bombard was persuaded that if he disrobed, the cold would surely kill him.

That said, by Sunday, October 26, after precisely one week at sea, Bombard's concerns over his provisions had been thoroughly allayed. He had all the fresh fish he needed and found the brackish Atlantic water not just serviceable but delicious. While he still worried about the strength of his mended sail, the thing was holding together better than Bombard had feared, and he was careful to lower it in high, squally winds to preserve the stitching from undue strain. His wet clothes kept him adequately warm, and Bombard's leading complaint, after seven days on the open Atlantic in a rubber boat, was undue chafing.

Far more troubling was the fact that Bombard had already lost track of his longitude and had resorted to estimates and speculative corrections. He'd misjudged both the horizon and the accurate time on his first sight and would prove to be off by a full ten degrees, the equivalent of six hundred nautical miles. His latitude he could readily establish with his sextant by measuring the height of the sun above the horizon at midday, but calculating longitude is a bit more complicated and calls for a relative measure of the change in the sun's zenith from noon to noon. Bombard was insufficiently experienced in seagoing navigation to recognize and remedy his error and so persisted in the mistaken belief that he was well to the west of his actual position, an assumption that would have a substantial psychological impact in the coming weeks.

In an attempt to remain the master of events throughout the duration of his voyage, Bombard had adopted early on a schedule of activity that he kept to daily. He rose with the sun and collected the flying fish that had collided with his sail in the night (between five and fifteen every morning). He would eat the two largest for breakfast and then would fish for an hour, using the others for bait. He could reliably haul in the day's food in that time and would divide the catch into lunch and dinner portions. Given the curious nature of his diet—raw fish and plankton sluiced down with either seawater or rainwater—Bombard had decided to observe a strict dining schedule on the theory that his stomach had "acquired the habit of secreting certain gastric juices at certain times in order to digest the food it received."

Every morning after fishing, Bombard would pass an hour in inspection of his boat. He had reason to fear that friction might wear the coating off the canvas (a layer of paint over a layer of rubber), so he took pains to examine every inch of the craft above the water line each morning and did discover on one occasion a tiny bubbling leak that he succeeded in patching with a substance of a "physiological nature," which is to say a dab of yesterday's transmogrified dorado lunch.

Boat inspection was evermore followed by thirty minutes of exercise, after which Bombard would deploy his conical net to collect the two spoonfuls of plankton he took daily as an antiscorbutic. At eleven-thirty he would break out his sextant and practice with it in the pitching boat for a half hour before taking his noon sight. After a couple of weeks of this, Bombard was rarely more than a mile or two off on his latitude. Lunch followed and was succeeded by a seagoing medical checkup at two o'clock. Bombard took his blood pressure and temperature daily and then examined the state of his "skin, nails and hair, condition of the mucous membranes; noting the sea and air temperatures, humidity and weather conditions." He customarily closed out the session with an assessment of his "state of mind and morale" and then would turn to his books and read or translate until the sun had finally passed behind his sail and he was afforded a bit of shade.

Come evening, Bombard would perform a urinalysis and record the day's activities, including a description of the fish he'd caught and eaten, the taste and quantity of the plankton he'd choked down, and a catalog of the seabirds he'd spied.

Dinner followed, and Bombard usually capped off the day by listening to his radio for a couple of hours. In the course of what turned out to be a sixty-five-day trip, Bombard heard broadcasts of Schubert's Seventh Symphony no fewer than six times, often enough to grow to consider it the "signature tune" of the voyage.

Driven by northeast trade winds in a craft that proved surprisingly stable, Bombard made steady and, given the possibilities, rather untroubled progress. He endured the occasional squall; was menaced by an infuriated swordfish for a full twelve hours; suffered (to his great surprise) from the crushing effects of solitude on the open ocean; hooked one evening a "long, thin, villainous-looking fish, with a mouthful of vicious teeth," which he learned only later to be the not-so-elusive snake mackerel; all while engaging in wildly optimistic speculation on his progress.

On October 31, Bombard recorded in his log his assumption that he was covering eighty miles a day. The *Kon-Tiki*, on her best day, with appreciably more canvas, made seventy-two miles. More usually, Heyerdahl's raft managed forty to fifty miles a day, while *L'Hérétique* was probably covering thirty-five to forty. But Bombard's "stupidly optimistic" estimate was buttressed and confirmed by his faulty longitudinal calculations. After less than two weeks at sea, Bombard was convinced he'd already traveled a quarter of his route, almost seven hundred miles.

Although he troubled himself to note in his log, "Navigation is by no means a simple affair," Bombard hardly seemed to believe it, and he grew to be emotionally invested in his wayward prediction that he would reach the West Indies by the third week in November, specifically the twenty-third. On Wednesday, November 5, Bombard looked on as a flock of shearwaters attacked a school of flying fish, and he remarked how curious it was to find such birds so far out to sea. At the time, however, he was hardly sixty miles north of the Cape Verde Islands off the coast of Mauritania.

While Bombard aimed to prove that castaways could survive adrift without provisions other than those the ocean offered, his voyage was wanting in a key element of the castaway experience: stark uncertainty. Bombard had a chart of the Atlantic, a sextant, a wireless receiver, and faith enough in his calculations to believe that he would reach land (Guadeloupe) on a specific date. So he was essentially a man making a trip in a perilously small craft, a doctor out actively testing his theory of foraging at sea. It wasn't until the third week of November had come and gone with no land in sight that Bombard's experiment took on a more authentic cast.

On November 22, Bombard confessed in his log, "In spite of myself, I do nothing but scan the horizon." He believed he was within one hundred miles of land, though he was very probably not within one thousand. Bombard pledged to himself he wouldn't lose heart unless he had failed to see land by Tuesday, December 2. "If nothing has happened by then," he wrote, "I shall be completely baffled." He carried several pertinent reference texts with him, including a pilot book and a castaway's handbook, and Bombard scoured sea and sky for what the authors of each assured him would be signs of landfall in the offing. A large barracuda off the stern of *L'Hérétique* impressed Bombard as confirmation that Guadeloupe was at hand, as did the appearance of frigate birds and shearwaters, which Bombard's handbooks informed him never ventured more than a couple of hundred miles to sea.

But still the days passed with no sight of land. *L'Hérétique* was by turns becalmed and storm-battered, and Bombard suffered an ongoing bout of diarrhea, some of it bloody. By December 5, he pronounced himself "completely baffled" as to his position and elected to concentrate his accumulating ire on the offenders he had at hand:

> If the dinghy is thrown up with me as a corpse, I have only one request, and that is that someone goes and boxes the ears of the author of this Castaways' Handbook. It only serves to demoralise anyone who has been unfortunate enough to buy it.

He was equally irritated with the author of his pilot book, whose information on the strength and persistence of the trade winds impressed Bombard as so terribly unreliable as to suggest that the man had never set foot on a ship without an engine.

Finally, Bombard's simmering rage and his open ignorance of his true position served to make of him a castaway at last. He took in his log increasingly malicious delight in pointing out inconsistencies from text to text and in waxing corrosive on the demoralizing effect of authoritative misinformation. When Bombard caught a triggerfish, he was reluctant to eat it, since one of his handbooks pronounced the creature edible while another insisted it was poisonous. "You would think," Bombard wrote, "that those who have studied the problems of castaways would agree about something." He cataloged exhaustive evidence of seabirds ranging far more widely across the water than

his texts allowed, and in noting that the various claims and limits in the books were "tripe," Bombard went on to observe that
such faulty information only served "to lower one's morale."
He confessed in his log that he must have been mad to put his
faith in books written by "specialists."

Even though he was holding his own physiologically, Bombard's continued drift into December confounded all his expec-
tations, and his spirits flagged to the point that he recorded his
last wishes in the event that he was dead when *L'Hérétique* finally washed ashore. But Wednesday, December 10, brought
what Bombard took for a miracle. He awoke to find a British
steamer, the *Arakaka*, a mere two miles off his starboard quarter. Bombard signaled her with his heliograph, and when she
eased alongside him, Bombard asked for his exact longitude,
only to discover that he was six hundred miles east of Barbados.
It was a shocking bit of news, and Bombard considered abandoning the voyage on the spot. He'd been at sea fifty-three
days, and he tried to convince himself that "that must prove
something." He couldn't help, however, but suspect that his
critics would write off the entire expedition as a failure if Bombard allowed *L'Hérétique* to be taken on board the *Arakaka* and
he accepted passage the captain offered to the port of Georgetown in British Guiana.

Instead Bombard permitted himself only a shower and a light
meal. He sent a reassuring telegram to his wife and then slipped
over the rail and climbed down to *L'Hérétique*, his home for
what he anticipated to be another two and a half weeks at sea.
In his log entry for the day, Bombard wrote, "I have to admit I
very nearly stayed on board." He added, "Morale high, but I
still have it in for the specialists."

In what proved to be the twelve days he needed to reach land, Bombard suffered a quartet of swampings from following seas and so knew occasion to perfect his technique of bailing with a shoe, which came in especially handy once a large fish (probably a shark) had rubbed its rough back on the underside of the raft, thereby stripping away the waterproofing and causing the membrane to seep. Most significantly, Bombard suffered pronounced ill effects from the meal he'd taken on the *Arakaka*. Though only an egg, a small piece of liver, and a bit of cabbage, the shipboard snack constituted such a radical departure from Bombard's seagoing diet that his stomach became "prey to a sort of despair."

In accepting a more normal form of nourishment, Bombard had tempted his system to believe that the deprivation was over, and he described himself as "rather like an athlete who stops in the middle of a race and finds he cannot start again." Bombard simply lost his taste for fish, had difficulty choking it down, and suffered, as a result, malnourishment for the first time in his voyage. He lost more weight in the final twelve days of his trip than in the first fifty-three, endured the brand of hunger pangs and cramps he'd not known since his shakedown cruise, and became anemic. He dreamed of food and hailed a passing Dutch cargo ship almost within sight of Barbados simply "to see if they would give me something to eat—not fish."

At half past midnight on December 22, Bombard spied the reflected flash of a lighthouse in the night sky. At last he was actually approaching land, the north coast of Barbados. By daybreak *L'Hérétique* was only a few miles off the island. Bombard located an inviting stretch of beach on the eastern shore and made for it through the surging breakers. Three native fishermen leaped from their own boat and climbed aboard Bombard's as if to offer assistance. Instead two of them picked through Bombard's possessions while the third tried to talk him out of his wristwatch. Bombard escaped into the surf with *L'Hérétique*'s anchor in hand and hauled his boat and new crew to shore.

Bombard claimed that the voyage of *L'Hérétique* demonstrated that "the sea itself provides sufficient food and drink to enable the battle for survival to be fought with perfect confidence." The weight loss and anemia he suffered following his meal on the *Arakaka* were, by Bombard's reckoning, the greatest dangers to his health and "very nearly fatal." He endured a two-week attack of diarrhea in the course of his journey, effectively lost consciousness twice, and registered a curious correlation between his blood pressure and his state of mind. As his despair heightened, his blood pressure plunged dangerously, making his psychology far more of a threat to his survival than was any want of supplies. Bombard closes his account of his ordeal with an invitation to those sailors tempted by the promise of fame to set off in a raft on an ocean crossing. "Come see me first," he writes, fearing they might not realize "how desperate is the fight for life until it is too late."

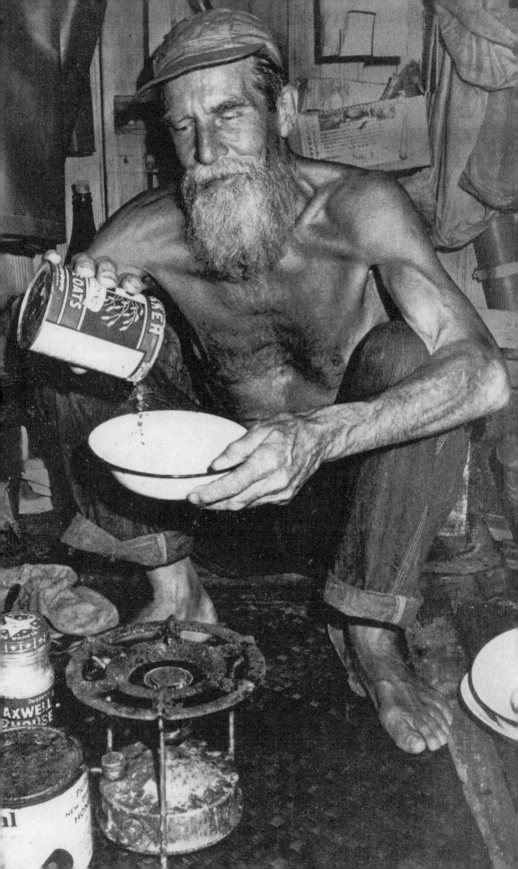

6

Calamities

WITH HIS RAFT SAILING away from him before a brisk wind in the rolling open Pacific, William Willis had all he needed of desperation. He made a brief, fruitless attempt to close the distance by swimming and was beginning to yield to grim resignation when he felt a tug at his shoulder and discovered that his fishing hook had snagged on his shirtsleeve. Willis took a quick turn of the leader around his right hand—his good hand—and waited for all two hundred feet of the line to play out.

This was a chance at salvation, but it was only a chance and perhaps no more than a slim one. While Willis had shipped new, stout fishing line from New York, it was still coiled and stowed on the raft. The line he held on to now, the line that would save him if anything could, had been given to him by a tuna fisherman in Callao. It was worn, even visibly frayed in places, and the fisherman had effectively discarded it in Willis's direction, convinced that the next striking tuna would likely snap it in two. Ever thrifty, Willis had decided to use the line until it broke, and now he had reason to fear that it just might.

At over twice the weight of the average yellowfin, Willis couldn't simply reel himself in, hand over hand, without running an overwhelming risk of parting the line. He had to kick and swim, gathering slack as the raft crested each swell, pausing before its descent. He'd been dressed against the chill air, and his clothing was leaden, so the task of reaching the raft would have been sufficiently daunting without Willis's wound to complicate matters:

> My left hand was gashed, and streaming with blood, dyeing the water around me and leaving a broad, red trail. Where was Long Tom? I wondered.

Where indeed? Long Tom had been at the aft corner of the *Seven Little Sisters* for days by then and was surely lurking somewhere nearby. In the few weeks he'd been at sea, Willis had seen enough sizable sharks—"any one of which could take off a leg with one snap of the jaws"—to be persuaded that the Pacific was fairly alive with them. And there he was thrashing in the water and "spouting blood" at the business end of a fishing line, bait personified.

The condition of the line demanded that Willis work toward the raft slowly, deliberately, creeping forward foot by foot, while his blood in the water all but guaranteed sharks. He took occasion to settle on a response if attacked, deciding he would kick at the beasts with what strength he could muster and pound their snouts with his fist. "I had fought sharks," Willis wrote, "and I knew them to be cowards but strong, cunning, and persistent." He realized, though, that he could hope to fend off only a shark of middling size: "A big one like Long Tom would of course make short work of me."

At an almost glacial pace, Willis closed on the raft. He was careful to keep steady force on the weakened line—no mean chore in the rolling Pacific—and after what seemed an age to him, Willis finally reached the spot where the line slanted out of the water, angling up to the raft's rear cross log, to which it was attached. Willis succeeded at drawing close enough to grab on to the iron rudder, and he worked his fingers into the lengths of the chain that controlled it. With what strength remained in his hands, he heaved himself onto the raft and collapsed to the deck.

Willis was hardly in fit shape, however, to sprawl and relish his salvation, since blood still flowed freely from his nicked artery. He wrapped a length of the frayed fishing line around his forearm, made a tourniquet with a marlin spike, and lifted his arm above his head until the blood had slowed. Willis then examined his wound and discovered that the artery on the underside of his wrist had been "grazed but not severed." He stitched it closed as best he could with a sewing needle and thread, slathered on a coating of Vaseline, and wrapped the gory mess in a bandage before moving on to other complaints. "I lay down flat on my back," Willis wrote, "and worked a few minutes pushing in my rupture."

At that moment Willis recalled a promise he'd made to his wife, the same wife who'd asked him to take a radio course he'd never completed and carry a rubber lifeboat he'd shunned in favor of a far less seaworthy dugout canoe, the wife who routinely "begged me to cut the line and forget about the hook." Willis had promised Teddy "to keep a rope or two trailing from the raft at all times," knotted float lines he might have used to haul himself back on board with ease. Now he finally got around to attaching a couple of lines to serve for salvation in a pinch.

By July 14, two days later, Willis calculated that he'd cleared the Galápagos Islands and was over one thousand miles from Callao. He set a southwesterly course in a bid to avoid the equatorial doldrums and complained of the difficulties of taking a serviceable midday sight. The weather continued overcast, and Willis noted that the "incessant movement of the raft and its low position in the sea" made a level horizon elusive. His remedy was to shoot twenty to twenty-five sights every noon with his sextant and then calculate an average. (Compare that to Alain Bombard's process of practicing for fifteen minutes before each noon hour and then shooting a solitary sight, and Bombard's compounded miscalculations seem almost inevitable.)

Willis's experience both as an able-bodied seaman and as a recreational sailor proved sufficient to drive the uncertainty from navigation for him. So day by day he remained confident of his position through either informed calculations or dead reckoning, though it turned out nobody else had any idea where he might be. Willis had been suspicious of the usefulness of his transmitter even before he'd launched and was convinced that the radio aerial on his mast rode far too low (only thirty feet above the sea) to project or receive a signal of any worthwhile gain. He'd dutifully switched on the set every evening and tapped out his position, but Willis had raised no response and had concluded that the only properly functioning feature on his Marconi Salvita III was its brightly glowing indicator lights. Convinced he was sealed off and out of touch with the rest of the world, Willis chose to believe that his wife had by then "steeled herself to the silence that had swallowed me."

Possibly so, since on June 24, following forty-eight hours

without contact, Peruvian authorities had officially declared William Willis lost at sea.

* * *

Like Bombard and Heyerdahl before him, Willis had discovered that gathering food on a low-lying craft in the open ocean wasn't terribly much of a challenge. He had intended all along to supplement his *máchica*-and-*raspadura* diet with whatever fish he could catch, only to find that the fish were, likely as not, apt to catch themselves. Flying fish in particular were plentiful and more than a bit of a hazard. Willis complained of being struck in the head and chest by the creatures on several occasions, and he was obliged to compete with Meekie the cat for every specimen that came aboard.

The thump and flop of a flying fish would frequently bring Willis forward from the tiller and Meekie aft from the coil of rope where she slept, and they would race to the spoils. If the cat won, she would carry the fish beneath the deck and feast on it atop one of the main logs, out of Willis's reach. If Willis triumphed, he would attempt to cook the thing on his balky stove. After little more than three weeks at sea, Willis was down to his single-burner spare, since his two-burner primary stove had already given out. Sometimes the spare lit. More often it didn't. So, unlike Bombard, who ate raw fish and drank fish juice by design, Willis ended up dining on uncooked fish flesh far more frequently than he'd intended, though he grew to savor it.

Willis was hardly condemned to flying fish exclusively, even among those creatures delivering themselves up for a meal. As opposed to a hulled craft, or even Bombard's Zodiac with its solid bottom, Willis's balsa raft was more *of* the sea than *on* it.

The construction, with lashed balsa timbers of imperfect fit beneath split-bamboo decking, allowed for the free movement of water up from below and down from above and made for a vessel that, while unswampable, was often slightly beneath the waves. Accordingly, it wasn't uncommon for fish to wash onto the deck and get stranded there once the sea had drained away.

Ordinarily, this sort of thing made do as welcome and labor-saving, but in sizable swells the leavings could get a little out of hand. Willis remarked, as had Heyerdahl before him, the curious sensation of riding his raft into a trough and seeing, in a wave looming before him, assorted substantial marine specimens head-high or higher. Heyerdahl was reminded of gazing into an aquarium, and as the swell rolled by and the sea hissed through the bamboo and drained between the logs, the craft would occasionally function as a sort of strainer and catch the odd swordfish or ray or man-size shark.

So fresh food quite frequently supplied itself, leaving Willis largely free to sail the raft, which was proving far more of a chore than he'd anticipated. "This was not sailing according to the rules," he discovered. "I covered miles on the deck in brief minutes, climbing and jumping from one end of the raft to the other." Willis carried three sails—a main, a jib forward, and a mizzen aft—and he had passed his first weeks at sea in an ongoing attempt to perfect the rigging so that he could more readily adjust his sails to the wind or drop them immediately with the onset of squally weather. Single-handed, Willis was having a trying time with the wallowing raft and found he was increasingly put upon to tend to mischief, was evermore trading off between adjusting his trim and manning his wayward helm. (And this in fair weather.)

Willis didn't meet with his first full-bore Pacific squall until the night of July 16. The sea went black, and the wind came up in such a frightful hurry that Willis was slow to drop sail, and the rising squally blasts had soon fouled his lines and frustrated all his attempts to lower the main from the deck. Ever mindful he'd shipped but the lone set of sails, Willis knew he couldn't stand by and risk his main blowing to tatters, so he began climbing the forward mast to gather the sail by hand. He ascended on a rope ladder that was attached at one end to the deck and at the other to the masthead, and from earlier experience in relatively calm seas, Willis knew the thing to be devilish to climb. It was insufficiently stout and taut to support a man's weight without swaying and twisting mercilessly, and with the raft pitching beneath him in the heavy seas, that ladder subjected Willis to fresh and unanticipated spasms of violence. The thing whipped and darted "like a battle flag in a gale," and it was all Willis could do to hang on. He was obliged to grip not just with his hands but with his elbows and knees as well, in what was an agonizing ascent to a fouled block that he succeeded in clearing. He returned safely to the deck but remarked that his rupture had endured "quite a time of it" and felt as if "another stitch or two had come loose."

Consequently, on the following afternoon, when Willis felt a sharp twinge in his stomach, he laid it off initially to his hernia, remembering the strain he'd put upon it the night before. But when the pain persisted and impressed him as something separate from his rupture, he decided it was probably some variety of stomach upset and took two doses of bicarbonate, to no discernible effect. If anything, what had commenced as a twinge was growing more acute. Willis noted a "continuous, contracting pain, increasing steadily," that was a "strange and entirely new" experience for him. "The whole front area of my body," he observed, "seemed to be drawn slowly but relentlessly into an ever hardening knot."

Willis had no history of stomach complaints and had soon ruled out indigestion or food poisoning. He returned instead to the suspicion that the general strain of climbing to the masthead the night before was likely the cause of the discomfort, which shortly began to flag and ebb but returned the following afternoon with renewed intensity. Again Willis tried bicarbonate, this time followed by a slug of brandy. The pain only increased, and soon Willis was sprawled on the deck "assuming different positions in the hope of finding relief." At length he began "rolling around in ever increasing agony."

He was mystified and, soon enough, utterly debilitated. The raft was left to sail itself in high winds under a reefed mizzen while Willis, writhing on the deck, resorted to hoping "the pain would become so severe that I would become unconscious and that during that time the muscles would relax and the pain disappear." But senselessness eluded him, and Willis remained agonizingly aware of "a steady, awful tightening" in his gut.

With some difficulty he broke out his various medicine kits. He had one from the *Santa Cecilia*, several donated by "wholesale drug houses," and a few supplied by acquaintances in Lima. Willis hoped to find morphine but turned up only aspirin instead, which he took in heroic doses, intending to "bring on oblivion." Still awake after an hour, he heaped aspirin tablets on the deck, "pounded them to a paste with water and drank it down." The pain only worsened, intensifying to the extent that Willis began to fear for his life and contemplated transmitting an SOS on the 500-kilohertz frequency in the forlorn hope that the signal might reach a ship in the vicinity.

Willis was sailing, however, along the third parallel south, where the westerly winds were strongest and merchant traffic almost nonexistent. His transmission would likely have to travel hundreds of miles to know even the slimmest chance of being received, and Willis's doubts about his radio and his reluctance to end his voyage in the event of his survival combined to leave him "twisting in agony" on the deck, where he occupied himself with a spasm of self-pity. "I saw no fairness here," Willis wrote. "I felt I had broken no law of nature for which I had to pay."

He gave passing thought to exploratory surgery with his long, thin fish-gutting knife and even contemplated suicide. He took still more aspirin and was writhing on the deck when the sun rose. Willis passed in and out of consciousness throughout the following day, yet he managed to drag himself to Eekie's cage in the tiny cabin to fill it with all the corn it would hold before spilling onto the deck a bucketful of flying fish he'd collected so that Meekie could get to them once Willis had expired. By now he fully expected to die, and soon.

Willis wrote a note giving the date, his last position, and the best explanation he could manage of what had befallen him. He then penned a separate letter to Teddy and tacked the pair of them to the cabin doorway. After an hour of resolutely not dying, however, Willis decided to send an SOS over the marine-disaster frequency. He cranked the dynamo of his Salvita III with his left hand while feebly tapping out the message with his right and then retired to the cabin for more aspirin, pounding the pills into an "enormous amount of paste" that he choked down to no palpable effect. It was by now the night of July 19, and Willis sat staring out the cabin doorway at the starry sky—still not dead, still not even agreeably unconscious. Then he drifted off, started awake, and realized he'd been dozing for a time. He noticed straightaway that the pain in his solar plexus had diminished appreciably.

Gingerly, Willis probed his stomach with his fingers. He was sore, but not acutely so, and though weak and a trifle addled, he found he could move around the deck relatively pain-free. Persuaded that the worst was over, he sent out a message retracting his SOS. He then ate for the first time in two days, celebrating his survival with a meal of rye flour mixed to a gummy sludge with water, a spoonful of raw sugar, and a cup of cold instant coffee. He capped off the evening by adjusting his long-neglected rupture while sprawled on the pitching deck.

Willis was later informed by his doctor that the cause of his attack had been a perforated stomach ulcer, which Willis had all but buried in aspirin after the initial twinges, thereby exacerbating a condition that is ordinarily repaired with surgery. (And not the long-thin-murderous-fish-gutting-knife variety.) That the symptoms abated, leaving Willis to face merely the perils of the open Pacific and the latent threat of a strangulated hernia, was construed by his doctor as a bit of a miracle.

The ordeal, however, left Willis with barely strength enough to stand. While he was incapacitated, the *Seven Little Sisters* had been driven west, chiefly on the prevailing current, since Willis had carried only his mizzen, and that reefed. The southeasterly wind remained brisk and favorable, and Willis knew that his best chance for survival, given his condition, was to race before it under as much sail as he could carry and so diminish his exposure to the heart of the Pacific hurricane season and bring himself with all possible speed into the general vicinity of landfall. With the Galápagos Islands already well to his stern, there was no earth for Willis to strike before the Marquesas, some three thousand miles ahead. He had a raft beneath his feet that was sure to lose buoyancy and sink in time, a mysterious crippling illness that was just as mysteriously in abeyance for the moment, a lone set of sails growing weaker at the seams with each passing day, and the ever-increasing likelihood—the longer he stayed on the water—of ordeal by typhoon.

So Willis had no leisure to be an invalid; he lurched around the deck—walking when he could, crawling when he couldn't— and made an all-day job of raising and trimming the mainsail and unreefing the jib. Too weak and distracted to trouble with his temperamental stove, Willis was obliged to effect his recovery on meals of rye flour and raw sugar. The flying fish to which he beat out the cat were soaked in lemon juice and taken raw.

*   *   *

Toward the close of July, Willis calculated he was over six hundred miles west-southwest of the Galápagos Islands. While he had yet to recover entirely from his two days of agony, he'd suffered no relapse, was regaining strength, and had come to be philosophical, in his way, about his prospects:

> I had never felt happier. I had come through a great ordeal, had been brought to the very edge of the end and been lifted up again. Nothing could really happen to me now to keep me down. How could anything be worse? I could fall overboard but that was all.

Though he was slow to regain his stamina and feared a relapse with every twinge and eructation, Willis's ulcer failed to
plague him further, and he entered August well on the mend.
The weather had lapsed into a welcome pattern of clear skies
and fair wind, and Willis's native optimism was beginning to
seem prescient, even a little sage, when, on the morning of August 6, he set about making coffee. As had Heyerdahl, Willis
stored his fresh-water cans under the bamboo decking of his
raft, resting securely between the mangrove crossbeams, where
they were lapped by the sea. This arrangement kept the cans
both ocean-cooled and out of the way and would surely have
been as successful a strategy on the *Seven Little Sisters* as it had
been on the *Kon-Tiki* but for Willis's penchant for misguided
corner cutting and senseless economizing.

While provisioning his raft, Willis had purchased cheap tin
cans to hold his crucial drinking water. Indifferently constructed, these thin-gauge containers had never been intended
for water storage. Willis allowed he had planned to coat the
seams and outer surfaces with tar, but he had "taken the easier
and faster way out, by painting them with a thin composition
not meant for the purpose."

So on the morning of the sixth, when Willis broke the seal
on a fresh five-gallon water can and took up the container to fill
his coffeepot, he was alarmed though not entirely surprised to
find the thing empty. When a second can, still under seal, be-
trayed by its weight that it was empty as well, Willis scrambled
to shift the decking and expose his entire water supply. He
moved frantically from container to container, only to discover
that almost all of his drinking water had leaked away. The bulk
of what was left had been contaminated by seawater, and only
two of the five-gallon tins remained uncompromised and full.

"The moment I had touched the first can and found it empty," Willis wrote, "I knew it was all my fault, knew the whole story. I knew they had to rust for they had been lying in pounding seas." This was altogether typical of Willis's pattern and technique. He would intend to see to a detail and carry out a job to its proper conclusion but would elect at the last to skimp in the execution, even while mindful of the perils of skimping. Only once the wages of his shiftlessness had been visited upon him would Willis acknowledge what he should have done and how he should have done it, embrace the blame, and steep briefly in regret before, most assuredly, repeating his mistake in some other arena at some other time. He wasn't remotely the sort to mine instruction from calamity or indulge in more than passing contemplation of his failings.

Fortunately for Willis, he had seen fit to stow an emergency supply of springwater in containers stout enough to hold and keep it. Unfortunately for Willis, those containers were paint cans that he had "prepared" by shoving a lit torch into each of them so as to scorch the residue. The cans had originally held lead-based paint, and somehow exposure to flame alone had been insufficient to sanitize them. Willis unhappily discovered that the water they held was tainted, was so foul, in fact, that he couldn't even bring himself to rinse his hands with it. He confessed he'd considered shipping a fifty-gallon wooden keg to hold his water, had planned to lash it behind the deckhouse in the stern of the raft, but procuring the thing from a chandler in Callao had turned out to be more bother than Willis could endure. "I had been in too much of a hurry to get started," he wrote, "being two months late."

Tardily and from a distance, Willis characterized the episode with his usual clear-eyed precision:

This had to happen to me, I who knew the sea and the laws of the sea, who knew that it is a crime to sail with all one's drinking water in frail cans, cans intended only for limited use ashore. I should have had strong, heavy tanks or kegs. That was the custom of the sea. At sea you only last as long as your water.

After sifting through his flimsy cans and tasting what liquid remained, Willis discovered he had but nine gallons of potable fresh water left. In his original estimate, Willis had predicted he would require two hundred days at sea to cover the distance between Callao and Pago Pago, and he had allowed two quarts of drinking and cooking water for each day of sailing, or one hundred gallons. By the morning of August 6, the *Seven Little Sisters* had been under way for only forty-five days, and Willis suddenly found his fresh-water supply reduced to a mere thirty-six quarts. He'd seen virtually no rain in his month and a half at sea and, given the season and his latitude, had no reason to expect downpours of any significance in the coming weeks. So he'd likely have to survive on the diminished stock at hand, which rationed out at little more than one cup a day, most of it Willis's, since Eekie drank little and Meekie seemed to draw her fluids from flying-fish juices, in the style of Bombard.

Worse still, Willis's emergency food rations had been stored in similar cut-rate canisters under the decking with the water tins, and the seams on those containers had also rusted through, permitting seawater to seep in and spoil the contents. So Willis was quite suddenly faced with surviving a potential five additional months at sea on the barest of provisions. While he was confident his meager rye-flour-and-raw-sugar diet would sustain him, he feared the effects of sailing under the tropical sun on eight ounces of water a day. Inspired by Bombard, Willis contemplated squeezing liquid from the fish he caught before a different and easier solution came to him: "Salt water—I would drink salt water!"

Willis claimed to have been drinking the stuff off and on since childhood and boasted of an almost unnatural tolerance for it. He theorized—correctly, as it turned out—that the want of salt in his diet over the years made the ingestion of ocean water far less of a physiological threat to him than it otherwise would have been. Moreover, Willis couldn't help but recall the cook on the *Henriette* with his crippling constipation. Sailors on board had advised young Willis to "keep his bowels open" with regular cupfuls of salt water, and he had long observed the practice with no ill effects.

So he readily reached for his enameled mug and dipped out a cupful of seawater that he drank down in a gulp. "I had no qualms," Willis insisted, "didn't even shudder. It stayed with me, too." He had heard that cattle and goats on the Galápagos Islands lived primarily on salt water and was aware that many Polynesians of the day made do with a brackish slurry from shallow, hand-dug wells, which he took as a sort of endorsement of his chances for survival. Even still, Willis couldn't quite forgive what he termed his "carelessness." His predicament was due entirely to his own misplaced thrift. Moreover, he hadn't shipped enough kerosene to keep his increasingly unreliable stoves going for the duration of the voyage, and he remained one violent storm away from tattered sails and a helpless drift on the current. "I could only tell myself that I had wanted shipwreck conditions," Willis noted, "and now I had them."

Faced with the very real prospect that his journey could, in one squally moment, become an extended ordeal in survival, Willis pronounced himself prepared and unafraid. "More and more," he wrote, "I looked upon my voyage as an experiment for all mankind." Even given his shortage of provisions, his equipment failures, his rupture, his gastric ailment, his lone set of ever-weakening sails, Willis was serene nearly to the point of bliss. "Nature had made me a part of her," he claimed. "Sometimes I felt as though my thinking had almost stopped."

Willis decided to preserve his fresh water for coffee, which he took cold, and for *máchica* paste, and he permitted himself two mugfuls of seawater a day, probably eight or ten ounces. Alain Bombard had calculated the daily human threshold for seawater consumption to be a pint and a half, so Willis stayed below the danger line. And while he suffered no ill effects, Willis was never tempted to pronounce Pacific water "absolutely delicious," as Bombard had, and seemed to consider it instead a point of ongoing pride that he could keep the stuff down.

As Willis negotiated the vast expanse of open ocean between the Galápagos Islands and the Marquesas, a fetch of almost thirty-two hundred landless miles, he felt the same oppressive sense of isolation that Heyerdahl had remarked on his passage. "I was in solitary," Willis observed, "in my vast cell of heaven and sea, lighted by the sun and at night by a thousand candles of the stars; I was a prisoner of the universe." Like Alain Bombard, Willis was left after weeks without human contact or any sign of civilized life to wonder if he wasn't perhaps abandoned on the planet. "Perhaps all people had died," he proposed, "and I was left alone."

Time became all but irrelevant. Each morning Willis wound

his clocks and marked off the previous day from his calendar, but only for purposes of navigation. He consulted no chart and employed only plotting sheets (generic and reusable) to keep apprised of his lumbering progress on the trackless ocean. Driven by wind and current, he covered on average seventy miles a day and noted that he was sailing the *Seven Little Sisters* like a yacht, "was knocking off the longitudes, running my westing down."

The constant demands of single-handing a ten-ton raft—adjusting the trim and centerboards, manning the tiller—offered welcome distraction to Willis, who was increasingly dogged by loneliness and remarked that he felt, on occasion, "quite forlorn." He had hoped the companionship of his cat and his parrot would compensate, and they made every now and again for diverting, even alarming crewmates. After six weeks at sea, Eekie the parrot suddenly uncorked one afternoon "the pitiful wail of a baby getting its first spanking." This after a fairly steady repertoire of profane barroom banter in Spanish, leavened with girlish giggles. The bird hadn't, Willis concluded, "been around a church much." One of Eekie's masterpieces of mimicry was a drunken lady "cackling so volubly that her head and teeth rattled, winding up with a screech that shook the masthead."

But Eekie was no command performer. He would sit silent in his cage for days before cutting loose with some manner of raucous palaver, all too frequently when Willis was napping. Every now and again, Willis would attach a line to the bird's foot and allow Eekie a spot of relative freedom in the rigging, where he would sit "flapping the stumps of his wings, gazing over the sea, no doubt dreaming of green forests and the snow-capped Sierras far away." The bird served as an object of near-constant scrutiny for Meekie the cat, who had taken to sleeping on the motor box hard beside Eekie's cage. "I was afraid," Willis confessed, "Meekie would get him some day."

Willis didn't permit Meekie free run of the raft either. She spent a fair part of each day tethered in the bow and tended to pass the bulk of her confinement sleeping in the hollow of the coiled mainsheet. When loosed, she would compete with Willis for flying fish, enjoy the occasional crab belowdecks on the main balsa logs, and feast on barnacles and seaweed attached to the centerboards. Evenings Meekie would customarily join Willis in the stern and sit on his lap as he steered beneath the stars before retiring to the motor box in the hut, where, with her gustatory leer, she would drive Eekie to the far reaches of his cage.

Long Tom, the sleek brown shark, remained a constant companion as well. "I think I would have felt a little sad," Willis confessed, "if one day I had looked into the sea and did not see his long, brown torpedo shape trailing along like part of the *Seven Little Sisters.*" At night the shark would sink to a depth of six feet or so. By day he traveled hardly twelve inches beneath the surface, knifing through the water with an entourage of pilot fish. Willis fell into the habit of sprawling on his stomach and watching Long Tom over the edge of the raft. Willis was mystified by the fact that the creature never seemed to feed. He slept while swimming and was a tireless, reliable associate, watching Willis with his "dull eyes."

Cat, parrot, and shark, however, could not provide sufficient company to put Willis's creeping sense of desolation entirely to rout. He had been warned by Ecuadoran fishermen and Peruvian naval officers that he was foolish to attempt a Pacific crossing alone. Not because of the dangers of storm and sea but due instead to the unrelieved solitude of the journey. To a man, they insisted that "madness would be the inevitable outcome."

Willis, for his part, had been anticipating the isolation of the passage with some savor. He felt he was in need of the sort of "cleansing" and "lifting up" that months alone at sea were likely to provide. In his best shrine-of-my-philosophy vein, Willis declared, "I needed to go back to the bourne whence I had come, to stand before the reckoning and receive new strength before going on. I knew that I had gone far astray, as men will." But Willis soon discovered, once he'd been agreeably lifted and scoured, that the solitude of long-distance, single-handed rafting was still making him, if not mad outright, at least profoundly blue. He required a consoling distraction from the isolation and happened upon one by chance.

"I started singing," Willis wrote, "and I realized that my soul had been hungering for this." Having spent much of his adolescence on merchant sailing ships, Willis was acquainted with a full catalog of sea chanteys, and he was pleased to discover that he could dredge one up when his spirits waned:

> A wild mood would sweep over me as I toiled all alone, wrestling with the ropes, or swinging aloft to clear running gear, or working with the flapping sail and barely able to manage it. I would burst out singing, roaring some old sea chanty learned long ago and long forgotten, now coming out in the wildness of the moment.

Willis proclaimed singing a "miracle that worked for me at all times," and he wondered if song might do the same for others adrift at sea. Bombard had certainly found the music he listened to nightly on his radio consoling, notwithstanding that he was all but plagued by Schubert's Seventh Symphony. Willis's favorite was "My Old Kentucky Home," which, oddly, he'd learned as a teen on the *Henriette* from a seasoned German sailor who spoke no English but for those lyrics.

His spirits buoyed by song, Willis drove before the trades in the finest fettle he'd known since his mysterious intestinal attack of some weeks before. By August 29, he was seventy days out of Callao and closing on the Marquesas. His daily intake of seawater over the past three weeks had produced no ill effects. He was thriving on a diet consisting largely of pasty *máchica*— he ate up to five servings a day—and he devoured the occasional raw dolphin liver as a vitamin-rich supplement, the odd flying fish (most of them ended up in his canoe), and every now and again a bonito tuna.

Far and away Willis preferred the flesh of the Pacific dolphin, or dorado, but landing and butchering one was frequently a tremendous ordeal. In his account of the voyage, Willis describes one particular five-foot specimen that he hooked with a flying fish removed from the belly of a bonito as bait. Willis fought to keep the creature from sounding under the raft, where it was sure to be set upon and ripped apart by sharks. As the dorado breached, trying to shake the hook, Willis managed to jerk the fish onto the deck. With no gunwale on the raft—no lip of any kind, in fact—Willis couldn't simply allow the fish to flop on the bamboo decking until it tired, since it would be certain to find its way back into the sea. He was obliged instead to fling himself bodily onto the creature and attempt to hold it in place until he could stun and then kill the fish with an iron bolt that he professed to be almost ashamed of employing.

For his trouble, Willis earned about thirty-five pounds of fish flesh and a rather thorough coating of dorado slime. He was obliged to spend the bulk of the afternoon cleaning first himself and then the deck of the raft so that the footing, treacherous as a rule, wouldn't be further compromised. Afterward Willis and Meekie enjoyed together a feast of raw dorado flesh, and Willis suspended the dressed fish by the tail in a shady quarter of the raft, a piece of canvas wrapped around it to keep off the sun. Willis's practice, following a day or two of all the sweet, fresh dorado that he and Meekie could stand, was to strip away the remaining flesh and dry it on the roof of the cabin into a kind of fish jerky, which man and cat would share until the next catch. (It's little wonder that Meekie had no appetite for the tinned cat food Willis had carried, and as little use for the evaporated milk.)

As with Bombard in the Atlantic, Willis noted that fish were ordinarily in plentiful supply around the raft. Though when flying fish turned scarce, or managed anyway to avoid the sails and glide past Willis's canoe for a night or two, he always seemed a touch reluctant to cast his line into the water and snatch out dinner. He remained throughout the voyage sensitive to the grace and beauty of Pacific marine life and felt a pang of remorse with every fish he landed and ate. Hooked dorado inspired special regret. The fish were beautifully colored in the water, a shimmering, iridescent green and gold, but turned a dull gray almost immediately when fetched into the air. "It always made me sad to catch one," Willis confessed, "and for that reason I postponed my fishing as long as possible."

On his passage between the Galápagos and the Marquesas, Willis had sailed two thousand miles virtually due west. His centerboards, saturated and weakened and taxed throughout the crossing by the prevailing southeasterly winds, had begun to break in numbers enough to deplete Willis's spares and prompt him to salvage planks from his bowsprit and under his decking for replacements. As Willis sailed out of August and into early September—spring in the Southern Hemisphere— the weather became more unsettled, the sea more violent, and he was obliged to go with little sleep, catching what naps he could at the helm before the raft would begin to wallow and threaten to go up into the wind.

Accordingly, Willis was profoundly weary, and his eyes were suffering the strain of contending with the afternoon sun day after day as he sailed west along the fifth parallel. Taking sights became an increasing chore. Even reading his compass heading could be a trial in poor light. So Willis rigged up a canvas canopy by the tiller and began to retire to the shade of it as often as his duties allowed, in hopes of sparing his vision.

As he closed on the Marquesas, passing well to the north, Willis's raft was covering from sixty-five to slightly over ninety miles a day, depending on wind and drift. He estimated that the prevailing current alone propelled him fifteen to twenty miles each day, and by September 1, Willis had enjoyed for several weeks a fairly steady twenty-mile-per-hour wind out of the southeast. Belting out sea chanteys continued to serve him as a means of putting despondency to rout, though for variety he would occasionally recite poetry from a volume he had self-published a few months before his trip. The collection, entitled *Hell, Hail and Hurricanes,* runs to seventy-eight pages and is comprised almost exclusively of what can only be classified as doggerel. The briefest, least excruciating selection among the eleven poems included is "Toilers of the Sea":

> *The stars on countless thrones are keeping*
> *Eternal court in silent night,*

While deep below where seas are sleeping
The sailors praise the august sight.

The stars in endless drifts are bringing
Their caravans thru time and space,
While deep below where winds are singing
The sailors watch with lifted face.

The tempest smites with crashing thunder,
The night is black with flame and wind—
On seas aroused to slay and plunder
The sailors to their vessels cling.

The sun her light is skyward sending,
Flooding the spheres with golden day,
While deep in depths, dark and unending,
The dead drift silently away.

Willis considered the collection something in the way of a "tombstone." The poems were intended to survive his trip even if he didn't. "I wondered," Willis wrote, "if Teddy ever read any of them." (She must have been mercifully silent on the matter.)

Willis's route had carried him 150 miles north of the Marquesas, and he was a good fifty miles clear of the islands to the west before he set a new course to the south-southwest for American Samoa, still two thousand miles away. As the *Seven Little Sisters* closed on the Tuamotu Islands, Willis couldn't help but remark that he had covered virtually the same distance as the *Kon-Tiki* in only three-quarters of the time, since Heyerdahl had needed 102 days to reach Raroia. "I had been sailing through the winter with its stronger winds," Willis allowed, and he theorized that "the construction of my raft also accounted for my greater speed."

With no recurrence of the mysterious gastric symptoms that had felled him in June and no ill effects from his daily intake of Pacific water, Willis was in rather good shape for a sixty-year-old man after three months at sea. Meekie the cat was just as fit and appeared to be thriving on her diet of fresh fish and occasional barnacles. Willis noticed, however, that Eekie the parrot seemed to be suffering curious effects from the extended voyage. The longer they were at sea, the more profane Eekie became, swearing prodigiously in Spanish throughout the afternoons. Willis counted three vulgarities for every civilized utterance, and he claimed to recognize in the way Eekie watched the drifting clouds a pronounced longing for land.

Willis had decided against carrying a barometer, his thinking being that no matter how the pressure might plunge, there was nothing he could do on his plodding raft to avoid an approaching storm. So he was obliged to depend upon his seagoing experience alone, and he found himself troubled by the hue of the sunrise one September morning. "It had a coppery tint," he noted, "that generally meant wind and bad weather." Willis remarked that the wind and sea were both "moderate," and as the evening sun begin to sink, he noticed the same coppery hue to the sky that had troubled him in the dawning.

Whether he could avoid it or not, Willis was left to wonder if a storm were brewing, and during the evening the raft was beset by a series of squalls. None was so strong as to trouble Willis until just after midnight, when the fury of the storms increased. The sea rose, and the wind was soon "moaning in the darkness." Though Willis couldn't see much, he noticed that a "solid black wall was making up that looked really ominous," and soon the seas were "running mountainously."

Willis decided to shorten sail, but it was a decision late in coming. The storm was already upon him, and the wind was blowing a gale as he attempted to lower his main yard, the mangrove spar from which his mainsail was suspended. "I hoped everything would run clear," Willis wrote, "sheets, braces, lifts and downhauls. 'Don't foul up—any of you,' I told them."

Hoping wasn't enough, however, and the yardarm had dropped only a few feet before the wind wrenched it about and hung it up. No amount of force Willis could manage on the downhauls would free the thing, so his weathered mainsail was left exposed to the gale, and the fabric began to rip almost immediately. The wind, Willis wrote, "came through the rent in a demonic blast of victory. My beautiful white sail was fluttering in shreds before my eyes." This was the moment he had dreaded, the prospect he had anticipated back in Callao Harbor when he had decided to carry but a lone set of sails. He'd known then what he was chancing, had been fully aware of the risk he ran of a helpless drift on the current, and yet had persuaded himself that one set of sails would likely see him through.

What Willis had feared and failed to guard against had come to pass in an instant. His fragile expanse of sun-baked Orlon was "a sail no more, only a mass of angry white rags in the darkness."

7

Samoa

THE STORM BLEW FOR two full days, and the *Seven Little Sisters* rode monstrous seas under a jib and a reefed mizzen. But for these two scraps of sail, the raft would have surely gone broadside in the swell and very likely been destroyed. As it was, Willis feared on several occasions that she'd "go clean over." The raft's bow would plunge into the sea, and only her porousness kept her afloat. Water passed through the decking from breaking seas above and rose in jets between the logs from beneath. In the throes of the storm, Willis abandoned the helm to lash the cabin into place. The structure was in danger of getting raked off in breaking seas, and it contained everything Willis owned, from cat and parrot down.

The wind had shifted out of the north and was blowing the raft south toward the Marquesas, but Willis was confident he had sea room enough to ride out the storm without piling up on the islands. His sails permitted him nominal control, and even with the battering they were enduring, Willis's seven balsa logs looked to be firm in the their lashings and gave him no reason to fear they would pull apart in the heavy weather. After his seventy-day ordeal—overboard, perforated ulcer, loss of fresh water, bothersome rupture—Willis still professed surprise that a forty-eight-hour gale succeeded in taking the starch out of him. "I found," the sixty-year-old Willis conceded, "that I was not quite as strong as I used to be."

He proved strong enough, however, to last out the storm, and with the wind still high and the seas still running with some violence, Willis attempted repairs on his tattered sail. He'd carried needles and twine for that purpose but, typically, suspected he was insufficiently provisioned. When a roll of Willis's sailing twine had gone missing in Callao, Teddy had encouraged her husband to send off to New York for another one. "Of course," he admitted later, "I had done nothing."

Willis began by erecting a canopy against the sun. He suspended three blankets above the deck to provide reliable shade and spare his compromised vision to the extent possible. He left the remnants of the mainsail attached to the yardarm, unrigged the arm completely, and laid the whole assembly out on the deck beneath his awning. The sail was torn across horizontally just a foot below the yardarm and ripped vertically along numerous of its sun-baked, weakened seams. Willis anticipated three full days of steady stitching to make the repairs.

Unfortunately, he was still the helmsman and lone hand aboard, and given the running seas and the tendency of the raft to go up into the wind, Willis knew he'd be obliged to dart between his work on the sail and the stern wheel. The *Seven Little Sisters* was making headway under jib and mizzen but was moving at only slightly better than half speed and could be expected to cover no more than forty to forty-five miles a day. In the wake of the storm, Willis had also noticed a troubling loss of buoyancy in the raft. He calculated that she was sitting at least four inches lower in the water than she'd ridden in late April when he'd launched her. The bow was now only slightly above the sea, and if the raft sank further and began to plow through the water, Willis's progress was sure to slow profoundly and the raft would become appreciably more difficult to steer.

It was imperative, then, that Willis make short work of his repairs, rehang the mended mainsail, and drive with all deliberate speed southwest toward Samoa, which, even if he failed to reach the island, would return him to trafficked waters, where he could know a realistic hope of raising a ship in an emergency. Recognizing his peril, Willis wanted to sew around the clock, but in assessing the state of his equipment, he found that his lantern cast insufficient light for his weak eyes to see by, that his flashlight batteries were in low supply, and he feared that if he used his generator to power the lone electrical searchlight he carried, the thing might break down and leave him no way to run his radio in an emergency.

So Willis's work on the sail would have to be confined to daylight. He stitched for hours at a time with only brief interruptions for steering adjustments and snacks of dried fish and pasty *máchica*. He sang to entertain himself and dispel the tedium of the work. He was capable by then of a solid fifty minutes of song, a repertoire that he warbled through daily to keep up his spirits. He'd expanded upon his original clutch of sea chanteys and now sang "songs from everywhere, bits from all corners of the earth. . . . I sang songs of men lying under shellfire thinking of home and loved ones, songs of sailors when their ships went down, songs of the exiled."

Willis's midday sight on September 5 revealed him still to be slightly north of the Marquesas though safely west of them in the event of further squalls, and while the weather in the area did remain unsettled, the storms were hardly of gale-force variety. Willis complained of a series of squalls bringing high winds and heavy swells and thereby compounding his labor. It was difficult enough, given the state of his vision, for Willis to stitch his tattered sail effectively. A pitching, storm-tossed raft only slowed and complicated matters. Worse still, the squalls were all dry. Willis had yet to see a drop of rain since leaving Callao in June, and he knew that rainfall collected from one tropical downpour would likely be sufficient to supply him with fresh water for the rest of his voyage.

The twine held out, and Willis finished his stitching in three days. With the wind still moderate to high, he was reluctant to raise his mended mainsail to test his handiwork, but squall followed squall with such regularity that Willis soon decided he had no choice and so hoisted the sail under far worse conditions than he would have preferred. It billowed out and held. "I had patched it up in good shape," Willis wrote, "and it seemed to be as strong as ever." But he was quick to lower it whenever the wind rose to a troubling pitch, until he'd gained enough confidence in his stitching to leave the sail unfurled and drive with it before the fierce winds. Willis estimated that the raft was making nearly six miles an hour under her mended main, and he figured he was more than doubling the daily progress he'd experienced while he stitched.

On September 7, Willis enjoyed an actual tropical downpour. After months of dry weather, he was caught unprepared for the storm and had to hustle about the deck setting up containers to catch the rain. He had known the foresight to patch a couple of his leaky water cans, and he attached them to either corner of the mainsail, where they collected runoff. Willis then stripped out of his clothes and scoured clean his salt-encrusted body. By the time the rain stopped, he had caught seven gallons of fresh water. "I was rich," he crowed.

Alternatively becalmed and storm-driven, Willis made slow, inefficient progress southwest toward Samoa. Long Tom had abandoned him just north of the Marquesas after over four thousand miles at the raft's aft corner, but Willis was compensated and consoled in a fashion by a sea "brown with sharks." During one windless lull, Willis stretched out on the deck for a sunbath at the edge of the raft, dozing until the *Seven Little Sisters* began to roll in a rising chop. Willis startled awake. "A big sea stood right above me," he wrote, "with the sun shining through it and the brown body of a huge shark inside it, within a few feet of my naked body, seemingly ready to attack." On the spot, Willis formulated a new bylaw for napping: "I decided to lie a few feet farther from the edge next time."

In keeping a close eye on his mended sail, Willis had noticed a separation in the stitching, a tear of little more than six inches that he allowed to go untended with the coming of evening on September 8. A squall in the night ripped the seam further, and Willis found an eight-foot rent in his sail come dawning. He lowered the main, stitched the tear, and was attempting to raise the arm and reset the sail when a topping lift fouled in a block and frustrated the effort. Willis's only recourse was to climb his perilous rope ladder to the masthead and clear the block by hand.

The wind was brisk and the swell rolling vigorously as Willis scaled the ladder. He spent much of his energy in gaining the masthead and untangling the topping lift, and he was only halfway down when his strength abandoned him and the pivoting, whipping ladder succeeded at bucking him off. He dropped ten feet to the rolling deck, landed on his shoulder, and struck his head on a mangrove plank, a stout three-by-twelve centerboard. The blow knocked him senseless, and he awoke—nauseous and shivering—under the night sky. He immediately passed out again and came to only the following afternoon.

The raft was wallowing along on her jib and mizzen. Willis was numb all over but tested his joints and could find nothing broken. He crawled to the cabin, where he kept a tin of fresh water, and drank from it. Willis knew he should set the mainsail but lacked the strength, and he dropped off again and slept through the night. He awoke the following afternoon with a sore head but no broken skin or bones and dosed himself with aspirin sluiced down with cold coffee as he grappled with what sounded suspiciously like embarrassment. "It was hard for me to believe that I could be knocked unconscious by a blow that didn't fracture my head," Willis allowed. "That hurt my vanity. Maybe I wasn't as tough as I used to be."

The day was September 10, and Willis was approaching tiny, uninhabited Flint Island. Perhaps still feeling the effects of his fall, or simply weary of uninterrupted sea travel, Willis began to entertain the notion of calling at Flint Island for no other conceivable reason than it would soon be convenient to call at. Consulting his sailing directions for the area, Willis learned that the island was two and a half miles long, hardly one thousand yards wide, and offered, by way of amenities, two brackish ponds. It was protected by a reef, was fairly carpeted in birds, and the authors of the description Willis had at hand could not have been more discouraging of a visit. "Even under favorable circumstances," Willis read, "anchorage is not safe."

Nonetheless, Willis confessed that the "idea of sailing to Flint Island had taken solid hold," and he put himself on a course for the place even while mindful of the considerable dangers. The mends he had made on his mainsail kept pulling apart, and he was regularly obliged to repair them. The weather continued squally and still by turns, and the raft had lost such buoyancy that the bow was very nearly plowing the water, sure to slow Willis on his final eleven hundred miles to Samoa. And yet he was still capable of "wondering whether it would be wise to go to Flint Island in such uncertain weather," which, in the annals of wisdom, paled by comparison to his declaration that he still might go on to Australia or New Guinea. "I had been thinking along these lines since the beginning," Willis noted, "and now felt that if I reached Samoa it would be too early an ending of my voyage."

That Willis could entertain such a thought, given the state of his mainsail, the diminished flotation of his logs, and the fact that the manufacturer of the rope he'd used for lashings had cautioned him not to depend on it for more than six months submerged (it had been in the water since April in Guayaquil) suggests that Willis was either out of his proper mind or obliquely suicidal. So calling at Flint Island for an afternoon among the bird droppings and the brackish water seemed nearly the height of good sense by comparison.

Considering the limited control Willis could exert over his raft and the ongoing pattern of unpredictable stormy weather and swirling wind, he was endangering his craft and running the authentic risk of making himself a castaway simply by closing within sight of a reefed island. He owned up to ambivalence about his plan and conceded that he was "a little worried" about his course, but he continued nevertheless on a tack that was sure to put him on the lee side of Flint Island but harder upon it than he had any rational reason to be.

On September 18 around midmorning, Willis spied land a few degrees off his port bow. Only then did he swing off a point or two to starboard to give the island a wider berth. He would pass Flint Island to the north, and with the wind blowing out of the south, Willis still couldn't entirely dispense with the notion of landing the raft and feeling for the first time in eighty-eight days solid ground beneath his feet. Such was the temptation, the almost irresistible pull of tiny, barren Flint Island. "It was more than just Earth," Willis insisted, "it was the Earth; I heard it say quietly: I am the Earth, I am the real master on this planet."

The immediate trouble was that the "real master on this planet" was largely surrounded by a coral reef, and Willis, mindful of the fate of the *Kon-Tiki*, couldn't expect to be plucked off Flint Island by friendly natives from across the lagoon. If marooned on the island, he would very probably die there, given the unsavory aspect of the place and the unambiguous prohibitions of the sailing directions for the area. The baleful likelihood of this prospect managed finally to worm its way even into Willis's hard head as he closed to the point where he could hear the crash of the surf over the reef. "The siren song of land was sounding through my blood," Willis finally admitted. "Swing off more, Bill—westward and clear it. Clear it!"

Willis swung just in time, appreciating at the last moment his utter recklessness and all it could have cost him. But the idea of land, of Earth, had taken hold of him. "Its loneliness," he said of Flint Island, "was appalling; it affected me." Willis permitted himself a final glance at the place as he pursued a southerly course. He waved, "just as if someone were standing on the shore watching me sail away."

*   *   *

Samoa would be Willis's next landfall, and it was just over one thousand miles away as the *Seven Little Sisters* drove south-southwest with a favorable wind. Thinking more sensibly now, Willis recognized that his mainsail was beginning to fail, not just at the mends but tearing anew, and might not even last to Samoa. His intent was to ride it as far as it would carry him and with as much speed as he could manage until it finally blew to irreparable tatters, when he would limp along the last leg of his voyage on his jib and mizzen.

By the end of September, Willis had cleared the uninhabited island of Suwarrow and was making steady progress toward Tau, the easternmost of the Samoan Islands, when eyestrain from the constant glare became more painful than he could endure. He lowered sail and retired to the dark cabin to recover, complaining that the sunlight "stabbed my eyes like a hot iron." For three days Willis's raft would drift on the current, its sails unset, its helm untended. Willis would admit to no alarm over his condition, telling himself that "even if blinded I would eventually drift to some beach."

Eekie the parrot convalesced alongside Willis, having lately fallen victim to the designs of the cat. The door to Eekie's cage had been snapped off by a flailing dolphin, and Willis had replaced it with a square of cardboard that Meekie had managed to dislodge. Willis had found the cat "half inside Eekie's cage and trying to take him apart." The bird had lost some feathers, suffered a few scratches and (Willis's diagnosis here) a dislocated leg. As Willis convalesced in the hut, Eekie passed the bulk of his time suspended by his beak from a bar of his cage to take his weight off his injured leg. He looked, Willis wrote, "like an acrobat in green tights hanging by his teeth."

By October 10, the pain from his eyestrain manageable now, Willis was sailing a course direct for Tau. His noon sight put him at just over one hundred miles from the island, and he tapped out a message on both seagoing emergency frequencies requesting a boat to stand by to assist him in landing. He received no reply. Willis had retired to the cabin to plot his position when he heard Meekie "give out an agonized miaow." Willis stumbled onto the deck to find Meekie washed overboard. She had gone off the bow and was drifting aft a good four feet out of reach.

In the wake of his own mishap, Willis had attached two float lines to trail behind the raft. One was tied to a stern cross log and the other to a bamboo jib boom that jutted out on the starboard side of the raft. There was Meekie, Willis wrote, "looking at me, yowling for help, and drifting past the raft." Immediately, instinctively, Willis went over the side. He succeeded at grabbing the boom line just before he hit the water, and Meekie proved resourceful enough to save herself by climbing onto the top of Willis's head. Willis noted that "she dug her claws deep into my scalp. I felt she wouldn't come loose until my head came off too."

Drawing himself and his cargo along the length of the rope,

Willis regained the raft and succeeded at prying the cat from the crown of his head. Meekie, for her part, shook once and returned to the bow, her favorite napping spot.

Willis's late-afternoon sight of October 11 put him within fifty miles of Tau. By six o'clock he had spied the island, and at six-fifteen, the traditional time for ships and shore stations to monitor for disaster signals, Willis broadcast a message giving his position and asking once more for a ship to usher him safely to shore. Again he raised no reply.

The following morning at seven forty-five, Willis sent out another message on both emergency frequencies. He was not twenty-five miles from Tau and still in need of an escort to see him through the reef to safe harbor. By now Willis had stopped listening for responses. He was far too busy with the work of managing his raft and confessed that he "did not have enough training to pick up code at average speed." Willis was now 112 days at sea, and by late morning, and with the weather fair and aided by a strong wind, he was within a half mile of the northern coast of Tau. Expecting to land most anytime, Willis broke out his rather ambitious assortment of flags and hoisted them all—the Stars and Stripes, the flag of Peru, the flag of Ecuador, and the Union Jack. This last was flown in honor of Sir George Nelson, who'd contributed the transmitter that had served, so far, exclusively as ballast.

The chart Willis consulted as he skirted the northern shore of Tau was homemade. He had been obliged to draw it hurriedly and freehand from the printed description in his sailing directions for the area. "It was just like me," Willis allowed, "not to have gotten a special chart of the Samoa group while buying my other charts at the Hydrographic Office in New

York." He could see the twin islands of Olosega and Ofu, a mere six miles to the northwest, and when no chance of landing presented itself at Tau and no boat came out to meet him, Willis steered for Olosega in hopes of better luck there.

The twin islands, however, were steep and inaccessible on their northern faces and surrounded entirely by a reef. Unadvisedly, Willis attempted to sail between Olosega and Ofu, since his sailing directions located the only villages on opposite sides of the treacherous dividing channel. He found the sea choppy as he forged a route partway through the passage. Knobby reefs protruded into the waterway like jetties, and the crosscurrents were so potent as to challenge Willis's control of his raft. Twice his mainsail went aback, and he fairly lost control of the *Seven Little Sisters*, which drifted on the current toward destruction. But he managed to recover and finally persuaded himself that the danger was too great, that he would be wise to head back out to sea while he still could and make for Tutuila, some fifty miles away. By early evening Willis had cleared Ofu to the northwest and had set a course for the main island of American Samoa.

That night, which would prove to be the *Seven Little Sisters'* penultimate one at sea, Meekie saw to its grim conclusion a bit of business she'd clearly been committed to throughout the course of the voyage. Long hours of feline frustration passed on the motor box in devoted study of succulent Eekie the parrot met, at almost the last conceivable opportunity, with full compensation. The cardboard door Willis had rigged up on Eekie's cage had become saturated with spray in the violent chop of the channel between Olosega and Ofu. Meekie tested it with a paw and, finding it limp and yielding, pushed her way into the cage while Willis dozed at the helm.

Willis was awakened by the moaning wind of an approaching

squall, and though he heard Eekie squawk loudly once, the rough weather kept him at the helm until the storm had passed. Only then could he slip away to the cabin, where he found the cage upset, the cardboard door torn away, and both Eekie and Meekie inside. He had arrived too late. Eekie was dead.

The dawning of October 13 found Willis stitching his gnawed parrot into a square of canvas for burial at sea. "I sewed him up, as should be done with a shipmate," Willis declared. He then returned the bird to his cage, weighted the thing with a spare shackle, tied shut the broken door to keep Eekie from floating out as a shark hors d'oeuvre, and then dropped the cage over the side of the raft and watched as it sank from sight.

> The day before, he had squawked with joy as we sailed close to the green slopes; he had seen land and trees again after the long voyage from Peru. He hadn't quite made it, the little comedian with his hooked nose and green coat who had helped so much to make the journey pleasant. Good-bye, Eekie!

Meekie, Willis noted with a hint of condemnation, "sat nearby, not even looking."

Willis spied the island of Tutuila off his port bow at nine in the morning and keyed over his Salvita III a request for assistance at nine-fifteen. Given that help had yet to come his way, Willis had no reason to believe that any of his previous messages had been received, so he was increasingly persuaded he'd need to make it to shore on his own.

As he approached eastern Tutuila, Willis was obliged to negotiate a heavy sea whipped up by squally weather. The prevailing wind was out of the south, and he sailed as close to it as possible—no easy task on a keelless raft—in hopes of keeping within striking distance of the northern shore. By late afternoon he had fought his way close enough inland to spy out an inviting stretch of beach, where he attempted a landing but was driven off by wind and current.

He could get no nearer than five hundred yards and, sailing close-hauled, went up into the wind on several occasions and lost all headway. As evening fell, Willis attempted an approach on a flat, reefless bay, but again wind and sea were against him, and he was driven off. With rocks ahead to the west, Willis was obliged to interrupt his crawl along the shore, clear the danger, and then approach afresh. He found this new bit of coastline well protected by a reef, and he sailed along the length of it in what was now utter darkness, looking for a place to land. Fighting wind and swell, Willis could get no closer to Tutuila than 150 yards before gusts from the island's peaks would whip down to bedevil him and drive the raft away.

By two in the morning, Willis was frustrated to the point of defeat. Fearing the real prospect of piling up on a reef, he decided to head back out to sea and make for British Samoa. The island of Upolu was but thirty-six miles away, and Willis was determined to approach it in daylight. He would ready his canoe in the course of the crossing and attempt his landing in the dugout if need be. Given the wind, he would again be obliged to bear in from the north, but he was encouraged by the fact that the main port and the most favorable anchorages of the island lay on that side.

The morning of October 14, 1954, saw nine-fifteen come and go without Willis's sending an additional emergency message over his Marconi. He had decided that "the transmitter did not work, for no ship or plane had come out from American Samoa looking for me." Instead he occupied himself on the passage by shaving—his scrupulous practice each day at sea—and tidying up his appearance with a self-inflicted haircut and a fresh set of clothes. He thought he had "better spruce up a little for the British," he wrote, "knowing that they are greater sticklers for form than we." The crew of the *Kon-Tiki* and Alain Bombard had reached their destinations not just unshaven but shirtless, ragged, bedraggled, and thoroughly salt-encrusted. Photos of Willis at the helm of the *Seven Little Sisters*, after an ocean crossing of almost seven thousand miles, show a man nappily attired in street clothes who looks for all the world like someone on his way to the bank.

Willis had only just finished shaving and dressing when, turning for one last look at Tutuila, he saw a ship following several miles behind him. Through his binoculars he could make out the vessel's white hull and its buff masts and stacks—American Coast Guard colors. Willis assumed that the craft was on its way to Apia, the main port of Upolu, and that his encounter with it was a mere coincidence, but it turned out that one (and only one) of his innumerable radio transmissions in the course of his voyage had actually been received.

Willis's morning emergency message of the previous day had been picked up not by the Coast Guard on Tutuila but by an amateur radio operator on Rarotonga in the Cook Islands, over seven hundred unlikely miles away. The operator had relayed the message to a station in Wellington, New Zealand, and news of Willis's position and predicament had been forwarded to authorities in Pago Pago. The *Manuatele* had been dispatched immediately on October 13 but was driven back to

port by heavy weather. The ship had put out in better conditions on the morning of the fourteenth, and after a search of
several hours, the *Manuatele*'s radioman had spied Willis's sail
at eleven-thirty.

The bridge was lined with well-wishers snapping photographs as the ship closed on the *Seven Little Sisters*, and at first
Willis was tempted to believe that the *Manuatele* "might be a
Hollywood studio ship; maybe a movie company was shooting
a film in Samoa and had come after me for some fun."

But soon a voice shouted down, asking Willis, "How does it
feel to see human beings again?"

Willis thought for a moment and responded, "Fine."

"What else," he wondered, "could I say?"

Under tow, the *Seven Little Sisters* made the sixty-mile return
trip to Tutuila and Pago Pago in heavy seas. She traveled reluc-
tantly, snapping the towline three times along the way. Willis
elected to remain on the raft, which he shared with several of
the *Manuatele*'s crew, who informed him, to his great surprise,
that he had been officially considered lost at sea for 113 days of
his 115-day voyage.

Five hundred flower-bedecked Samoans lined the harbor to
greet Willis as the *Manuatele* returned to port just after midnight on October 15. "This seemed to be a moment of holiness
for the people waiting for my raft to touch their earth," Willis
proposed, and then added, "I, too, felt the sacredness of the occasion." An Associated Press reporter on the scene described
Willis leaping "briskly to the dock" and recorded his comments
to the crowd:

> The trip at sea was fantastic and it was also a nightmare,
> and yet it was a dream which changed from day to day.

Prompted by shouts of "Where's the cat?" Willis returned to the raft and fetched Meekie to show him off.

Willis was officially welcomed to Samoa by the provincial governor, Richard Barrett Lowe, whose wife placed a lei of flowers around Willis's neck. Later that same day, Willis was the guest of honor at a *kava*, a traditional island ceremony attended by local chiefs and dignitaries, where Willis was acknowledged as *Tautai 'o le Vasa Laolao* or "Captain of the High Seas."

On the following day, the sixteenth, Willis composed a letter in which he formally presented "to the people and the Government of American Samoa my raft the *Seven Little Sisters* and all its equipment." He made the gift with the explicit understanding that the raft would be "protected and exhibited" and would not be "sold or transferred without the permission of myself or my heirs." Governor Lowe was pleased to accept the raft, arranged to have it hoisted from the water, and was quick to assure Willis that the "terms of the gift will be upheld." Willis includes in his book-length account of his voyage a rather forlorn photo of the "future site of the museum and final resting place of the *Seven Little Sisters*," which features little more than a patch of raw ground with a half dozen logs placed upon it by way of prospective raft supports.

The agreement, unfortunately, was between Willis and the governor and not between Willis and the native Samoans. Their innate sense of the "holiness" of Willis's venture notwithstanding, the locals had hardly seen Willis and Meekie off on their flight home when they set about chopping up the *Seven Little Sisters* for firewood. Unlike the *Kon-Tiki*, with its proper museum in Oslo and its permanent, curated display, no splinter of Willis's craft remains.

Five days after his landing in Pago Pago, Willis embarked on a journey east, with calls at Canton Island, Honolulu, San Francisco, Dallas, and, finally, Idlewild Airport in New York. It was a four-day excursion that put him on the ground in Queens on October 24. He remained in the cabin of the plane until Teddy had joined him, sobbing. When Willis asked if she had thought he was lost, she shook her head but assured him that "everybody else thought so." Then they departed the plane together, Willis and Teddy arm in arm, with skittish Meekie straining against her leash.

A *New York Times* reporter was present as Willis descended the gangway, and he provided a few telling details Willis neglected to mention in his brief description of his homecoming. On hand to greet Willis were both the Bronx borough president, James J. Lyons (the Willises lived in the Bronx at the time), and Willis's brother-in-law and Teddy's employer, Charles V. Yates, who had personally arranged for the *Times* reporter to attend Willis's triumphal return to New York.

When the reporter's questions threatened to elicit from Willis more details about his voyage than Yates believed should be volunteered without pay, Yates stepped in on Willis's behalf.

> The interviewing, arranged by Mr. Yates, was interrupted for a whispered conference and terminated with the announcement that a "very important" engagement had to be kept shortly.

Under Yates's direction, Willis then declared that there were "a few points he wished to clear up." He went on to announce that various news reports suggesting he'd intended to sail to

Australia rather than Samoa were "erroneous." Willis added that similar reports "that he had spent forty-four years as a seaman were also untrue." He then claimed to be a "theatrical writer" who was working "in collaboration with my brother-in-law, Mr. Yates."

Instead of responding to further questions, Willis supplied the reporter with a handwritten statement, a chunk of which was cited in the article.

> It was a voyage to the clouds amidst the roaring of the seas. I had stormy weather throughout. The voyage was fantastic, changing from nightmare to overwhelming dream. I had, I think, experiences surpassing the imagination. So far I have released just a few facts to satisfy the immediate curiosity of the world. Now I can tell my almost incredible story.

Willis informed the reporter he intended to write articles about his voyage, "show films he had made on the trip and then write a book." Willis entertained no further questions and departed the airfield in the company of his wife, his cat, and his agent.

The course and tone of Willis's public homecoming gave rise to a rather unfortunate headline the following morning in the paper of record: 115-DAY RAFT HERMIT FLIES IN WITH SCRIPT, SAYS HE'S THEATRICAL WRITER, NOT SEAMAN.

8

Progeny

WILLIS DID, IN FACT, write articles about his trip, did show films he had made on the crossing in the course of countless speaking engagements, and did produce a book-length account of the voyage of the *Seven Little Sisters*. The articles appeared prominently in the *New York Times*, running in the front section of the paper on five consecutive days from November 15 through 19, 1954. They were illustrated with Willis's photographs and served as the foundation for the book he produced, *The Gods Were Kind*, which was published by E. P. Dutton and Company in October of the following year.

In his review of the book, Orville Prescott professed admiration for Willis's bravery, passing distaste for his fulsome prose, and what would prove, critically anyway, a fairly commonplace ambivalence about the fundamental nature of Willis's excursion:

To read about such a voyage is to feel a mixture of contradictory reactions: humble admiration for Mr. Willis' courage and resourcefulness, blank astonishment at his folly. After all, he left behind a wife who loved him. He had no reasonable purpose to justify his lonely expedition one-quarter of the distance around the world. He was not searching for Cathay, or trying to prove the possibility of a controversial theory, or discovering unexplored islands.

In Prescott's view, Willis's was a "voyage undertaken for the sheer joy of doing something fantastically difficult" and little more than that. Willis, for his part, was given to describing the crossing as an "adventure of the spirit" and seemed to share Prescott's assessment that the voyage had served no scientific purpose or accomplished anything beyond satisfying Willis's appetite for ordeal.

By his own admission, Willis had embarked on his expedition as a means of trolling for hardship, but that hardly disqualified him from practical accomplishment. Even if inadvertently, Willis's experiences had complemented conclusions drawn both by Thor Heyerdahl and Alain Bombard. With the *Kon-Tiki*, Heyerdahl had set out to prove that a primitive balsa raft could leave sheltered coastal waters and survive in the open Pacific for months at a time. Willis had surely demonstrated that a primitive man could. Willis's native adaptability had led him to depend on unprocessed Andean grains and raw sugar to sustain him, and the failure of his kerosene stoves had ensured that his diet would be strictly ancient Peruvian in nature.

When the bulk of his fresh water seeped away, Willis was put upon by necessity to rely on seawater in the fashion promoted by Alain Bombard. Unlike Bombard's, however, Willis's predicament was not experimental. Willis had no sealed store of emergency rations to fall back on were things to take a direr turn and only a layman's instincts to dictate the quantity and frequency of seawater he might best tolerate. As did Bombard's, Willis's extended isolation and his shipwreck conditions functioned over time to all but poison his disposition. Bombard resorted to petulance and self-pity, unfreighting his ire on the "experts" whose books he'd been foolish enough to consult. Willis, sensing the steady erosion of his frame of mind, resorted to song and found in his fifty-minute repertoire a reliable antidote to sinking spirits. Like an authentic castaway, Willis was obliged to improvise throughout his voyage to keep himself and his craft fit and serviceable, and he gained shore after 115 days at sea in remarkably fine condition, far healthier than Bombard, who was twenty-eight years old at the time of his voyage (Willis had turned sixty-one en route) and whose entire journey, including the Mediterranean leg, lasted only seventy days.

So though Willis could well have boasted a scientific pedigree for the voyage of the *Seven Little Sisters*, he never got beyond characterizing the trip as a seagoing test of his pluck and fiber touched with quasi-religious mysticism. Coverage of Willis upon his return, the initial *Times* story aside, generally took the form of two parts "humble admiration for Mr. Willis' courage and resourcefulness" to one part snickering ridicule of his methods and habits.

Willis's embrace of an organic diet in the form of local South American grain and sugar supplemented with raw fish might be perfectly normal today, but it qualified as the height of eccentricity in the mid-1950s. Willis spoke and wrote openly of his faith in telepathy; of his enthusiasm for yoga and rhythmic breathing; of his queer, pantheistic religiosity; and, given the want of an overarching ethnological theory of Pacific migration to inform his voyage (and the inclusion of a parrot-eating cat), there always seemed to be room in an interview or print portrait of Willis for at least a bit of sneering.

Willis was essentially an extreme sportsman well in advance of the phenomenon, and in the context of his era he made for a gaudy curiosity, a sort of accomplished crackpot, and proved an irresistible subject for press reports. Accordingly, news of Willis's voyage and Willis's eccentricities traveled widely, and though he can't be said to have directly spawned two of the more significant Pacific raft expeditions that followed hard upon his crossing, Willis's celebrity must surely have goaded their organizers. These ensuing undertakings were represented as ventures, unlike Willis's, with legitimate points to prove and significant theories to illustrate, even if one of the theories was (to be kind) controversial and the other (to be honest) utterly harebrained.

* * *

Controversy first. A hydrologist by training and a Frenchman by birth, Eric de Bisschop had long been a resident of Polynesia, primarily Papeete, where he was living during the spring and summer of the *Kon-Tiki* expedition, which seemed to awaken in de Bisschop a vigorous strain of Tahitian chauvinism. While acknowledging, like Heyerdahl, the remarkable similarities of tribal customs, artifacts, and horticulture between the western Polynesian islands and mainland South America, de Bisschop refused to subscribe to either the conventional ethnological thinking on the matter or Heyerdahl's more recent minority theory of Pacific migration. In short, de Bisschop rejected the "semiofficial theory" that Polynesians arrived originally from Southeast Asia, and he asserted that cultural cross-pollination between Polynesian islanders and South American mainlanders had originated from west to east in the first century B.C., rather than the other way around some six hundred years later, as Heyerdahl had proposed.

De Bisschop was exasperatingly coy about the basis and evolution of his thinking on the matter and seemed delighted by the likelihood that his theory of Polynesian migration would "probably horrify most of the Pacific ethnologists." He offered a concise, three-point summary of what he identified as the conclusions of his "research":

1. The civilization of Polynesia, unlike all other known civilizations, was essentially a maritime one.
2. This maritime civilization could not have arisen or developed anywhere except in the Pacific itself.
3. Several centuries before Christ this civilization was widely dispersed—westward by voyages of migration, eastward by voyages of exploration and trade.

De Bisschop proposed that the Polynesian islands were the birthplace of Pacific civilization and that ancient Polynesians were mariners by cultural disposition. First-century Peruvians and Southeast Asians were, to de Bisschop's way of thinking, more in the way of navigators, the sorts of seamen given to coastal sailing, preferring to "go from A to B, to travel toward a known or accessible destination." The mariner, as de Bisschop described him, took to the sea "in a spirit of adventure and discovery." While the open ocean may have been "dreaded by the mere navigator," it exercised "on the mariner's spirit a kind of obsession, haunting, powerful, magnetic." Simply put, ancient Polynesians were bold, intrepid seamen; mainlanders to their west and east were not.

De Bisschop suggested that first-century Polynesian mariners, traveling principally on rafts, had sailed west to Java and south and east on inconstant winds and changeable currents to the coast of South America, whence they returned to the islands along Heyerdahl's route—with the North Equatorial Current and before the trade winds. De Bisschop characterized these as "primarily trading voyages" that "resulted in the exchange of numerous cultural traits, certain plants, and so on," and he explained away the want of Polynesian influence on the tribes of mainland South America by the fact that the mariners were too few in number to make any sort of significant cultural impression.

As pet theories go, de Bisschop's is sufficiently vague and self-serving to horrify not just ethnologists but even a benighted layman. The man's entire supposition seems, when scrutinized, to have its origins in the proper Polynesian use of adjustable *guaras* that were employed on the rafts of island mariners (mainland navigators, too, for that matter) as both keel and tiller. De Bisschop professed "astonishment" to learn that the *Kon-Tiki's guaras* had been fixed into place. Heyerdahl and his crew came to understand their full usefulness only midway through their voyage, when a few of their *guaras* broke loose and minor adjustments in the set of the boards had a sizable effect on the raft's heading. Willis, for his part, studiously adjusted his *guaras* daily on the *Seven Little Sisters* and depended upon them as an aid to steering rather than a substitute for it.

As proof that a properly fitted, competently sailed raft wasn't constrained to travel exclusively before the wind and with the current, de Bisschop mounted the *Tahiti Nui* expedition. His intent was to follow the route he believed ancient Polynesian mariners had forged. He would embark from Papeete Harbor and travel south, planning to reach the vicinity of the fortieth parallel—instructively known as the "roaring forties"—before steering due east to pick up a free lift north on the Humboldt Current and then on to the east-flowing equatorial current and, with following trade winds, back to Polynesia, thereby describing a complete counterclockwise circuit of the Pacific. De Bisschop's craft would be constructed of Tahitian bamboo and would have deployed along its centerline fourteen adjustable *guaras*, six forward and eight aft, which would permit the raft to hold a course in conditions far less favorable than any the *Kon-Tiki* could have managed.

That, anyway, was de Bisschop's fond hope. Doubters suggested that the weather and running seas at forty degrees south would be so violent as to tear the raft apart, and Bengt Danielsson, a member of the *Kon-Tiki* crew—and a friend of de Bisschop's—wondered if a raft was the appropriate vessel for de Bisschop to launch in the first place. The Polynesian archaeological record suggested that island mariners took to the seas only in outrigger and double-hulled canoes, which de Bisschop knew from experience to be altogether capable craft. He had already built and sailed a double-hulled canoe, the *Kamiloa*, from Molokai, Hawaii, to France by way of Cape Town. Perversely, de Bisschop insisted that all the rafts employed on the fringes of the Pacific were degraded versions of an original Polynesian model, long dispensed with before Europeans arrived on the scene. He felt free, consequently, to borrow the rigging for the *Tahiti Nui* (Polynesian for "Greater Tahiti") from Indochina to the west and the movable *guaras* from Peru to the east. Danielsson confessed that he found it difficult to "take this method of reconstructing a prehistoric type of raft really seriously." De Bisschop, for his part, hardly cared.

At the time of his voyage in November of 1956, Eric de Bisschop was a sixty-six-year-old curmudgeon with stubborn if not outright ossified opinions about most everything. If he had decided that a junk-rigged Tahitian bamboo raft with Peruvian *guaras* was somehow historically authentic, then it was. And if he were convinced that ancient Tahitians had traveled on such craft east along the storm-whipped fortieth parallel, then they had, and he would as well. So the *Tahiti Nui* expedition, in the end, was far more an act of intractable will than it was the pursuit of plausible science.

The raft was launched on November 8 with a crew of five. De Bisschop was joined in his experiment by two French brothers, a naturalized Tahitian, a Chilean to serve as cook, three cats, several chickens, and a pig named Panchita. Amid a throng of well-wishers in canoes, the *Tahiti Nui* was towed out of Papeete Harbor by a naval launch, through the channel between Tahiti and Mooréa, and ten miles beyond the last spar of land, where the tow rope was dropped and the raft was left to wallow aimlessly on a calm sea. "So there we were," de Bisschop noted, "at the outset of our voyage, moving neither forward nor back, bobbing about like a cork. It was a situation that had not yet begun to bore us."

After two weeks at sea, the raft was making sluggish progress south on inconstant winds. One of the cats, sickly from the start, had died, and another of the two remaining had taken to using de Bisschop's bunk for a litter box. Occasional squalls had "aroused a bit of sea" and permitted de Bisschop and crew to gain confidence in their craft, which they were able to steer almost exclusively with its *guaras*. They had caught and feasted on their first dorado, a fifty-pounder, and de Bisschop had already wearied of the near-incessant chatter over their radio. "How can you be a self-respecting deep sea sailor," he asked, "if you are constantly tied to the land by all this umbilical nonsense?"

Progress south was erratic. Favorable following winds would give way to headwinds, and the raft would yield hard-won progress, which meant the *Tahiti Nui* needed all of seven weeks to reach thirty-three degrees south. Here the crew was pleasantly surprised by a steady westerly wind and so set a course due east for South America a good deal farther north than they'd expected. As the raft was effectively self-steering and the wind reliable and following, the crew had little to do in the way of actual sailing for their first weeks of easting. De Bisschop occupied himself reading and making notes for his book on Polynesian navigation. Others of the crew fished and, by turns, monitored the radio, which brought messages from as far off as Syria and Norway. Juanito, the Chilean cook, practiced his French and basked in the company of Panchita the pig, of whom he'd grown inordinately fond and who'd been spared butchery by what the crew decided was "the hand of fate."

For several weeks running, Panchita had been slated for death only to be spared by one of the crew's landing a sizable fish, a rather rare event in the opening weeks of the voyage. For almost a month, every the time the butcher knife was produced, a dorado took the hook, so the crew decided their pig was charmed somehow, and they elected to spare her. This was no trifling decision, given the amount of food the sow required and her custom of devouring chunks of bamboo decking whenever she felt peckish.

But the *Tahiti Nui* hardly needed a pig to take it apart, since it appeared to be gradually disintegrating on its own. After a couple of months at sea, the raft began shedding bamboo. The craft's buoyancy depended on bundles of Tahitian bamboo strapped together to make floats, so the sight of loose sticks of the stuff drifting away in the *Tahiti Nui*'s wake was bound to be a little alarming, particularly given the vessel's sluggish progress. The first leg of the trip—five thousand miles from Papeete to the coast of South America—was taking far longer than de Bisschop had estimated. On February 23, 1957, the *Tahiti Nui* cleared the 117th degree of longitude, the halfway point of the opening phase of her trip. Slowed by intermittent contrary winds, she had traveled but twenty-five hundred miles in three and a half months, glacial progress when compared with Willis's six thousand miles in what was virtually the same amount of time. Worse still, the crew had seen no rain in over six weeks and so were running short on water, and though their raft was maintaining its buoyancy, the men knew that the gradual loss of bamboo was bound to tell in the coming weeks.

When the wind was favorable, the *Tahiti Nui* typically covered upwards of seventy miles a day, but she was frequently blown west or, in one instance, so far north that de Bisschop contemplated calling at Easter Island (they got within three hundred miles of it) in order to make repairs. But the southerly wind shifted, and the crew had no other choice than to steer for

Valparaíso and hope they could make it. By early May they'd
been at sea for seven months and were still over a thousand
miles from the South American coast. The raft had been blown
all over the place and had finally found a steady westerly wind
that, over the course of a few days, increased so in ferocity as to
force the crew to sail under bare poles or risk having their raft
torn to pieces. Even with sails down, what had become a gale
blow pressed forcefully enough against the windward side of the
cabin to cause the *Tahiti Nui* to list a good forty-five degrees.

As violent as the storm was, it had come out of the west and
thus had blown the raft toward her goal. The squall that followed it, more ferocious still, kicked up out of the east and
roared with such tenacity as to prompt de Bisschop to quip,
"We were on our way back to Tahiti." Together the storms battered the raft so that one of the crossbeams was crushed and a
fair amount of bamboo splintered and broken. In examining a
shattered scrap of bamboo, de Bisschop discovered it to be riddled with shipworms, a very bad sign indeed. When the chunk
was tossed into the sea, it sank immediately.

The teredo borer is, in fact, not a worm at all but a bivalve
mollusk, a sort of elongated clam with a pair of shells attached to
its forward end. The shells' leading edges are employed as exca-
vators, and the teredo can auger its way through even the stoutest
wood, leaving a channel about the size of a man's finger. Infesta-
tions have brought many a timber ship to grief. Christopher
Columbus was said to have lost his entire fleet to shipworms on
his fourth voyage to the Americas in 1502, and it was a dead certainty that even a modest dose of borers would make short work
of de Bisschop's bamboo raft. So the crew was obliged to suspect
that they would never reach Valparaíso, still eight hundred miles

away, and would be lucky to make landfall in the Juan Fernández Islands, a little over three hundred miles distant.

A thorough survey of the raft revealed additional damage from both storms and borers, and it was decided that the *Tahiti Nui* would likely sink from beneath the men without a tow. Accordingly, a radio message requesting assistance was relayed via Tahiti to Chile, and the naval cruiser *Baquedano* was dispatched to the raft's coordinates. In the small hours of the morning on May 22, the crew spied the lights of the ship in the east, and the *Baquedano*'s captain agreed to attempt a tow, though his clear preference was for de Bisschop and his men to abandon the raft.

The tow went as poorly as the captain had feared it might. Seas were high, and the ship, which normally traveled at twenty knots, had a difficult time keeping to the three knots the raft could tolerate. The towrope parted on several occasions, and in one bit of ill-advised maneuvering, the raft collided with the ship and was heavily damaged on her starboard side, with "masses of bamboos" coming loose. As a result the *Tahiti Nui* listed acutely and became even more of a chore to tow. At this point Más Afuera, the closest landfall, was still 150 miles away.

On Sunday, May 26, the towrope broke yet again, and the captain of the *Baquedano* sent a radio message to the raft informing de Bisschop and his crew that he had decided to dispense with any further attempts to tow the *Tahiti Nui*. The ship was low on fuel and could reach Valparaíso only if she proceeded east immediately under normal speed. The sea was running so heavily at the time that the *Baquedano* couldn't even lower a boat for the men. Instead the plan was for the ship to draw alongside the *Tahiti Nui*, which would permit the crew to leap onto the *Baquedano*'s quarterdeck once lifted by the swell.

Ropes were thrown to the crew, some to secure the raft to the ship and others to attach to the crew's possessions, which would be hauled on board the *Baquedano*. After the kit bags had gone up, Juanito, the chef, drew the crew's attention to one final bit of cargo—Panchita the pig. He had fed her the *Tahiti Nui*'s last bottle of wine, so she was in no state to resist the trussing inflicted upon her as prelude to the crew's flinging her into the sea so that she could be drawn, hand over hand, onto the deck of the ship. Given her bulk and dead weight, the seamen manning Panchita's rope assumed she was an injured crewman and shouted out for the *Baquedano*'s doctor, who came charging across the deck to find a drunken sow instead.

The cats were stuffed in a sack and carried shipboard by Juanito as he jumped with the rest of the raft's crew onto the pitching quarterdeck of the *Baquedano*. None too soon, as it turned out, since the raft rolled violently into the hull of the ship, parting her mooring ropes all at once. The *Tahiti Nui* drifted astern, already sinking, as the *Baquedano* throttled up and made for Valparaíso.

Two days later the crewmen of the *Tahiti Nui* were carried in the ship's launch to the quay of Valparaíso Harbor, where they were greeted by thousands of well-wishers. It's probably a bit difficult today to appreciate the pitch of worldwide interest that attended expeditions like de Bisschop's and Heyerdahl's, even Willis's, notwithstanding its paucity of practical scientific ambition. In the case of the *Tahiti Nui*, radio operators across the globe had eavesdropped on the raft's transmissions, and many of them had passed along garbled scraps of misinformation to news outlets that had reported them as fact. So almost anytime throughout the course of the *Tahiti Nui*'s 199 days at sea, people around the planet could hear passably unreliable word of the crew's progress and condition. In mid-May the men on board the *Tahiti Nui* had even picked up an American news bulletin that reported the raft badly damaged and three of the crew suffering from serious injury.

So interest in the expedition remained high, thanks to assorted alarming, inaccurate news reports, and de Bisschop and his crew were global celebrities by the time they reached solid ground. It hardly mattered that their raft had all but sunk from beneath them well short of their goal. If anything, that seemed to make the entire ordeal more romantic, and shared feelings of failure among the crew were soon put to rout by shouts from the crowded quay of *"Viva la* Tahiti Nui! *Viva Francia!"* A military band struck up the "Marseillaise," and someone surely shouted, "Where's the pig?" as de Bisschop and crew were hustled to the nearby town hall and ushered onto the balcony so that the crowd might see them and cheer.

By then de Bisschop had already decided to build a new raft and continue with his expedition. Or rather he had decided that his crew would build a new raft while he retired to a villa in the highlands to write his account of the first leg of the voyage. Money being short, there was no budget for having bamboo harvested and shipped from Tahiti, so the crew would have to depend on local resources and local generosity. A shipyard in Constitución came to the expedition's rescue. The owners offered to finance and assist in construction of the raft and boasted of some experience in raft building—limited, calamitous experience as it turned out.

Some years before, the shipyard had fulfilled a government contract for a large raft intended to ferry cars across the Maule

River. Constructed of oak, the raft was launched with high ceremony, and a band played stirring military music as the ferry was released to slide down her slip into the water, where she sank altogether from sight and settled onto the river bottom. Too heavy to raise, she was there still. Wisely, de Bisschop and his men decided against oak for their new raft and settled on cypress instead, which enjoyed the advantage—aside from buoyancy—of ready accessibility, since there was an extensive cypress forest hard by the town of Constitución. Fifty trees were felled, their trunks measuring an average of eighteen inches across, and hauled to the shipyard harbor, where two of the original crew members—Juanito and Alain Brun—oversaw the construction of the raft. The other two crewmen had given up on the expedition by then and had returned to Tahiti, while de Bisschop would descend only occasionally from the uplands to check on the raft's progress without troubling himself to contribute to it.

With no plans to work from, Brun and Juanito were forced to puzzle their way through construction problems on the fly. Finding it all but impossible to lash the giant cypress logs together in any satisfying fashion, they resorted to attaching the logs, each to the next, with wooden pegs driven horizontally through the members. Three such layers of cypress trunks constituted the platform of the raft, which was then fitted with masts, a raised deck, and a cabin, which, in what would prove a stroke of bluff good fortune, was built with a flat roof. Like its namesake, *Tahiti Nui II* would be junk-rigged and steered by a combination of fourteen maneuverable *guaras*.

By the end of the year, the work was all but complete, and de Bisschop returned to Constitución in January of 1958, having finished his account of the first leg of the voyage. Various Santiago newspapers had reported that the *Tahiti Nui II* would embark on February 15, which de Bisschop identified as a "baseless rumor" but added, "Let's help the papers be right for once in a way by making this our sailing date." That left no time for a trial voyage of any consequence, and de Bisschop decided that the opening leg of the trip, a fifteen-hundred-mile jaunt to Callao, would serve as the craft's shakedown cruise. He then introduced Brun and Juanito to their new crewmates, a German-Chilean mining engineer named Hans Fischer and Jean Pélissier, a French oceanographer. Neither had any practical sailing experience.

The raft was launched on February 14, was released down her slip to meet the water in a ceremony attended by thousands who expressed their pleasure and astonishment by crying out, "She floats! She floats!" when the *Tahiti Nui II* failed to join the oaken car ferry on the riverbed. The crew was helpless against supporters and well-wishers thronging onto the deck, and there were soon upwards of sixty people on board. The raft sank to its upper layer of cypress, but the crew was pleased to observe that the deck remained a good foot and a half above the waterline.

On the morning of the fifteenth, the *Tahiti Nui II* was towed by five rowboats out of the protected waters of the Maule River, through the breakers, and into open sea, where a cutter was waiting to take up the chore of hauling the raft to deep water. The wind freshened out of the west, however, and the raft was soon blown back toward the breakers, dragging the five rowboats with her. De Bisschop ordered the towlines dropped to save the rowers, and the untrained, disorganized crew, along with the French ambassador to Chile (on board for the occasion by special invitation), hectically raised the sails and set the *guaras*, and the *Tahiti Nui II* was all but miraculously carried out of harm's way.

Though his initial destination was Callao, due north, de Bisschop decided against riding the fast-flowing Humboldt Current the fifteen hundred miles to harbor and directed instead that the raft should sail west-northwest for two hundred miles and only then veer north, chiefly in a bid to avoid adverse winds and heavy shipping traffic along the coast. As had Willis, the crew complained of cold, cloudy weather when they crossed the Humboldt Current and saw the sun only after a full week at sea. The two new hands were comprehensively seasick for ten days running, and then they went from eating nothing to eating everything in sight (which was a bit of a chore, given the quality of the food).

Before departure Juanito had informed de Bisschop that he no longer wished to be the raftboard cook, and de Bisschop had responded by promoting Juanito to what he insisted was a new position, namely "superintendent of food supplies," which, as it turned out, called for Juanito to prepare meals. The uncanny similarity between Juanito's previous position on the *Tahiti Nui* and his new position on the *Tahiti Nui II* failed to escape his notice, and Juanito responded by "superintending" meals that were only passably edible at best. His specialties were "half-cooked rice mixed with an enormous quantity of bitter onions and a kind of pancake which was regularly burnt on one side and sticky on the other."

Only once extended sulking and a spate of wretched dinners had failed to get him demoted did Juanito accept his lot and become a "tolerable cook and jolly shipmate." In fact, the spirits of the entire crew rebounded after the raft had cleared the frigid Humboldt Current with its gloomy, oppressive weather and had gained warmer waters and bright tropical sunshine. Jean Pélissier soon demonstrated a welcome deftness with a spear gun that kept fresh fish on the table almost daily, and the raft handled about as well as the crew might have hoped. After three weeks at sea, the *Tahiti Nui II* was a solid eight hundred miles up the coast and halfway to Callao. Her average speed worked out to forty miles a day, and the crew had no substantial complaints beyond wireless-radio failure. None of the crew's transmissions had raised a response, which, given the incessant chatter that had marked the first leg of the voyage, was a source more of delight than disappointment.

By March 20, the raft was back in sight of land, specifically the towering peaks of the Andes. Her course had remained a steady due north all along, but the continent—bulging to the west at the frontier between Chile and Peru—had effectively come out to meet the *Tahiti Nui II*. With the proximity of the coast as a fresh danger and an increase in shipping traffic to guard against, watches were set around the clock, and by March 27 the crew had closed within ten miles of Callao. A navy patrol boat raced out of the harbor and bore down on the raft. The launch swung around. A crewman tossed down a towline without query or comment, and the boat headed back for Callao with the *Tahiti Nui II* in tow. "It seemed evident," Alain Brun remarked wryly, "that Peruvian patrol boats were accustomed to towing rafts of prehistoric model."

On the voyage up from Constitución, de Bisschop and Brun had been troubled by a gradual loss of buoyancy in the raft. After only six weeks at sea, the deck was a full foot closer to the water. A cursory inspection revealed no trace of shipworms, and seawater had saturated the cypress logs to an average depth of only an inch, yet the raft had sunk sufficiently to prompt de Bisschop to advertise in local newspapers for balsa logs by way of additional flotation. He bought the twelve largest that turned up and secured them in a hollow beneath the stern. From a Lima chemist, de Bisschop procured an assortment of forty-gallon aluminum tanks and stowed as many sealed empty ones beneath the deck as he and the crew could make fit. Satisfied by the increased freeboard, de Bisschop set a departure date of April 13, and at eleven o'clock on that Sunday morning the *Tahiti Nui II* was towed out of Callao Harbor and into the powerful northerly sweep of the Humboldt Current. (The *Kon-Tiki* had embarked from the same anchorage eleven years earlier to the month.)

As had Willis, de Bisschop set a westerly heading, which, given the force of the Humbolt Current, actually resulted in a north-northwesterly course that carried the *Tahiti Nui II* past the Galápagos Islands and into the South Equatorial Current. Suddenly the water was bluer and warmer and fish were more plentiful, including the ever-so-rare snake mackerel, which for a few weeks was a nearly pestilential presence on board. The creatures would throw themselves onto the raft's deck at night and did so in such numbers that de Bisschop felt no compunction in gutting and cooking one of these "extinct" fish as a kind of experiment. The crew pronounced the flesh "quite excellent."

The opening month of the voyage resembled a "holiday cruise," with uninterrupted fair weather, a favorable following wind, and a steady current. Among the books in the raft's library was a copy of *Kon-Tiki*, which the crew took to consulting for comparison's sake, and they were pleased to find that they were matching Heyerdahl's progress. Since de Bisschop's intention was to reach Tahiti specifically rather than Polynesia generally (Heyerdahl's goal), the *Tahiti Nui II* kept to a more northerly course than had the *Kon-Tiki* but was still equaling Heyerdahl's daily runs of thirty-five to fifty miles. Once Alain Brun had rigged an extra square sail from two foresails stitched together, the *Tahiti Nui II* began to regularly outstrip the *Kon-Tiki*'s progress, which left the crew little to complain of but for the ongoing failure of the raft's wireless transmitter to raise a response.

On May 26 the crew did, however, succeed at making contact the old-fashioned way, hailing a passing ship, the Tahiti-bound steamer *Pioneer Star*, and requesting that the captain "tell our friends in Papeete that all are well on board *Tahiti Nui II*." Alain Brun noted that the meeting took place at a point precisely halfway beween Callao and Papeete, a distance the raft had covered in an economical six weeks. Given the strength and reliability of the south-bending current and steering winds, the crew had every reason to expect that they would reach Tahiti on or before July 14, an islandwide festival day.

Trouble, though, started in early June, when the raft began, ever so slowly, to lose buoyancy once again and sink. Soon enough the deck was awash in several inches of water, and, to make matters worse, the south-flowing current deviation the crew had been led to expect at 120 degrees west never really took hold, and the *Tahiti Nui II* continued on a westerly course at 4 degrees south. The island of Tahiti lay in the 17th degree of southern latitude and was fast becoming unreachable. When a whale shark (the largest of the fishes) began to follow the

Tahiti Nui II in much the same manner one had followed the *Kon-Tiki*, Alain Brun observed waggishly that they seemed to be "copying the *Kon-Tiki* expedition in everything—except the raft's ability to float."

By the middle of June, with water eight inches deep in the cabin, the crew took up residence on the structure's flat roof, where they suffered from exposure to the near-constant wind. De Bisschop was especially affected. His strength had begun to ebb, and though his crewmates could discover no telling symptoms of any specific illness, he weakened steadily and suffered from the cold, damp conditions on the cabin roof.

By June 20, Alain Brun, the raft's navigator and the only able-bodied, legitimate sailor on board, recognized that without a miraculous shift in wind and current the raft had no prospect whatsoever of reaching Tahiti, and even the Marquesas (four hundred miles away) would remain out of reach without at least a quartering of the prevailing wind. To make matters worse, during Brun's watch on the night of the twenty-sixth, the raft quite suddenly and inexplicably sank three feet in one abrupt go. With the dawning came a general inspection to discover the cause, and when Brun sawed off a chunk of cypress in the bow to examine it, he discovered the wood to be riddled with teredo borer holes.

The crew attempted to lighten the raft by tossing overboard every disposable item that came to hand, but the improvement in buoyancy was only marginal and short-lived. As a further complication, the deeper the raft sank, the more difficult it was to steer and the more inclined to yaw and pitch, to the point where the crew, at de Bisschop's suggestion, fitted the *Tahiti Nui II* with an outrigger in what proved a successful bid to stabilize her. Feverish and growing weaker by the day, de Bisschop then officially passed command of the raft to Alain Brun, who set up a schedule of watches and a plan for rationing out the food that remained. With de Bisschop too weak to function effectively, the working crew was down to four, and short rations and long hours had soon taken a toll on the general mood on board.

Juanito was the first to grow sullen and shirk his duties. During his watches at the helm, he repeatedly allowed the raft to run up into the wind, to almost disastrous effect. Juanito resented the extra measure of honey that was permitted de Bisschop in his suffering, and he began to speak of an escape craft he intended to build in which he would take his chances on the open ocean alone. Water was growing scarce, as no rain had fallen for months, and the *Tahiti Nui II* had drifted into such a desolate quarter of the Pacific that salvation was beginning to look increasingly uncertain.

On the morning of July 14, festival day in Papeete, the crew spied a cargo ship a few miles astern of the raft and crossing perpendicular to her course. They succeeded in lighting a signal fire, but the smoke it released was contained by a relentless downdraft, and no amount of yelling and arm waving could attract the notice of the ship's crew. So Brun was already disappointed when he climbed off the cabin roof to take his watch at the helm and discovered that the sea was up to his calves and the raft was sinking rather more quickly with each passing day.

As a further complication, Juanito had decided that the time was ripe for him to build his escape craft, and he took up the raft's ax and proceeded to hack loose the eucalyptus bowsprit. Brun intervened, and de Bisschop, so weak as to be immobile by this point, found the strength to draw up a document (in duplicate) codifying Juanito's rights and privileges as decided by the rest of the crew:

1. to let Juanito Bugueño build his raft on condition that he does not thereby diminish *Tahiti Nui II*'s already much reduced buoyancy;
2. whether he will nor not, to compel our former comrade without hesitation or compassion to cast off—having first received his share of the provisions and water—as soon as his raft is completed.

But before Juanito could get much beyond constructing an oar, a storm blew up bearing rain, and the downpour lasted for several hours, during which the crew increased its water supply from three gallons to forty. But the cloudburst ushered in a period of storms and high seas that battered the sinking raft and her crew for days thereafter. By the time the wild weather had ended, the *Tahiti Nui II* was another four inches below the waves. The crew gave in to despondency. Juanito's escape craft was forgotten. The only remaining hope was that the wind and current would continue driving the raft toward tiny Starbuck Island.

By August 6, conditions were still favorable for landfall, but the raft had 250 miles yet to cover, which, by Alain Brun's calculations, would likely require ten days, and it hardly seemed possible that the raft would stay afloat for that long. Consequently, it was decided that a new raft had to be built from the remaining sound timbers and aluminum drums that were at present keeping the wreck of the *Tahiti Nui II* above the waves.

De Bisschop, in between bouts of fever, had sketched a plan for the new raft that was inspired by Melanesian canoes with their double outriggers. Corralled aluminum barrels would provide the flotation, and the crew would ride on a tiny deck of Masonite salvaged from the walls of the *Tahiti Nui II*'s cabin.

The trick would be to dismantle the sinking *Tahiti Nui II* and construct the new craft (not very creatively dubbed the *Tahiti Nui III*) while keeping both afloat. Uncompromised timber proved scarce, and more than a few of the aluminum barrels beneath the *Tahiti Nui II* turned out to be full of seawater, but the crew succeeded at constructing a new raft, along the lines of de Bisschop's sketch, in seven days, from August 7 to 13. The deck was only five by six feet, and the raft lurched and bobbed violently, but it promised to stay above the waves, and the men abandoned the half-sunk *Tahiti Nui II* 180 days out of Constitución, thereafter setting a course for Starbuck Island on a craft known to them simply as "number three."

With but one centerboard, the new raft was helpless against current deflection and shifts in the following wind and so could hardly be steered in any useful sense. Accordingly, as the raft approached Starbuck Island on a course bound to carry her slightly to the south (twenty-nine miles as it turned out), there was nothing the crew could do to compensate. Even worse, though the crew couldn't know it at the time, most of the open ocean surrounding the Line Islands (Starbuck's group) was closed to shipping due to ongoing British nuclear-weapons tests on Christmas Island. An atmospheric device had been exploded in April of 1958, and another was scheduled for detonation on August 22, so there was no chance at all of meeting a ship. By the sixteenth the *Tahiti Nui III* had passed just south of

Starbuck Island, and Brun steered for Penrhyn Island with only modest hopes of making landfall there.

By this time de Bisschop was lapsing in and out of consciousness, and the crew was increasingly restive in the face of further rationing of both food and water. Ten gallons of the latter remained, and the available food stores consisted primarily of rice and lentils. When the raft sailed well wide of Penrhyn to the north, a sort of apathetic fatalism took hold of Juanito and Jean Pélissier, and they became even less useful to Brun and could hardly be relied upon to man their watches.

By the afternoon of August 26, the wind had shifted out of the northeast and was blowing the raft toward the northern end of the Cook Islands, specifically in the direction of Manihiki and Rakahanga. By the thirtieth, Brun's calculations confirmed that the raft was but ten miles off Rakahanga, and at quarter after five in the evening the crew sighted the island straight ahead. By eight o'clock the raft was little more than a mile from Rakahanga with its surrounding reef, and a full moon had risen to light the *Tahiti Nui III*'s way in to the breakers when no navigable gap in the coral presented itself. De Bisschop insisted on sitting atop the sleeping box that had been constructed to keep him dry, and Hans Fischer and Jean Pélissier joined him there—one on either side—to protect and support him.

The fragile, jerry-rigged raft was at the mercy of the waves now and was soon lifted and driven into the reef, where following breakers tipped it forward and swept the deck clean, driving the crew into the roiling water. Upon surfacing, Brun immediately sought out de Bisschop and found him floating unconscious. Assisted by Jean Pélissier, Brun struggled with de Bisschop across the lagoon to the beach, where the men determined that de Bisschop was dead (of what would prove to be a broken neck). The rest of the crew survived with only scratches and gashes from the coral, and they were fed and nursed by the natives of a nearby village until they could be returned to Papeete—along with de Bisschop's body—on a French gunboat dispatched for that purpose.

If de Bisschop had only intended to demonstrate it was *possible* to make a counterclockwise circuit around the Pacific Ocean from Tahiti to the western coast of South America and back to Polynesia, then his expedition could be thought a marginal success, even given the hardships and the great personal cost. Instead, however, he'd insisted that it had been historically practical to do such a thing, that he was following a route Polynesians had forged on craft like his own for trading purposes, which hardly seems likely, for a host of reasons. The crew's experience in the tempestuous southern latitudes would seem to confirm that a bamboo raft is a poor match for such reliably violent winds and seas, and the dawdling breezes and inconstant currents of the northern Pacific made a return to Tahiti far less of a sure thing than de Bisschop had expected. Throw in teredo borers, infrequent rainfall, and the vagaries of human psychology, and one can only wonder who exactly would have left ancient Tahiti on such a business trip as that.

*   *   *

If de Bisschop's proposition was controversial, even marginally mad, it was still more credible than a theory hatched by one DeVere Baker in another quarter of the Pacific at along about the same time. Baker was a shipbuilder by profession and a Mormon by religious disposition, and he'd had a curious epiphany while visiting the ruins of an Aztec city in Mexico. Impressed by the sophistication of the crumbling structures and the ambitious layout of the city at large, Baker reasoned that the natives were insufficiently sophisticated to have possibly built such a civilization unassisted.

After studying a nineteenth-century English translation of a fifteenth-century Aztec document, the Works of Ixtlilxochitl, in conjunction with the Book of Mormon, Baker concluded that ancient Israelites, led by the prophet Lehi, had come to Central America in 600 B.C., "bringing with them their gospel and precious records." According to Baker, these intrepid Israelites had "fled Jerusalem at the time of the Tower of Babel and the confusion of tongues" and had crossed the wide waters to the New World. Wide indeed, since the Middle East and the western coast of Mexico are separated by two oceans—let's call it twenty thousand miles—which Baker proposed Lehi and his followers crossed on rafts and primitive barges.

Working backward, Baker promoted the heightened state and sprawling scope of Aztec urban ruins as proof that Lehi and his band of Israelites had arrived in the New World and had civilized it before being driven out by the natives. "The people of one nation were white, delightsome, cultured and peace-loving, living within the cities," he wrote, while "the other people"—read "natives"—"were fierce, warlike, and given to wild paintings of the body, weird firelight ceremonies and waging war upon their more peaceful brothers." In short, the delightsome white Israelites had been driven out by the dusky undelightsome Central Americans.

As ethnological propositions go, this one is more than a little bigoted at bottom and boasts, for a foundation, a preponderance of Mormon wishfulness largely untroubled by fact. More curious still is the means by which Baker intended to "prove" his theory of Israelite influence (and not just throughout Central America but along the western coast of South America as well). He suggested that when warring natives drove out the delightsome Israelites in A.D. 34 (which, Baker claimed, prompted a visit by the resurrected Christ to Mexico, but we'll leave that for another day), the descendants of Lehi took to their rafts and barges and set a return course for the Middle East. Due to the vagaries of Pacific currents, however, some of these craft were driven west and made inadvertent landfall in the Hawaiian Islands, where, according to Baker, the wayward Israelites visited a bit of their delightsomeness on those inhabitants as well.

Accordingly, in order to prove that men had sailed from the Middle East to Central America in 600 B.C., DeVere Baker proposed in 1954 to construct a raft and sail it from San Francisco Harbor to Hawaii. Essentially, then, by following the course the Israelites would have taken by accident if lost on their way home, Baker hoped to establish that they'd actually come in the first place. As an added value, he also intended to mount his expedition in promotion of world peace and against the scourge of godless Communism.

Using his own money—thirty thousand 1954 dollars— DeVere Baker constructed his raft in the yard of the Sausalito Shipbuilding Company. He used fir timbers and planking and, with the help of his brother-in-law, manufactured over the course of twelve months precisely the sort of raft a shipbuilder would build. The platform was shaped something like the base of an electric iron, and the cabin atop it was a squat rectangular slab. The craft carried a lone mast forward, which was rigged for a large, square sail.

The crew consisted of Captain DeVere Baker (and from this point forward he would doggedly and quite seriously refer to himself as "Captain Baker"), his wife's brother, a merchant marine radio operator, a college student, and a journalist. The raft was christened *Lehi I* on July 2, 1954, with Miss California, Lee Ann Meriwether, presiding. The craft was launched, Baker wrote, "amid the cheers and doubts of hundreds of curious people."

Baker and crew sailed the *Lehi I* out of San Francisco Harbor and into the teeth of a coastal storm that battered the raft for a solid week, until—as Baker observed graciously—in "the midst of the ocean's fury our radioman broke down and radioed an SOS for help." Baker was hoping for a tow, but the captain of the responding Coast Guard cutter gave the raft's crew the option of either abandoning their craft or riding out the storm. The crew clambered onto the cutter, and the *Lehi I* was left to drift. Thereafter Baker claimed to get occasional reports on her progress, and he even gave credence to one that had her passing, entirely unmanned, through the Panama Canal in 1956. "She had caught the Humboldt Current off Panama," Baker proposed, "and was headed for Tahiti." (Actually, all abandoned rafts passing through the locks of the Panama Canal catch the North Equatorial Current and head for Japan.)

Undeterred (wouldn't you know it), Baker almost immediately set about the construction of *Lehi II*, a raft built along the same lines as its predecessor but with the addition of an aft mast. Ten months and forty thousand dollars later, the *Lehi II* was towed to sea without Baker's "permission or knowledge, in the face of regulation flag storm warnings, by a publicity-blinded deck hand," he reported, a revelation firmly in the growing tradition of Captain Baker's talent for delegating blame. The *Lehi II* was abused by heavy seas throughout the night, took on an acute list, and had to be abandoned the following day.

Hardly the sort to be stifled by embarrassment, Baker began work on *Lehi III* with an ill-advised but necessary redesign, given his diminished circumstances. Out over seventy thousand dollars and no longer welcome at the Sausalito Shipbuilding Company, Baker drafted plans for a vessel he could build in the garage of his home in Petaluma, California. What he came up with was little more than a floating cabin encircled by a narrow walkway. The entire vessel was sixteen feet long and maybe seven feet wide. There was hardly room enough in the cabin for the crew of Baker, his first mate, and his two hands, whom Baker identified as "Brandt Pierce—Master Sergeant in the Army" and "Larry Foglino—Psychology Major."

Baker's plan, inasmuch as he had one, was to sail the raft south from Bodega Bay, north of San Francisco, to the port of Los Angeles, from where he would contemplate a crossing to Hawaii. Baker set out on March 19, 1957, with just his first mate on board, and the pair soon found the action of the "perilously tilting cabin" at sea to be more than a little unsettling. They bobbed and lurched about for a month, making deliberate progress south, until the first mate (a butcher from Oakland), quite done in by the chill weather and the violence of the ride, asked to be set ashore before Baker's scheduled call at Avila on the Central Coast, where the *Lehi III* was to take on the master sergeant and the psychology major.

Baker was forced, consequently, to sail alone for the three additional days it took him to reach fresh crew in Avila. He couldn't afford to sleep, given his proximity to the coast, and in a bid to keep awake and alert, he began to take a food supplement he'd been given by his brother-in-law, pills marketed by the Abundavita Corporation of America. Apparently, the product was a blend of vitamins, minerals, and roughage (Nutrilite, a similar item of the time, included alfalfa, parsley, and watercress), and the stuff had a conspicuously stimulant effect on Baker. He took six pills a day in two doses of three and straightaway felt so downright perky that he pressed the supplement on both the master sergeant and the psychology major, and soon they were all eyeing their watery world with "fresh enthusiasm," which resulted, at length, in seagoing high jinks: "We shot films of Larry trying in mock desperation to find an electric outlet so that he could use his electric razor." (Ah, the fifties.)

The good humor eroded, however, when the raftboard supply of pills was exhausted, and "the drop in bodily fitness and mental good fellowship was almost immediately apparent." Baker responded by tacking toward the coast—"into port went the little cabin and into our galley that morning went another supply." So there they were, three overstimulated men on a raft the size of a Chrysler, a vessel with all the oceangoing virtues of a buoy. With many thanks to the Abundavita Corporation of America, Baker and his speeding crew rode the tiny, bucking *Lehi III* all the way to Los Angeles in three months' time.

Even though, as one headline writer put it, LEHI RAFT SKIPPER STILL HOPES TO ESTABLISH EARLY WHITE RACE, Baker had known quite enough rough treatment from the rolling sea on his puny raft to have cultivated a reluctance to venture west into deeper waters. At least not until he'd applied a supplement to the vessel as well. Baker's plan was to mount the *Lehi III* on a larger platform and so employ the craft as the cabin on what would become the *Lehi IV.*

After blundering down the coast, the *Lehi III* had been put on display in a Redondo Beach car lot, where it attracted the notice of one Keith Ackerman of the local chamber of commerce. Upon learning of Baker's plans for the *Lehi IV,* Ackerman persuaded the city council (the vote was unanimous) to designate Redondo Beach as the home port and official sponsor of the *Lehi IV.* The relationship seemed exclusively to entail an obligation on Baker's part to build his raft on a beachfront lot along the town's main street (just across from the Rexall drugstore), where he would be available for gawkers and kibitzers and leisured passersby with questions and comments or, more likely, invaluable nuggets of raft-building advice.

As there was no financial support involved, Baker raised money by lecturing on both his seagoing travails and his singular theory of the influences behind the Aztec Empire. He also sold film footage of the coasting voyage of the *Lehi III*—presumably including the electric-shaver gag—to the NBC television show *I Search for Adventure.* At this point even Baker had to recognize that he no longer enjoyed an "allowance for failure" and needed to reach Hawaii on the *Lehi IV* or give over the effort entirely. To that end he resorted to intensive prayer:

> I believe that there is *Unlimited Knowledge* in this universe, *knowledge* which can only be tapped by the vibratory power of prayer. Mistakes made in the past *Lehi*

ventures were made because I had failed to draw heavily
enough upon this *Universal Knowledge* and to act upon
the help I did receive at just the right time for it to jell
into success.

Success, in this instance, was to take the form of an eighteen-
by-twenty-four-foot timber platform with the *Lehi III* centered
upon it and bolted to it. July 5, 1958, was both departure day
for the *Lehi IV* and "Neptune Day" in Redondo Beach. Baker
had been named King Neptune for the annual parade, which
wound through the streets of the town and came to a halt at King
Harbor, where the raft was moored. Civic elders had organized a
showy leave-taking for Baker and his crew, which called for the
four of them—stripped to the waist like Polynesians—to pile
into a launch, motor out to the raft, raise her lone square sail, and
make for the open ocean. While the four men managed to shuck
their shirts quite splendidly, they couldn't get the launch motor
started and so, while waving to throngs of well-wishers, drifted
aimlessly into the harbor.

Upon finally reaching the *Lehi IV*, the men secured her to a
towline and raised her sail, so from shore she probably appeared to be sailing out of the harbor but was in fact attached to
the *Crest*, a pleasure boat owned by friends of Baker's. Preoccu-
pied with filming their own departure, the crew failed to notice
the rising wind, and the raft bore down precipitously on the
towboat, ramming her with its bowsprit. All in all, it was a fairly
inauspicious beginning. Fortunately, the whole pageant was
largely for show. Once the crew had lowered the raft's sail, the
battered *Crest* towed the *Lehi IV* into nearby San Pedro Harbor,
where the raft tied up for a week to be provisioned.

The day before the *Lehi IV* was to embark in earnest for Hawaii, Baker's wife and younger daughter decided the raft needed a mascot. Captain Baker accompanied the two to a Torrance animal shelter, where they selected a terrier mutt from a pen of dogs scheduled to be destroyed the following day. Baker dubbed the creature Tangoroa, the name of the Polynesian god of the sea, and during the first days under way, little Tang more than held up his end of a raftwide dose of near-debilitating seasickness.

The crew for the voyage consisted, once again, of Larry Foglino, who had graduated in rank from mere psychology major to first mate and navigator. He'd enlisted a student friend, Don McFarland, to come along, while Baker had recruited an authentic Polynesian, Ed Kekaula, who made up for his want of sailing experience with a deep, pleasing baritone, a talent for the ukulele, a "white-toothed smile, broad as were his strong brown shoulders," and an abiding faith in Mormon doctrine. He was "our morale booster," Baker insisted, by which he probably meant "*my* morale booster," since Baker had soon identified a troubling strain of heathenism in Foglino and McFarland. Both were well into their college degrees at the time, and Baker concluded that their fine educations were leading them "from full knowledge of God." The young men were chiefly guilty, as it turned out, of a flirtation with Darwin's theory of evolution, which Baker and Kekaula considered blasphemy. "I made a mental note," Baker wrote, "to watch how the two seemingly different trends of thought would blend or conflict."

There would not be terribly much room for blending or conflicting. The raft's cabin was only seven by ten feet, and the outer decking around the perimeter was but three feet wide. (Throw in a vomiting dog and you've an ordeal in the making.) The *Lehi IV* was, however, towing a fifteen-foot rubber raft as her lifeboat. It had been provisioned in the event of a calamity, and the crew took turns sequestering themselves in it when nothing but a little privacy would do. Baker, conditioned by experience to expect the worst, had also nailed a handsaw to the bottom of the raft in case she were to turn turtle in high seas. His plan was to cut his way back in and "finish the trip upside down if I had to."

Unsurprisingly, given Baker's luck thus far, the towboat hired to haul the raft clear of coastal currents experienced engine trouble and had to cut the *Lehi IV* loose near enough to land to leave her in a south-flowing current and so make a real hazard of Guadalupe Island. Baker was obliged to depend on makeshift sea anchors, an ineffective ten-horsepower outboard motor, and dumb luck to stave off yet another catastrophe. But after two nights sufficiently close to the rocky island coast to hear the surf breaking, the *Lehi IV* finally cleared the danger to the southwest on July 23.

After nine days at sea, the raft had traveled little more than 250 miles, which makes the calculations Baker indulged in at the time all the more curious:

Lehi I averaged forty miles a day.
Lehi II averaged forty miles a day.
Lehi III averaged forty miles a day.
Heyerdahl's Kon-Tiki averaged forty miles a day.
And Lehi IV averaged her forty miles a day.

The *Lehi I* was but a week under way, and that in a gale, while Baker and crew were aboard the *Lehi II* only twenty-four hours, and that lone day in a storm as well. The *Lehi III* was a coasting voyage south in a strong-flowing current, and by the time the above was included in Baker's log, the *Lehi IV* was making, at best, twenty-eight miles a day. The *Kon-Tiki*, to be precise, averaged closer to forty-three miles a day.

Nonetheless, Baker's faith in his figures encouraged him to extrapolate on the voyage that he believed the prophet Lehi and his followers made in the sixth century B.C. from the mouth of the Red Sea to the coast of Central America. That trip required, Baker determined, precisely 344 days at sea, because his experience and attendant calculations now confirmed that "they would have had to average forty miles a day."

In truth, the *Lehi IV* was more than a bit of a wallower, essentially a ten-ton floating dock that could usually be counted on for about one knot an hour in a following wind and with a westerly nudge from the Kuroshio, or Japanese, Current. Adjustments to the sail were minimal in most conditions, and the tiller was lashed into place, which rendered watches fairly perfunctory. Baker recognized early on "that just plain monotony would be one of our worst enemies." Baker and Ed Kekaula had their faith to distract and occupy them, discussing Scripture most evenings and holding a weekly two-man prayer meeting, which often featured Ed's "rich baritone" and Baker's "tuneless monotone," applied to "Jesus Wants Me for a Sunbeam," a particular favorite.

The heathens, on the other hand, fished, at first with erratic success, and the entire crew suffered from the persistent damp chill of the open Pacific. After two and a half weeks, seasickness was largely a thing of the past, even for little Tang, so appetites improved and cooking became a priority. A raftboard specialty was bread made from freshly ground whole wheat—the loaves were baked in a canned-heat oven—and supplemented a diet of steamed rice, tinned fruit cocktail, and the occasional fresh fish.

The heathens proved the best fishermen on board, and they worked, with Baker's advice, to develop a pretty ridiculous technique for securing freshly landed dorado. Larry the psychology major would grab the fish by the head while Don, his college buddy, would grab it by the tail, and together they would fling the thing into the cabin, with Baker closing the door behind it. In their first attempt, the trio neglected to clear the premises and so tossed a frantic fifty-pound dorado on top of napping Ed. Tangoroa, for his part, barked indiscriminately at everything all day and most of each night.

As a hedge against unwanted drift, Baker employed leeboards rather than proper *guaras*. These were planks attached to the lee side of the raft and served as a makeshift keel, and more were added whenever navigational sights revealed undue slippage south. By the end of July, the *Lehi IV* was sailing virtually due west along the twenty-fifth degree of northern latitude. Holding that course meant that Baker could then afford to drift south as he neared the Hawaiian Islands, located closer to twenty degrees north. If he dipped too soon, he had no hope of recovering against wind and current to make landfall, and the raft would be carried well west of his target, conceivably to Japan.

With the tiller lashed, there was little actual sailing to do other than rigging the occasional supplemental mast in hopes of hanging more canvas and taking better advantage of the steady following wind. Storms, though fierce when they bore down, proved reliably short-lived and infrequent, which left a bit more leisure time than Baker thought good for the soul. He observed with sadness that Larry and Don spent more and more of each day in the trailing lifeboat reading books of "an agnostic nature." Who could blame them, given Baker's ecclesiastical relentlessness? One entry from Baker's log reads, "Had talk with Don and Larry about possibility of there being a God, a Personal Being. Got nowhere." Another records, "Ed and I discussed deep church doctrine tonight."

When one considers that the proselytizing was compounded and exacerbated by Ed's tireless enthusiasm for his repertoire of hymns and traditional Hawaiian songs—all accompanied by the ukulele—it's a wonder Don and Larry didn't retire to the raft one morning and throw off the towline. Given the circumstances, the two behaved remarkably well and were never openly criticized by Baker for their coal black godless hearts, but they did finally earn his overt disapproval with their ever-more-sadistic experiments on sharks.

The crew had tired of shark meat, with its sour, ammonia-steeped flavor, and had left off butchering the creatures for food—this didn't prevent Don and Larry from hooking and landing sharks in relative profusion and gutting them just to see what might spill out. In one instance they removed the beating heart from a tiger shark, tossed the carcass into the water, and were astounded to see the thing swim after the raft, following them for a good twenty minutes before sinking into the depths. Baker seemed to object less to the sadism than to a deck routinely awash in shark entrails. In his capacity as captain, Baker finally ordered an end to the pastime, but not before Don had sliced open an eight-footer to discover, among the contents of its stomach, "a long, pinkish object about one inch in diameter and roughly three feet long." Upon consulting a reference book on board, the crew established that "the queerest sight we'd seen yet" was (you guessed it) the elusive snake mackerel.

When he was not reading the Book of Mormon or discussing church doctrine with Ed, Baker passed no little time in contemplation of godless Communism. While in Redondo Beach, Baker had attended a lecture by Dr. Fred C. Schwartz, an Australian by birth and a Christian anti-Communist by zealous disposition. Schwartz considered Communism a disease, and he fretted in pamphlets and essays over the ongoing infection of America's youth. According to Schwartz, the Kremlin intended to achieve world domination by 1973 and the Russians were already, in 1958, six years ahead of schedule, because Communists knew to prey on the student mind, which was "vibrating and reaching out for new knowledge."

How, Baker asked, "do we protect our student minds or, for that matter, our adult minds against the doctrine of Godless Communism?" Baker believed that the only fitting response was to prove *scientifically* "that there *could* be a God." To that end, Baker construed the voyage of the *Lehi IV* a scientific endeavor, since he was convinced that a successful landing on the Hawaiian Islands would serve as confirmation that the prophet Lehi and his fellow pilgrims did travel to Central America and did get blown off course on their way back to the Red Sea. Since Baker held that a "revelation from God" had prompted Lehi to take to the sea in the first place, any evidence of Lehi's influence on Central American or Hawaiian culture functioned for Baker as solid proof of the Almighty's existence and, therefore, as a hedge against Communism.

Accordingly, Baker had sallied forth on the *Lehi IV* as a righteous Cold Warrior. Unlike de Bisschop and his crew, who'd been limping along in the southern Pacific thirty degrees below, Baker was well acquainted with the British hydrogen bomb tests on and around Christmas Island and considered them a useful contribution to the crusade to stave off the Bolshevik threat. The only concern Baker expressed about the detonations was passing and meteorological. His log entry for Monday, September 1, read in part, "Wonder if the testing of the H-bomb could influence the weather."

(Two nights earlier, on August 30, the *Lehi IV* had passed 140 degrees of longitude—two-thirds of the way to Hawaii—and the rigged and rickety *Tahiti Nui III* had struck the reef encircling Penrhyn in the moonlight, leaving Eric de Bisschop dead of a broken neck.)

On September 10, Baker noted in his log that the *Lehi IV* was a good one hundred miles farther north than he'd hoped or intended by this stage of the trip. The wind had been lifting the raft for some weeks now and had put the crew in real danger of drifting past the Hawaiian Islands without making landfall— they'd need an additional month on the water to make the Gilbert Islands or Midway. And yet Baker was close enough to his target to gloat a little, to recall the galling headlines that had greeted the failure of his first two attempts.

By September 13 a merciful shift in the wind had driven the raft to twenty-two degrees of latitude, which made Hawaiian landfall far more of a certainty. And that evening, a Saturday, the crew picked up Hilo on their radio receiver and were able to pinpoint their position. By now food stores were running low, specifically wheat, which meant fewer loaves of fresh canned-heat bread and more beans than four men confined to a raft should be allowed by law to eat. Don McFarland's twenty-seventh birthday was observed on the fourteenth, and his gifts included "a half hour of his favorite songs wrapped up in Ed's rich Hawaiian voice." By the fifteenth, Baker had posted a constant watch, certain that land was in the offing. To stay alert the crew popped Abundavita supplement pills "like popcorn." Fish refused to take Larry and Don's bait. Ed continued to sing, which, Baker noted, appeared to antagonize the dog.

On September 17, with the raft just seventy-five miles from the big island, Baker won a convert. Don approached him on the deck, his "eyes sparkling with a new light." Don confessed that he could now "see how world peace *could* be brought about by the teachings of Christ." Baker preferred to believe it wasn't just the food supplement talking. "Now that the seeds are planted," he wrote, "only time is needed to bring in the harvest."

At 6:00 A.M. on September 18, the crew sighted land off the port bow, which supplied Baker and Ed occasion to give extended praise to the Almighty for his admirable work through Larry, the navigator. "Modern science," Baker told the crew in his best Christian anti-Communist vein, "has provided facts by which to know how God makes known his will to man." Since they had received no indication from on high as to how they might land the raft, the *Lehi IV* was carried by a southerly breeze just north of both Hilo and Maui and was in genuine danger of making the Gilberts when a shift in wind suddenly threatened to blow the *Lehi IV* directly into the rocky coast of Molokai. Baker's plans to steer for the Pailolo Channel between Molokai and Maui were frustrated when the wind quartered to the north and blew the raft toward Maui. Baker feared that, without assistance, the crew might have to swim ashore and leave the *Lehi IV* (and possibly Tang the dog) to the mercies of the sea.

They were spared the choice, however, when the pilot of a

Hawaiian Airlines plane making for Honolulu spied the raft on his descent and circled back for a look. He called in the *Lehi IV's* position, which brought a Coast Guard cutter out of Kahului Harbor along with a local fishing vessel, the *Amberjack.* According to Baker, the cutter commander's first words, amplified across the water, were, "Congratulations, Captain Baker—you have proved your point."

Baker preferred to believe that the commander meant his *historical/religious* point, when it's just as likely (probably more likely) that the cutter's captain, aware of Baker's previous failed voyages, had more of a *nautical* point in mind. At any rate, Baker felt vindicated on both fronts, and he and his crew were towed triumphantly into harbor by the *Amberjack.*

In the ensuing days, Baker approached local museum officials in hopes of having his raft displayed for posterity and his theory of Polynesian migration (Israelites from Central America, lest we forget) embraced as a viable alternative to the more conventional view that the Hawaiian Islands were populated from the east, specifically from the Gilbert Islands. Baker was disappointed on both fronts. The Maui Historical Society, after soliciting Baker to donate his raft, decided against accepting it for display, and Baker's request to a Dr. Emory of the Bishop Museum of Natural and Cultural History in Honolulu to include his theory of east-to-west Polynesian migration in future museum literature and displays was met with a polite but firm refusal. Dr. Emory "flatly closed the doors on entering any theory into the museum other than the one written in the history books and therefore accepted as fact."

Baker was disappointed but, in his own colorful fashion, resigned:

There was nothing to do but to girdle my swollen ego
with a little humility and try to slip it through the slim
doorway of reason.

Which leaves only one pressing question: Where's the dog?
As the *Lehi IV* was being towed into port, Baker had learned
that the threat of rabies required all dogs arriving in the islands
be quarantined for 120 days at a cost to the owner of one dollar
a day. Naturally, it was this bit of business that captured the
public's attention rather than Baker's theory of seagoing Israelites, and on October 2, 1958, the mixed-breed terrier Tangoroa was officially inducted as a "seaman" in a widely reported
full-dress ceremony aboard the USS *Kawishiwi*, a thirty-eight-
thousand-ton Pacific oiler with a crew of 273.

With the help of Baker's wife, Nola, Tang wrote and published his own account of the voyage of the *Lehi IV,* replete
with canine wisecracks and wayward theological musings.
Even by lax Torrance dog-pound standards, the book is virtually unreadable, though the doctored photographs are pretty
arresting.

9

Age Unlimited

Given William Willis's ongoing interest in raft travel and the international press attention afforded de Bisschop's *Tahiti Nui* expedition and Baker's drift to Hawaii on *Lehi IV*, it's reasonable to assume that Willis was sufficiently acquainted with the competition to realize, by the autumn of 1958, that he'd been outantiquated by de Bisschop (sixty-seven years old at the time of his death) and outcrackpotted by DeVere Baker. In the wake of his voyage, Willis had mounted a modest *Seven Little Sisters* lecture tour, conducted largely in Europe, and he was disappointed that his book-length account of his trip to Samoa had performed poorly, selling fewer than ten thousand copies Stateside. Curiously, the book enjoyed success only in the Soviet Union, where it became a children's favorite and, by 1961, had sold in numbers approaching one hundred thousand copies.

As he neared seventy, Willis acknowledged that his body was "showing signs of wear," and he professed to be shocked that age was catching up with him:

Diabetes, arthritis, and digestion and kidney troubles began to plague me, not to mention other symptoms of

which one was consuming nervousness, which I felt was
an indication of some other serious and still hidden condition. . . . The man who I had thought was unbreakable
was breaking up.

In an attempt to engineer a recovery, Willis and Teddy retired (after a fashion) to Oceanside, California, where Willis existed exclusively on the vegetables he grew organically in a
garden plot by the house. "I tried everything in the way of
natural healing I had learned in my wanderings and studies,"
he wrote, which included breathing exercises, fasts and water
cures, and a diet, when he ate, of distilled water, cereals, and
raw vegetables. Teddy took it as her duty to remind Willis that
he was "an old man nearing seventy" and should temper his ex-
pectations accordingly. But Willis owned up to a certainty that
"my knowledge, my insight and will would carry me through."

He needed a full year to return to a condition he found satisfying, and once he had recovered his health and his stamina,
William Willis began to entertain thoughts of yet another
open-ocean rafting voyage, a full crossing of the Pacific from
South America to Australia. "I felt something stirring within
me," he confessed, and he recalled with fondness a severely
selective version of his first voyage, remembering "those glo-
rious days and nights when the whole world was mine, the sea
and sky from the highest star to the darkest depths." He kept
the scheme to himself while it evolved in his mind and finally
told Teddy, who responded as he'd expected: "She looked at
me as if I had lost my mind."

Willis worked on Teddy tirelessly, determined to convince her
that he was still a capable sailor and fit for the trip, and ultimately

she folded, telling Willis, "There will be no living with you if you don't do it—go ahead." Teddy's only condition was that Willis see a doctor for a thorough physical, and if he were judged sufficiently healthy for the trip, Teddy would raise no further objections. The physician she selected happened to be her cousin, who, after examining Willis and subjecting him to an ambitious array of tests, declared (according to Willis), "You are dramatically—let me say fantastically—healthy." The good doctor then packed away for safekeeping (again according to Willis) Willis's near-superhuman electrocardiogram results, preserving the readout as a kind of trophy.

Given the triumphant report, Teddy had little choice but to relent to Willis's wishes, and she could take only small comfort in the fact that he had decided against another trip to Ecuador after balsa logs. Though his memory of the hardships he endured in the course of the voyage on the *Seven Little Sisters* seemed to have evaporated, Willis could well recall the ordeal of harvesting and transporting the balsa trunks he'd employed for the raft's platform, and he was determined not to repeat the exercise. Inspired by a clutch of steel drainage pipes he'd seen on a beach near his California retreat, Willis decided that his new raft would be a trimaran constructed of three steel pontoons held together by a welded topside framework to which pine planks would be bolted to serve as decking. He described the raft as "a type of craft used since ancient times and very much in vogue now."

Upon returning to New York, Willis again petitioned deep-pocketed Werner Woehlk for funds (fifteen thousand 1963 dollars) and then located a facility able and equipped to manufacture the craft. The raft would be built at the Guyon

Fabricating Division in Harrison, New Jersey, on the Passaic River. In a *New York Times* profile of Willis that previewed his latest transpacific plans, Willis claimed that designers and engineers ordinarily hired out to NASA had a hand in designing his raft. So somehow it was to be both "a type of craft used since ancient times" and simultaneously "a 'space age' raft if such a thing is possible."

Presumably, Willis was referring to the use of polyurethane as buoyant filling for the hollow steel pontoons. The stuff was pumped in liquefied and then hardened into foam to protect against a damaged pontoon filling with water and sinking the raft. In its dimensions the new raft was virtually the same size as the old one—thirty-three feet long and eighteen feet wide. The stepped forward mast would carry a square sail, as had the *Seven Little Sisters*, and a mizzen would fly from the twenty-foot aft mast. A forestay running between the mainmast and the bowsprit would accommodate a jib when winds permitted, an arrangement that had served Willis well on his previous voyage. The new raft, in a departure from Willis's previous design, would be double-ruddered, and the small deckhouse (only five by seven feet) would have a steel superstructure concealed beneath slatted bamboo and banana leaves for a more traditional look.

Though the seventy-year-old Willis intended to keep daily records of his blood pressure and heart rhythm and monitor, as best he was able, the psychological effects of seagoing solitude over the course of, quite possibly, nine months under way, he had no overarching reason for making the voyage other than to prove to both himself and the world at large that a man's active life needn't end at the arbitrary retirement age of sixty-five. "I feel myself at least the equal of a man of 35 in coordination and reflexes and am in prime physical condition," Willis assured *New York Times* reporter John Rendel. "I feel fully able to face the hardships again without qualms."

On the afternoon of May 3, 1963, the new raft was hoisted onto the Grace Line ship *Santa Margarita* to make the passage to Callao secured to a forward hatch cover. With the coming of evening, the ship weighed anchor and steamed in growing darkness through the narrows of upper New York Harbor and into the open Atlantic.

The passage to Callao was leisurely, a thirteen-day voyage with stops at Norfolk, Panama, and Buenaventura in Colombia, which afforded Willis occasion to brush up on his plotting skills with the help of the *Santa Margarita*'s navigating officer. Willis claimed not to have touched a sextant or charted a course since his 1954 voyage, and, to complicate matters, this upcoming crossing would require him to establish his position east of Greenwich—beyond the international date line—for the first time in his experience.

The trip also provided Willis's prospective companion the chance to find her sea legs. In the ongoing tradition of rafting trips of the time, which saw cats and dogs and parrots, even pigs, dragooned into service as crewmates, and given his own experience on the *Seven Little Sisters*, Willis was determined to haul four-legged company on this crossing as well. He claimed, however, to have been instructed by his previous voyage, when there had been "bad blood," as Willis fashioned it, between Eekie the parrot and Meekie the cat. This time he rather curiously proposed that he would head off conflict by taking aboard "a young cat and a young dog which would become friendly."

Fortunately for Willis, suitable cats were far more readily available than suitable dogs. A few days before their departure on the *Santa Margarita*, Willis and his wife had scoured Manhattan animal shelters for candidates. Most of the dogs on offer struck Willis as "cautious," by which he seemed to mean cowering and defensive, and he very nearly failed to find a tolerable cat as well. However, at the last of the shelters he and Teddy visited, in a grim basement in lower Manhattan, Willis spied a two-year-old calico that leaped purring into Teddy's arms as soon as her cage door swung open. This would be his raft cat, and Willis named her Kiki in conscious echo of and tribute to Meekie, his former companion who, at the age of ten, was living a life of leisured retirement in Long Beach, California. After several more unavailing searches of shelters throughout the New York area, Willis decided to look for a dog in Peru.

The *Santa Margarita* docked in Callao Harbor on the afternoon of May 16, and Willis's raft was lowered into the water during the night. Back in New Jersey, as he was being towed down the Passaic River for his rendezvous with the ship, Willis had noticed that his raft rode disturbingly low in the water. The bow in particular showed a tendency to plow under the surface, which left Willis to fear what the craft might do in the rolling Pacific. He knew he had work ahead of him to make his raft reliably seaworthy, and once more the Peruvian navy volunteered whatever resources he might require.

Willis, Teddy, and Kiki moved into the Hotel Bolívar in Lima, and every morning for what turned out to be almost two months, Willis made the eight-mile commute to the harbor of Callao, where, initially, he worked to lighten the raft. Though the *Seven Little Sisters* had weighed close to ten tons and Willis's new "space age" raft was five tons at most, the three pontoons (even packed with urethane) were appreciably less buoyant than balsa and made for a craft that Willis feared might lumber under the best of circumstances. Though his options were meager, Willis did manage to reduce the load somewhat by replacing the steel superstructure of his cabin with timber framing before adding additional weight in the form of *guaras* that were held in place by specially forged collars.

To serve as decking, Willis nailed sheets of split bamboo directly to the underlying planks that had been spaced one and a half inches apart to allow the sea to wash through, and he sheathed the cabin in split bamboo as well. For a bit of greenery and as a purely cosmetic touch, he applied a layer of banana leaves to the cabin's roof and then turned his attention to the provisions he'd require for a voyage that Willis suspected might call for eight or nine uninterrupted months on the water.

With no recesses for storing cans of water beneath the decking as he had on his first voyage and no appetite for the calamity that had ensued, Willis resorted to three fifty-five-gallon wooden barrels for his drinking water. He lashed them to the port side of his cabin and calculated that the contents would see him through eight full months, even without additional rainfall. Though Willis had thrived on his previous seagoing diet of rye flour, raw sugar, and what fish he could catch, he opted on this second voyage for far different supplies:

My provisions were all staples—beans, lentils, rice, flour, oatmeal, dehydrated potatoes, dehydrated soups, lemon juice, prunes, raisins, honey butter, ship's biscuits, and shortening for frying fish.

Willis also laid in condensed and evaporated milk, canned lemon juice, boiled lime juice, ten dozen limes packed in sawdust, and assorted fresh vegetables, most prominently potatoes, which Willis employed as an additional antiscorbutic. He preferred them raw and claimed to enjoy his potatoes grated with onions and seasoned with lemon juice.

Ship's chandlers on City Island, New York, who were acquainted with Willis from his previous voyage and mindful of his tight budget, had supplied him with top-quality gear at a discount. This new raft would be rigged with fine Irish linen rope and would ship a wealth of extra buckles and shackles and blocks. Willis had also been given a pair of slightly used Egyptian cotton staysails to supplement the set of rayon sails he'd had specially made for the raft. He anticipated that these staysails would add sufficient speed to the raft to help in whittling away at the duration of the voyage.

On the canine front, Willis and Teddy were enjoying as little success in Peru as they had in New York. Lima and Callao boasted no end of available herding dogs, but the candidates all impressed Willis as too large and too active for the voyage. A creature with the size and energy of the animals he and Teddy were seeing would require more food than Willis could afford to ship and more water than he could possibly spare. Sensibly, he decided to take another cat instead, and he and Teddy were invited to pick among "a whole cat family" at a hacienda near Callao. They selected a four-month-old kitten—"gray with snow-white, downy belly and feet, and supposedly a male"— and decided on the spot to name him Aussie, "after the land he was bound for."

By late June 1963, most of the preparations were complete,

including the installation of an updated version of the Marconi Salvita III transceiver, an odd choice given Willis's experience on his previous voyage. Moreover, Willis apparently had little enough faith in his radio to suggest that he and Teddy attempt to communicate telepathically at specific times during the course of each day. "Thought travels faster than anything," Willis told his wife, "and thought is something definite just like electricity." (Somehow Teddy found the proposal a trifle less than consoling.)

At a modest ceremony in Callao Harbor in advance of a brief trial run, Teddy christened the raft *Age Unlimited*, calling out the name in both English and Spanish before smashing a bottle of Peruvian sparkling wine against the iron bowsprit. Willis had settled on the name as an expression of his "rebirth to health," and he'd had the letters stenciled on the big, square mainsail, which, during the course of his trial run, he never had call to raise. The seas were calm and the air still, so the naval tug that towed the *Age Unlimited* out of Callao Harbor and twenty miles into the Pacific failed to drop the line. Consequently, Willis gained no useful understanding of the virtues and liabilities of the raft under sail and passed the time instead, with the aid of a naval officer, working out his compass compensation to accommodate for the effect of the iron raft on his magnetic readings, which, after a day's worth of testing, proved to be negligible.

In advance of his symbolic departure date—the Fourth of July—Willis submitted to a spate of interviews, in which he was unfailingly asked both why a seventy-year-old man would attempt such a voyage and why he would attempt it alone. Willis frequently responded with a mild backhanded swipe at the well-manned *Kon-Tiki* and *Tahiti Nui* expeditions that had

enlisted crew enough to divide the day into watches. For him,
isolation in such a venture was the thing that truly mattered; it
was the quality that separated him from Heyerdahl, de Bisschop, even from the ancient Peruvians with their well-crewed
coastal craft:

> To me the real test of the voyage was the solitude and all
> it implied: man on his own, depending solely on himself
> under all conditions, with no one near except his Cre-
> ator, and every fiber—physical, mental, and spiritual—
> put to the test. I had been through it for 115 days in
> 1954 and, though near disaster more than once, had
> never felt so keenly and gloriously alive. For this I
> longed again. To go with others, even with only one
> man, would in my eyes have watered down the expedi-
> tion to a routine job, even to drudgery.

Willis also let it be known that he intended to keep a scrupulous record of his "physical and mental reactions" as a tool in
the study of "so-called senior citizens."

At half past two in the afternoon of July 4, 1963, William
Willis kissed his wife good-bye and left her on a pier crowded
with thousands of well-wishers as he climbed down to the deck
of the *Age Unlimited*. A launch towed the raft from its slip and
out into the harbor, where Willis took up a line from the *Ríos*,
the same naval salvage tug that had hauled him to sea on his
trial run. The sky was low and the air raw as Willis departed
the harbor in the *Ríos*'s wake with three Peruvian sailors raftboard to oversee the tow along with two cowering cats, tethered for their safety. The tug wallowed west hour after hour

with the *Age Unlimited* wallowing behind her. Shortly after midnight the two craft were suddenly tossed with violence on what had been a calm sea. Willis saw the *Ríos* deep in a trough before him, struggling to stay upright. The first wave was followed by a second and then a third before the surface settled out again into a gentle roll.

Somehow the towline held, and soon a walkie-talkie message from the bridge of the tug confirmed a tsunami generated by an undersea earthquake. The cities of Lima and Callao, Willis wrote, "had been shaken to their foundations," and the citizens had fled into the streets fearing a repeat of the massive 1960 Pacific quake that had left towns and villages along the western South American coast entirely flattened. Relayed reports from the *Ríos* suggested, however, that no such damage had occurred in this instance, encouraging Willis to assume that Teddy was safe and unharmed.

With the coming of dawn, Willis and his three temporary crewmates huddled on the leeward side of the raft's cabin to escape the wind and the chill spray. One of the seamen took occasion to ask if Willis was actually seventy years old. When Willis assured him it was so, the seaman responded, "My father is an old man, and he is only fifty-two." Though Willis snapped back that a fifty-two-year-old was but "a mere child," the seaman's reaction was understandable given the context. The average life expectancy of a white American male hovered around sixty-seven years in 1963 (it's closer to seventy-five today), and the Peruvian average was doubtless a few years lower. So a man of Willis's age with Willis's vigor and drive was surely an oddity in that place at that time, and photographs of him taken during the voyage show a man remarkably fit and youthful for his years, a sort of Centrum Silver poster child whose devotion to his health and conditioning, though eccentric in his day, anticipated a way of thinking about and by "so-called senior citizens" that has become unexceptional in ours.

For his part, Willis was given to thinking himself a rather miraculous ageless exception. "I often wondered," he wrote, "as I saw the years go by and the world change and people grow old and sick, why I should remain as I was." The fact of his seventy years meant nothing to him. His infirmities, his "breaking up," had been the element of shock that drove him to build his raft and mount his second expedition. He was more intent, at bottom, on proving that he was sufficiently healthy to make such an arduous voyage, rather than that he wasn't too old to undertake it.

And arduous it would be. Willis was enough of a salt to recognize, even under tow, that his trimaran was more than a little balky and awkward. She rode low in the water and yawed violently. Even before he'd raised sail, Willis already feared that the sluggishness of the *Age Unlimited* would add weeks if not months to his voyage. Accordingly, he must have had mixed feelings when the *Ríos* reached her target distance at half past eight on the morning of July 5 and, in the course of maneuvering in rough seas to take off her sailors, promptly collided with the *Age Unlimited*, not once but several times, before the captain saw the wisdom of lowering a boat.

Discovering no apparent damage, Willis could only wave the ship away, and she gave a blast on her horn as she steered east for Callao. The scene Willis described as the *Ríos* steamed from view was more than a little discouraging:

The sea had come up considerably and was full of whitecaps. Heavy clouds darkened the sky. The raft rolled as if possessed and sat low in the water, and I threw some sacks of vegetables, which I knew I wouldn't need, overboard to bring her up, but it helped little, and water kept coming over. . . . Kiki cried now and then and looked beseechingly at me, as the day advanced and the atrocious jolting continued.

Willis found he couldn't hope to stand without holding on to something, so the maneuvering required to raise and set the sails was punishing. In addition, the sea boiled up through decking and the temperature hovered around sixty degrees. The raft traveled under sail just as poorly as it had under tow— "like an empty drum dragged behind a steamer."

For his first meal under way, Willis prepared "something highly antiscorbutic." He mixed grated potato with chopped onion and lemon juice and took it all cold and raw, because the vitamin C would dissipate if the potatoes were cooked. Unfortunately, Willis's reliance on potatoes as his chief antiscorbutic was ill-advised, since raw tubers contain a toxic alkaloid, solanine, that can lead to gastroenteritis, diarrhea, heart arrhythmias, even death, and is thwarted only by cooking. Willis capped off the meal with a can of beans—all a far cry from the *máchica*-and-*raspadura* diet of his first voyage.

For the first few days, Willis kept Aussie and Kiki tethered for their own safety. The raft's action on the pitching Pacific was rude and jarring, and the deck was regularly swept by breaking seas, so Willis had reason to fear that if he turned the two loose, he would soon after find himself catless. But

Aussie and Kiki proved, from the outset, far bolder than Willis had expected. "They weren't a bit afraid of the sea," he noted, "and sometimes stood with their forefeet on the board I'd nailed to the edge of the raft, gazing into the foam streaking past and almost touching their noses." Though dousings were pretty routine for the pair, Willis remarked that they hardly seemed to mind.

As a favor to a Lima acquaintance, Willis had carried along two homing pigeons he had agreed to release on his second morning at sea. He performed the task in heavy weather, and the birds soared high overhead and circled the raft before breaking off due east. Willis made no secret of watching them a little jealously as they flew toward land. Even on this, his second full day at sea, he had already soured on the craft pitching beneath his feet and was contemplating "a better-designed raft with more sails." He went so far as to make a few sketches "which perhaps some time in the future I might make use of." For the moment, though, he was obliged to blunder along with the scow he had, even though working on the rolling deck was a ceaseless trial that called for acrobatic skill.

The winds stayed high for a solid week, with gusts often approaching gale force. Heavy seas battered the raft and assured that captain and cats remained soaked through in the chill air. Due to the heavy cloud cover, Willis navigated by dead reckoning and duly transmitted his position each evening over his Salvita III but received, as on the *Seven Little Sisters*, no reply. He ate hurriedly, usually canned beans and evaporated milk, and was far too busy manning the tiller and the running gear to know opportunity to fish.

So conditions were already trying by July 14, when Willis

noticed hairline cracks in both of his rudders where the tillers joined the blades. Only now while under way did he investigate the connecting rods closely enough to discover that they were made from hollow tubing rather than solid iron and so had been, from the outset, bound to break. Following seas pounded the raft to the extent that Willis couldn't hope to make lasting repairs even if he found suitable materials on board for mending the fittings. In considering his options, he immediately had to rule out a return to Callao (almost six hundred miles to the southeast) and briefly entertained the notion of steering for Punta Aguja (northeast) before deciding to make for Guayaquil, where he would either mend his rudders or build an entirely new raft out of balsa, "for I am far from being satisfied with my trimaran," Willis troubled himself to observe. So much for space-age New Jersey construction.

By the sixteenth, two days later, the cloud cover had broken sufficiently for Willis to take sights, and he discovered that Guayaquil was already out of reach, as he'd made no significant easting in the surging Humboldt Current. Worse still, Willis's present course threatened to bring him perilously close to the Galápagos Archipelago with its circular currents and stagnant calms that could well snare and maroon him. To make his peril complete, Willis discovered that his Marconi radio no longer functioned at all. While he'd doubted from the beginning that his transmissions were being received, at least the indicator lights and dials on the Salvita III had suggested there was some life in the contraption. Now, after only twelve days at sea, the thing was conspicuously dead, and Willis confessed, "I never thought it was rigged up right in Callao." Even under ideal circumstances, the transmitter's range was slightly less than five hundred miles, and, to judge by Willis's comments, he'd not bothered to test the transmitter since its installation in New Jersey, where, unsurprisingly enough, "it had worked perfectly."

Consequently, still shy of two weeks on the water, Willis was without even the illusion of a functioning radio, and with every rolling impact of a following sea, he ran the risk of seeing his compromised tillers shorn clean away. As with the *Seven Little Sisters* expedition, this new voyage was rapidly going to the primitive, and Willis was having to endure—almost as if condemned to it—shipwreck conditions once more.

Food and water were more plentiful and varied on the *Age Unlimited,* at least for the time being, but the raft was sluggish and unwieldy and rode so low in the sea as to keep the deck awash and the passengers soggy. What steering Willis could manage was affected more by adjustments in the centerboards (the traditional Peruvian method) than by any input to the increasingly frail rudders. There was little chance of rescue if other crucial features of the craft proved as fragile as the rudder arms, certainly no way to call for help given the dead Marconi. And if the raft sank beneath him, Willis's salvation depended on a kayak strapped to the cabin roof, a craft that would require the man to serve as a human stopper for two anxious, fully clawed cats loose in the hold. Cast the whole wretched predicament against unremittingly bad weather and steep seas and you have a fair picture of Willis's opening month on the water.

Willis, being Willis, refused to yield to self-pity or even indulge in passing complaint. Instead he chose to savor the challenge and embrace the conditions. He was very much where he wanted to be—alone on the open Pacific. His rudder trouble didn't preoccupy him in any meaningful way ("I wouldn't get excited about it"), and the brand of solitude that many might have found crushing wasn't simply welcomed by Willis but was cultivated by him. He carried a radio receiver—a legitimately functioning unit separate from the Marconi, on which Willis received his daily time signals—and he could easily have picked up broadcast radio on the thing but never permitted himself to tune in a station, even if only briefly, for the sound of another human voice.

Willis was effectively a connoisseur of solitude and a student of isolation, particularly the sort a single-handed sailor is bound to meet with at sea. Solitude generally, he wrote, "chastens a man, for he sees himself in his true little stature, whether he wants to or not." But isolation on land, in Willis's view, was reliably "gentle," while the experience of a sailor alone on the implacable ocean was certain to be more "absolute," like "a window opening into a naked space."

It was Willis's custom to observe a strict routine and thereby provide each day with at least a nominal shape and order, as he found solitude agreeable only without attendant listlessness. Given the raw, windy weather and the incessant yawing of the raft, all planned activities on the *Age Unlimited* qualified as draining chores, but Willis wasn't easily frustrated. Every morning he performed exercises on the rolling deck. He would twist and stretch and pummel his torso with his fists, inflicting what he chose to call a "rubdown." Afterward he would submit to a manner of ordeal by seawater. Willis would suck the stuff in through his nose until persuaded his passages were clear. He'd then rinse out his ears and gargle with it, before drawing up onto the deck a brimming bucketful of briny Pacific in which he would submerge his head and condition his eyes by opening them in the salt water and shifting them vigorously from side to side. Breakfast followed—bananas and prunes until he ran out of them, flying fish when the cats allowed him one, the occasional bowl of oatmeal—and served as prelude to Willis's inspection of his sails and rigging. He would tidy the deck as he went.

When weather permitted, he took multiple sights with his sextant at midday, usually twenty or more, from which he would calculate an average for use in plotting his position. Adjustments in course, now managed primarily through manipulation of the raft's centerboards, would often follow, and Willis always worked with an eye toward the water, ready to cast in a line if he spied dorado prowling about. On the rare sunny afternoon, he was given to napping on the deck, but he was frequently awakened by incoming seas bouncing him off the cabin.

When he had no fresh fish, a situation more common than not, Willis would often cook a vegetable soup on his Primus stove, usually a concoction heavy on potatoes, garlic, and cayenne pepper. The cats, for their part, would share between them a can of Puss 'n Boots. Every evening Willis would switch on his receiver for a time check, adjust his chronometers as needed (two ordinary wristwatches), and wind them. His nights were usually spent by the tiller, where he would sing and practice songs on the harmonica Teddy had given him and, sporadically, attempt to reach New York with telepathic waves.

Though he'd known to expect chill, gray weather while riding the icy Humboldt Current, Willis hadn't anticipated the relentless storminess that accompanied his progress north along the coast and then northwest as the *Age Unlimited* drove nearly two hundred miles south of Isabela Island, the largest of the Galápagos group. Sure now to avoid a spiraling drift around the archipelago, Willis anticipated improved conditions as he was handed out of the Humboldt and into the far warmer South Equatorial Current.

On his previous voyage, this portion of the crossing had ushered in clear, balmy days, a steady following wind, and splendid fishing. But Willis's poor luck continued as the storminess persisted and high seas hammered the raft, further damaging the cracked rudders to the point where they were of little practical use to him in steering. He was determined to attempt repairs, but strenuous following seas guaranteed a battering to a man foolish enough to enter the water astern. Fishing proved spotty at best in such conditions, and Willis's reliance on a diet of almost pure roughage had left him feeling "stuffy around the middle and sluggish mentally." Recalling the lessons of the *Henriette*, he began to treat himself with regular doses of seawater. He swallowed, on average, a cupful daily, with no discernible pleasure. "My technique of drinking," he revealed, "was to pour it quickly down my throat and then inhale quickly a few times with open mouth till the gall and salt taste had disappeared."

Unlike their captain, the cats were thriving. Kiki and Aussie had bonded and were fast pals. They wrestled and tumbled away a chunk of each afternoon and napped together in the box Willis had established for them in a corner of the cabin. They scarfed up virtually all of the flying fish that blundered onto the raft, reliably leaving scraps of fin and bone for Willis to tidy up in the dawning. They were peerless acrobats, had adjusted immediately to the yawing of the deck, and appeared to be benefiting from it. Willis noted that Kiki and Aussie became fitter as the trip progressed and remarkably well muscled due to the hectic motion of the *Age Unlimited* and the incessant demand of adjustments in balance.

By early August the strain on Willis had begun to show. In leaving the Galápagos Islands to his stern, he had passed into a vacant quarter of the Pacific and was several thousand miles from potential landfall should his trimaran fail him in some significant way and make of a dicey situation a dire one. He was getting no useful sleep to speak of, and high seas persevered to make even the most trifling maneuver deckside a strenuous undertaking. Erratic and unsuccessful in his early attempts to communicate telepathically with his wife, that all changed when Willis began to hear voices. Not just Teddy's but his dead mother's as well.

Moreover, he could see the women. "The impression of face and body was quite distinct," Willis wrote, "and I took their appearance for granted and was never startled." Ordinarily, they offered a "gentle warning" when he was faced with some dangerous task like climbing the mast or dropping astern in the roiling water to attempt his latest mend on the rudders. When entirely rational, Willis was prepared to "consider their voices echoes of my innermost craving for companionship." In the night, however, when the specters of his mother and wife awoke him from a sound sleep only to vanish like mist, his reaction was somewhat different and more telling:

Then invariably the knowledge of being so utterly alone came with a shock, followed by a definite feeling of having been unjustly abandoned by them. This always produced a sense of resentment.

By August 10, Willis had been blown a good seventy miles north of the equator and was beginning to fear being trapped in the doldrums on his wallowing raft when he finally enjoyed a bit of good luck: The wind veered suddenly and drove him south and west on a light breeze that steadily advanced to gale force. Weighing the potential peril of damage to his rigging and sails against this rare opportunity to drive hard on a favorable heading, Willis decided to take his chances and fly as much sail as he could manage.

His original set—a main, a jib, and a mizzen—were of rayon, and a misunderstanding between Willis and his City Island sailmaker had left the mainsail much briefer than it should ideally have been, a good eight feet short of the deck. Willis hit upon the notion of flying one of the spare, donated sails in the gap beneath the main by hoisting it with the jib halyard and attaching the foot to the foredeck. The other spare was perfectly suited to double up the mizzen, and Willis was soon running with five sails set before brisk winds in a bid to get at least within striking distance of land as soon as conceivably possible. Though his calculations confirmed that the additional sails earned him only an extra couple of miles a day, he decided that even meager improvement was worth the strain on his gear.

Willis's rudders, though, had become so unresponsive that he found he had no choice but to attempt repairs, even in less-than-ideal conditions. He hadn't the tools or supplies for anything other than temporary mends, since the sections of tubular steel were failing variously along their lengths, so when he slipped off the deck of the raft with pliers between his teeth and a wrench in his belt, he was only hoping to shore up the joints and tighten the connections sufficiently to make the rudders serviceable for a day or two, at which point he would either repeat the process or try some fix he'd hatched in the interim.

The immediate problem for Willis, in addition to the action of the sea, was that the tiller arms and the rudders themselves offered assorted jagged edges for him to cut and scrape himself on. Consequently, he ended up bleeding as he worked but thought little of it until he glanced down to see "a long dark shape within a few feet of my naked legs." Willis was inspired to scramble onto the deck and reconsider his approach to tiller repair. While the system he came up with didn't improve his handiwork, it did allow him to persist in flailing at the rudders with his lower extremities still attached.

Willis rigged one end of a sheet of split bamboo with iron to weigh it down and dropped it into the water off the stern of the raft once he'd tethered the other end to a cross brace beneath the deck. The thing then served as a makeshift protective screen and might only have hidden Willis's view of an attacking shark if he'd not worked further to improve his odds by offering bait beyond himself. It became his practice, whenever there was no help for it but to work on his rudders, to first hook a shark on his fishing line—they responded greedily to flying fish and hunks of dorado and were easily caught—draw it onto the deck and kill it, hack its flesh so it was sure to bleed, and then shove it back into the water, allowing it to trail behind the raft. Sharks in the vicinity were sure to be drawn by the blood and would feed on the carcass, leaving Willis to work unmolested behind his bamboo screen.

The diversion must have worked well enough, given Willis's survival, but he never managed to repair his rudders to his satisfaction and would have had no control to speak of over his raft but for his maneuverable centerboards. Even they snapped off with some regularity when wind and sea were high, but Willis believed (hoped at least) he had shipped sufficient spares to see him through.

On August 16, at two forty-five in the afternoon, Willis had an experience unique to his rafting career: He met by chance a ship in the vacant wastes of the mid-Pacific. More remarkably, the crew actually spied Willis's raft, and the ship steamed directly for him and circled the *Age Unlimited* twice. She was the *Whakatane*, a New Zealand steamer bound for Papeete. Willis owned up to having been tempted to ask for help in repairing his rudders, but he decided against it, blaming a heavy sea that might have brought a lowered boat to grief. Instead he only waved to indicate he was well and took comfort in the certainty that the Coast Guard would be notified of his position and condition and that this information would be passed along to Teddy.

Far less remarkable than the meeting, however, was the glacial progress of the news of it. Teddy did receive the following from the Coast Guard office in Washington, D.C.:

ON 17 AUG SS WHAKATANE/GRKY REPORT FOL QUOTE LAT 02.4 SOUTH LONG 108.6 WEST SIGHTED RAFT WITH NAME AGE UNLIMITED ON MAINSAIL FLYING UNITED STATES ENSIGN RUNNING BEFORE THE WIND AT COURSE 280 TRUE STOP CIRCLED AT TWO CABLES ONE MAN ON BOARD HEALTHY NO SIGNALS OF DISTRESS UNQUOTE.

But due to what Willis could only identify as "a mistake somewhere," the telegram didn't reach her until October 25, over two months after the sighting.

* * *

One can only wonder what the crew of the *Whakatane* made of the spectacle Willis must have presented. This latter was a very different enterprise from his *Seven Little Sisters* voyage. For its design and weight, the balsa raft had sailed well, had floated high on the water (at least for a raft), and Willis had made a point of keeping her as tidy as a yacht. With his austere fish-and-*máchica* diet and his favorable breezes and fair weather, that first voyage had the feel of a happy experiment in oceangoing nutrition. Even the loss of his fresh water was readily remedied and contributed to the general theme of the adventure. On the *Seven Little Sisters*, Willis had gone so far as to look the part of the jolly, untroubled voyager, bathing and shaving every morning without fail, and when he wasn't stark naked in the tropical sun, he was usually dressed like any upstanding, responsible American in 1954: pleated trousers, neatly buttoned shirt, and probably the only pair of lace-up oxfords ever to go to sea on a raft.

With the *Age Unlimited*, the general look and atmosphere of raft and skipper were something else altogether. A craft rigged for three sails was flying five with what must have looked like all the trim and nautical organization of laundry on a line. The deck was cluttered with produce, and Willis himself looked like a different and somewhat degraded creature on this voyage. Once out of the chill Humboldt Current, he had adopted the prevailing uniform of the Pacific rafter of the time—ragged shorts and nothing else. He had also decided not to shave on this crossing and so sported a luxurious gray beard and a degree of wiry muscle tone all but freakish on a man Willis's age, particularly in 1963.

In short, Willis must have looked like such a castaway in the making that it's a little surprising the captain of the *Whakatane*, hewing to etiquette, allowed himself to steam clear of the *Age Unlimited* on the strength of a simple wave.

By August 19, both of Willis's alcohol-fueled Primus stoves had corroded to the extent that they wouldn't reliably light. Therefore he ate his beans directly out of the cans more often than not and was obliged to take his potatoes raw in their least delicious but most antiscorbutic (and toxic) state. When he could get a flame, he often made a rather exotic concoction of no known culinary pedigree: He would chop three cloves of garlic and simmer them for ten minutes in a cup of evaporated milk mixed with water, which he would then drink down, usually for breakfast. He liked to believe that the garlic helped compensate for the lack of what he called "fresh food" in his diet.

Fundamentally, though, Willis's problem wasn't a fresh-food deficiency but a fish deficiency. Unlike the situation on the *Seven Little Sisters*, when the tropical weather was reliably fair and the raft was sound and well functioning, Willis's problems on the *Age Unlimited* were myriad and ongoing. Storminess was the rule, as were high, turbulent seas that made even simple tasks more time-consuming and demanding. The poor weather served to keep the raft in near-constant violent motion, and the blocks and shackles and stays and halyards suffered such accelerated wear and damaging shocks that Willis was kept busy tending to and repairing his running gear when the disintegrating rudders or broken centerboards didn't demand his attention instead.

He lacked, then, much opportunity to fish and so often went without the protein a fresh dorado would supply. As a result, Willis confessed that his "vitality seemed a little impaired," and he noticed a "slow drain" on his strength. Though there was shark flesh available to him with some regularity, the ammonia-steeped quality of it rendered it sufficiently unappetizing that he stuck to his potatoes and his garlic-laced evaporated milk while hoping for fairer weather and a bit of passing leisure.

By September 6, Willis had crossed the 134th degree of longitude and was three and a half degrees south of the equator. His calculations put Callao over four thousand miles to his stern and Pitcairn Island almost fourteen hundred miles due south. Still plagued by visions and visitations—mostly of and from his wife and mother—he had an experience of another stripe when he became, in an instant, convinced that Teddy had been killed in an automobile accident.

Willis had imagined himself docking his raft after a successful passage to Sydney, where a friend had approached to give him the news. The image seemed so real and the news so shocking that he had difficulty laying the episode off to mere imagination. "Was the isolation beginning to work on me and break me down?" he wondered. He decided the vision was an indication that Teddy was sick, "perhaps even struggling for her life" (which was better than dead and mangled in a highway pileup, but not much). The sense of doom and grief attending the vision settled in with Willis and would plague him for many weeks thereafter.

By the middle of September, Willis had made such scanty progress south that the prospect of his raft's breaking up on the Filippo Reef grew increasingly ominous. He knew that at the same point in his 1954 voyage he had passed the 140th meridian at a latitude of slightly over five and half degrees south, which put him less than two hundred miles north of Nuku Hiva in the Marquesas. At the same meridian, the *Age Unlimited* was over three hundred miles north of Nuku Hiva, and the raft's "almost useless rudders" gave Willis cause to be persuaded that he wouldn't succeed in dipping far enough south to escape the coral. Though it lay still six hundred miles to his west, the Filippo Reef served as a treacherous barrier spanning nearly one hundred miles of ocean. Willis needed a shift in wind to drive him well below six degrees in latitude, or he would surely be doomed to the kayaking excursion of a lifetime.

It's little wonder, then, considering Willis's catalog of nautical problems, his alarming presentiment about his wife, and his increased lethargy, that he would finally and openly own up to "a depressed and agitated state of mind." This was quite a confession from a man who was ordinarily almost blitheringly happy and had demonstrated in the past a ready capacity for defusing dire prospects and diminishing long odds with bulletproof optimism and rank wishfulness. Somehow, though, Willis was shaken by the realization of what a tiny (and rudderless) speck of humanity he was in an enormously vast and unpopulated space. Even the depth of the sea served to amplify his solitude. While still north of the Marquesas, Willis noted grimly that the Pacific bottom beneath him could be found only at a staggering thirty-six thousand feet.

The elusive snake mackerel did what it could by way of

repulsive distraction. A specimen washed onto the deck along about mid-September, and Willis took occasion to lay open its stomach, wherein he found a wealth of baby flying fish. But for the mackerel's revolting appearance—"with vicious-looking head and eyes and the undershot jaw of a barracuda"—Willis might well have filleted the thing, eaten it, and found it, as had de Bisschop, delectable. But he just tossed it overboard for the sharks and made do with his potatoes instead. For an occasional jolt of protein, Willis had come to prefer shark liver, which he took fresh from the carcass and ate raw.

In what for this voyage was a rare stroke of good fortune, the wind shifted to the northeast as Willis closed on the Filippo Reef, and it blew him just far enough south to avoid destruction. He did, however, spend a night clinging to his mast and scanning for breakers with his binoculars. Even though he'd been spared, Willis's gloomy mood persisted, and he soon discovered that a new voice had been added to the general imaginary chatter on the *Age Unlimited*. This one was unknown to him and wholly unexpected.

After a night of squalls, a weary Willis felt a presence on the deck and heard a voice say, "Get out of it! You can't make it—get out of it." He described how his gaze was forced to the rolling sea and he found himself prompted to consider, for the first time in his sailing life, not merely failure but suicide. "I fought this thing down, this all-pervading summons," Willis wrote, but then added, "The fact that it had appeared made me wonder at myself." The following morning he was ordered again, "Get out of it," and the day after that and the day after that. Willis had soon accepted the voice as a token of his isolation, which was bound to visit him "like a toothache or bellyache when conditions were right," but that hardly dispelled the shock of his vulnerability.

By early October, Willis had been driven before a favorable wind south to the twelfth parallel, which put him clear of Rakahanga, where the *Tahiti Nui* had crashed and Eric de Bisschop had died. In his log entry of the fifth, Willis recorded his longitude at 145 degrees west and remarked that he'd been under way for precisely three months, covering in that time fifty-seven hundred miles. "Weather continues bad," Willis added. "Don't seem to know the Pacific of 1954." Willis owned up to wondering "what the world was doing" and briefly entertained the notion of tuning in a Cook Island station on his transistor radio, but he decided against it, even given the intense international tensions of the day. "There wouldn't be a war," Willis wrote, "for the big boys were afraid of their own bombs."

By now Willis usually passed a portion of each day shoring up his rudders, tightening straps and bindings in hopes of getting some use out of the things as supplements to his centerboards. During one such session in mid-October while he was struggling with a lashing, he felt a hot, tearing pain in his left side, managed to clamber onto the deck, and had soon located a fresh rupture to complement the old, unrepaired one on his right side. Instead of a truss, Willis had packed a "rubberized bandage" in his medicine kit. It was intended for a potential sprain, but when he combined it with a dose of morphine and a nap, he found the pain manageable with the wrap in place and was able to go about the business of sailing his raft as long as he moved gingerly and was "especially careful," not an easy option on a lumbering trimaran in midocean.

At about the same time, Willis began to notice a change for

the worse in the quality of his drinking water. The wooden barrels in which the raft's water supply was stored had originally contained sacramental wine. Willis had gone to the trouble to scour them thoroughly but had filled the barrels with local Callao tap water to keep them from drying out while he waited for the shipment of Andean springwater he intended to take on his voyage. In a fashion that should be painfully familiar by now, Willis had proved less than scrupulous in replacing the tap water with the springwater, failing to dump all the tap water and clean the barrels again. Instead he'd only drained the barrels through their bungholes, leaving a couple of quarts of unpurified tap water in the bottom of each to mix with and contaminate the springwater as he added it. After three months at sea, the blend had ripened to the extent that Willis couldn't help but notice that the water had grown murky and had developed a smell that was "sort of sewerlike."

Short of rainwater, Willis cooked with and drank the tainted water, boiling it beforehand, but the bacteria felled him nonetheless, and he collapsed in a fever for two full days. "It was all my fault," he wrote, "and I had no reason to complain." He feared malaria or, worse, typhoid, but his temperature never ranged much over one hundred degrees, and he seemed more bothered by the lingering cloacal stink of the water on board than by the sweats and the vomiting. He once again took fistfuls of aspirin, drank seawater in a bid to drive out the sickness, and let the *Age Unlimited* go where she wished. "The raft would keep on her course," he wrote, "if one could call it a course."

Willis decided that his ideal cure would be a long steam in a sauna, followed by a "tumbler full of gin." He settled for intermittent naps on the pitching deck and the occasional mug of coffee made from a separate water supply he had stowed in his kayak by way of emergency rations. He'd forgotten the cache was there until forty-eight hours of fevered nausea had served to prime his memory.

By October 22, the wind had quartered again, and Willis was sailing to the northwest in the general direction of the New Hebrides. In consulting the sailing directions for the area issued by the U.S. Hydrographic Office, he was a little dismayed to discover that natives of the New Hebrides "used to practice cannibalism not so long ago and are still apt to stray." He couldn't help but imagine beaching his raft on some wild New Hebridean shore and soon thereafter watching a local feast "from the inside of a pot." Willis then expressed openly his first legitimate second thoughts about pressing on toward Australia with his broken rudders and his dwindling supply of center-boards.

October 27 saw Willis equal the duration of his 1954 voyage—115 days at sea. He'd covered far less distance on this excursion, however; he was still well shy of the Samoan Islands and not at all settled on where he should go and how he might get there. When the wind veered once more and drove him on a southwesterly heading directly toward Apia, Willis noted in his log that Samoa was "coming uncomfortably close," though by this time he must have considered landfall far more a temptation than a peril.

By November 1, Willis had finally concluded that Australia was simply out of his reach due to the condition of his raft. He resolved to put into port, make repairs to his rudders, collect new centerboards as swiftly as possible, and then continue on to Sydney. But the *Age Unlimited*'s almost utter helplessness before the wind guaranteed that Willis's options for landfall would be few and ever-changing. The Fijis, the Tongas, and the Samoa Islands were all before him, but quartering breezes had soon put the Tongas out of reach to the south, and, in consulting his chart of the Fiji Islands, Willis came to realize that any approach to Suva, the only harbor where repairs could be made, would require that he negotiate a "maze of reefs." That left Apia or Pago Pago, both of which were far closer and readily within reach. Feeling a bit of a failure, Willis steered as well as he was able for Samoa.

He largely held to a favorable course throughout the first week of November and was eight miles southwest of Swains Island on the sixth when a gale kicked up in the afternoon, and he elected to sail before it rather than reef and limp along. He even made rousing headway briefly until three centerboards snapped in half, sounding like cannon shots beneath him, and the *Age Unlimited* swung into the wind, backing the mainsail. The sail beat against the mast, Willis wrote, "with a fury that threatened to bring down the whole rigging. I threw the lashings over the wheel and jumped forward just as the sail was ripped from top to bottom."

With two aft and one midship centerboards broken and none to replace them, and with his mainsail in tatters, Willis's sailing decisions were suddenly all made for him. "Apia," he allowed, "if I was lucky." He now considered himself a man "forced to give up," and fifty miles east of landfall Willis made a rude attempt to stitch his mainsail back together and raised it for the final approach. With his rudders useless, his centerboards wanting, and his sail threatening to blow to rags, he limped toward Apia after 130 days at sea. As the wind freshened, Willis found he couldn't control the raft under even a ragged, seepy mainsail. The *Age Unlimited* would invariably swing up into the wind, so he would have to make harbor under a jib and a mizzen, and as he was blown toward the foaming reef protecting Apia Harbor, he raised the American flag he carried—the same one he had flown in the *Seven Little Sisters*—hoisting it upside down as a signal of distress.

Willis dallied as best he could, hoping he'd be spied from shore and for a boat to come out to offer a tow, but once he'd been blown past Apia around a spar of land toward the tiny village of Pui Paa, he concluded he was entirely on his own. In preparation for what promised to be a lively approach to shore (Pui Paa was protected by a reef as well), Willis closed up Kiki and Aussie in the cabin in the vicinity of a box he had prepared for them, a wooden crate secured in the hole of a Grace Line life ring. He seemed to think the cats would know enough to pounce into the thing if the raft broke up and ride it across the lagoon to the beach.

On his approach, Willis scoured for a break in the reef but couldn't discover one and so resigned himself to a collision. He took to the stern of the raft and held for support to the wheel as the *Age Unlimited* was lifted and flung into the coral. The remaining centerboards all snapped off at once, but the mast held upright and the raft stayed of a piece as it was washed by surging waves over the reef and into the lagoon. The jib and mizzen plumped with wind, and Willis was able to bring the battered trimaran to within twenty-five yards of shore, where he dropped both anchor and sails. "I feel suddenly lonely," he said of the moment, "as if something has been taken out of my life."

The locals who first came upon Willis, including an island

police officer, could hardly believe that he had brought his raft over the reef and had survived the experience at what turned out to be low tide. They provided him with fresh fruit and transportation to the telegraph office in Apia, a few miles away, where he notified Teddy of his arrival and was pleased to discover with her return cable that she was healthy and uninjured in spite of his grim presentiment.

With the coming of high tide, the *Age Unlimited* could be and was safely towed out over the Pui Paa reef and around the headland to Apia Harbor, where she was anchored a mere ten yards from shore. Willis decided to leave the cats on board but took a hotel room for himself, from where he intended to oversee repairs to the raft. Mechanics at the Apia public-works machine shop offered to fix and reinforce Willis's rudders, and one of the men, upon learning of Willis's rupture, encouraged him to see the local surgeon, a Dr. Goodman, who diagnosed hernias on both sides of Willis's torso and warned him of the "definite danger of strangulation" were he to continue his voyage without surgery.

When Willis asked Dr. Goodman, "Just what does a strangulation do?" he was informed, with no bedside manner to speak of, "It kills you if you are alone out there."

Willis wandered the hospital grounds as he considered his options. "Strangulation had sounded bad," he wrote, "but now, outside, it didn't scare me." He did, nonetheless, demonstrate the good sense to cable his wife and seek her opinion. Her response arrived the following day:

COME BACK TO NEW YORK FOR EXAMINATION STOP AM CA-
BLING PLANE TICKET TEDDY

Since his arrival on Apia, Willis had also learned that the Australian government would be bound by law to destroy Aussie and Kiki once he docked at Sydney Harbor. The ongoing threat of rabies meant that only dogs and cats traveling directly from the British Isles were allowed into the country, so a trip to New York would provide Willis the opportunity to carry the cats home with him. The local police chief took charge of the raft, promising to keep it safe in Willis's absence, and Willis was soon boarding a flight to Pago Pago, where he passed part of his layover on a visit to the Government House, specifically to a square of adjacent lawn that was to have been the permanent home of the *Seven Little Sisters*. The ugly rumors Willis had heard in Apia proved true. The raft had gone entirely up in smoke by then, and no trace of it remained.

10

Willis from New York

ONCE WILLIS HAD RETURNED to Manhattan with Kiki and Aussie, Teddy dispatched him to her cousin the doctor, who declined on this occasion to pronounce Willis "dramatically— let me say fantastically—healthy." His conclusion was more on the order of, "You need an operation." He concurred fully with Apia's Dr. Goodman about the threat of strangulation posed by Willis's hernias and then explained to Willis the risk he ran of having his intestine pinched off in one of the tears, which could well lead to gangrene, perforation, and "a hell of a fix."

When asked how he was otherwise, Willis chirped, "Ready to go," but he promised Teddy's cousin that, where it came to surgery, he would "sure think it over." And he did, for the balance of the afternoon and well into the evening, before informing Teddy that he'd decided against the operation. "I know myself pretty well," Willis assured his wife, "my insides, I mean," and he went on to add that he couldn't really warm to the idea of being "cut open and stitched up again, like a bag." He allowed that if his condition were "a real emergency," he'd have the surgery, which set Teddy to sputtering, since it all seemed urgent enough to her. But when Willis volunteered to "get a good truss," Teddy yielded and gave her blessing for the second leg of the trip, though she insisted he buy two trusses in case one of them failed. Teddy, Willis remarked, "was always practical."

Aussie and Kiki were adopted by well-heeled friends of the Willises, and they retired from rafting to an estate on Cape Cod, which left Teddy, in her view, sufficiently unencumbered to make the Samoa-to-Australia run on board the *Age Unlimited* with her husband. Now it was Willis's turn to sputter. "Impossible," he told her. "The reefs—the reefs, Teddy. It'll be a tough trip." When Teddy assured him she would prefer reefs to idle waiting, Willis produced a chart of the western Pacific and taught her how to track his progress on it from home. He also promised more and better telepathy, while insisting that the trip was his to make alone. Teddy relented. (Teddy always relented.)

In the spring of 1964, Willis returned to Apia via Los Angeles, Hawaii, and Pago Pago. Among his luggage was a bag of sails, used but refurbished, that had been given to him by a City Island sailmaker who had once counted among his employees one of Willis's former crewmates from the *Henriette*. Willis arrived in Apia to find his raft resting on the sandy floor of the lagoon at dead low tide. He walked out to it and climbed on board. Willis made a quick tour of the damage the intervening months had seen, all of it cosmetic, and then took his place at the wheel as the incoming tide washed into the lagoon and slowly floated the *Age Unlimited*. Willis was gripped so by a "feeling of exultation" that he broke into song and lingered belting out sea chanteys long enough to have to swim the three hundred yards back to shore.

Willis had quite a bit of work to do on his raft to put it in shipshape condition, and the locals proved as generous with their time and materials as had the Peruvian navy in the harbor of Callao. A dozen new centerboards—two-by-twelves, each twelve feet long—were provided free of charge by the owner of an Apia sawmill, and mechanics from the public-works department who had repaired and reinforced Willis's rudders assisted him in their installation. He had the raft hauled out of the water so that he could scrape and paint the rusty pontoons, after which he set about overhauling all of the running gear, replacing the lines, greasing the blocks and buckles, and stitching and patching his torn mainsail properly, since he lacked the money to replace it. The used sails he'd brought from home he planned to employ as wing jibs. Willis had drawn up designs for booms to be made from three-inch iron pipe—they would fly sails to either side of the main and were to be used to take full advantage of following winds.

Willis's water barrels had dried out in his absence and had gone largely to pieces, so he had new rings made, put the original staves back together, and filled the barrels with seawater to swell them and make them tight. In doing so, Willis drove out hordes of cockroaches that were living in the gaps and channels between the staves. A man full in the flush of reason might have opted for new barrels, but Willis only remarked, "Better cockroaches than rats or something else to foul the water."

When the barrels had swollen to the point of being leakproof, Willis dumped out the seawater and filled them with fresh water that, upon inspection, was visibly fouled with cockroach legs and wings and eggs. He took a sample to the Apia hospital lab for analysis and was told that the water was comprehensively contaminated and would be lethal after only a few days in the tropical sun. Willis returned to the raft, dumped the water, rinsed out the barrels, refilled them again, and carried off another sample for testing. "Better now, but still bad." This time he was offered chloride. He rinsed out and refilled the barrels again, treated the water, and returned to the lab with yet another sample. "It was still not safe," Willis revealed, "but I said I would watch it and, if it started to smell, put in more chloride."

In addition to his cockroachy water and the sorts of canned goods that had seen him through the first leg of his trip, Willis planned on the morning of departure to crowd the deck with "piles of coconuts, pineapples, papaws, and bunches of bananas," along with a wealth of lemons and limes.

Willis had announced a departure date of Saturday, June 27, and a sizable crowd was expected to see him off. On Thursday the twenty-fifth, however, Willis got some unsettling news. A waitress in the restaurant of the hotel where he was staying acquainted him with the particulars of a conversation she'd overheard: A local captain was planning to follow Willis out of the lagoon in his sloop and film him for several days in hopes of selling the footage to American television. This might have been an irritant but an otherwise harmless development, except for the fact that Willis was carrying a camera of his own and intended to film his voyage and then sell the documentary to recoup expenses. He therefore was in no position to tolerate a cinematic poacher and confided as much in the harbormaster, who helped Willis arrange for a surreptitious departure the night of the twenty-sixth.

The ruse was that Willis merely intended to move his raft away from its dock and deeper into the harbor in preparation for sailing the following day. A large tug had been enlisted to warp alongside the *Age Unlimited* around midnight, when the few longshoremen looking on saw a short line dropped to Willis as if the tow were to be brief and contained by the lagoon. To that end, Willis had been obliged to leave his produce on the wharf to avoid suspicion. Once cloaked by darkness, the tug steamed toward the harbor mouth, playing out towline as it went, and soon the *Age Unlimited* had passed entirely out of the placid lagoon and into the wind-whipped Pacific. A fierce storm was raging, replete with lightning and erratic gusts, and the raft banged along on the chop at little more than four knots.

Willis had been advised to leave no less than fifty miles of sea room between himself and landfall, so naturally, given his troubled relationship with advice, he motioned for the tug to stop at eight the following morning when they were but thirty-five miles north of Apia. He dropped the towline, set his jib and mizzen, and then went about the chore of positioning his centerboards. Finding three of the six boards too wide for their slots, he performed a spot of quick carpentry with an ax, and by 9:00 A.M. on June 27, 1964, a catless William Willis was properly under way, bound for Australia.

Or at least he was marginally under way. Willis still had to install his specially manufactured wing booms and then rig their sails and raise them, which required the balance of the day. The following morning he awoke to find himself becalmed. By noon he could make out the mountainous island of Savai'i to his south. He was drifting back to land on the swell and was helpless to do anything about it. The calm persevered, and by the morning of the twenty-ninth, Savai'i was alarmingly close. Willis was reminded of a story he'd heard in Apia about a

disabled Japanese trawler that had drifted 350 miles due south
to wreck on the reef at Upolu, Savai'i's sister island. Willis was
on a similar course, with only a tenth the sea room.

By the afternoon of the twenty-ninth, still windless, Willis
had decided to send an SOS. He was hardly twenty miles from
Apia and so had to believe that even his repaired but unreliable
Marconi transmitter would get through at that distance. The
dynamo required hand cranking, and as Willis knelt beside the
Salvita III and rotated the handle, he felt a sharp pain in his left
side. He rested a moment and then turned the crank again,
until he was stopped by the agony. Willis immediately knew
his hernia was the source of his discomfort, "but having had
pains there before," he wrote, "I didn't think it could be anything serious." He stretched out on the deck and massaged his
abdomen before making another attempt to send his SOS, but
the pain from cranking the dynamo was more than he could
bear. Here, it seemed, was the "fix" Teddy's cousin had spoken
of. Drifting toward the island of Savai'i in a dead calm, Willis
was incapable of mustering the strength to save himself. He
thought of his wife if he were to die, his embarrassment if he
were to live. He stretched out flat on the split-bamboo deck
and performed a blind and blundering examination, soon
reaching the conclusion that "it looked like strangulation."

"It seemed to be exactly what the doctors had warned me
against," Willis confessed. "There it was looking me in the
face—strangulation, gangrene, perforation, the works. Maybe
death on the raft within sight of Samoa." Willis lifted his legs
in the air and attempted with his fingers to massage and ma-
nipulate the exposed bit of intestine back through the tear in
his muscle wall. He noticed that his abdomen was growing

distended and hot, and he concluded that "the pinched-off piece of intestine was putrefying and sooner or later would burst open." He wondered how long that might take and contemplated surgery—not the safe antiseptic sort performed by trained professionals but spontaneous deckside surgery, a marriage of guesswork and marlin spike. "But, I realized, if I made a mistake and cut too deep or wide of the mark, not being able to see among the blood and inflammation—where would I be then?"

The swelling persisted. Willis grew dizzy and nauseous. He managed to light his Primus stoves and heated seawater on them so that he could apply hot packs to his hernia. He'd persisted at the cure for some hours before wondering if heat were really wanted in this circumstance. He felt that if he could only relax his muscles, the bit of protruding intestine might slip back through the tear, and that's when Willis hatched an inspired idea. He ran a length of half-inch rope through a block welded to a davit, tied one end around his ankles, and pulled on the other until he had hoisted himself upside down off the deck.

> I swung back and forth to the rolling of the raft, while trying every movement and twist and manipulation with the full weight of my intestines now on my heart and lungs. Sometimes I hoisted myself high until I stood almost on my head; sometimes I lowered myself. I also hung by one leg, the left or the right, always watching which position relaxed the abdomen most.

By eight in the evening, Willis had been dangling for a couple of hours. He'd dozed a little, vomited some, and finally "became aware of a feeling of relief." While his torso was still sore to the touch, the pinched-off bit of intestine seemed to have slipped back inside. Gingerly, he lowered himself to the deck and lay still, reluctant to believe that, at least for the moment, the danger had passed.

Willis felt well enough, in fact, to indulge in a poetic apostrophe: "How beautiful the night looked to me suddenly, how like a divine fluid the silent sea in which I lay" (a marked improvement on the earthly fluids he'd been manufacturing for some hours). Then he took up a bit of belated practical business. "Still lying," he noted, "I put on my truss."

Willis awoke the following morning, weakened but without pain. Becalmed, he was drifting more to the east now than the south and so was no closer to Savai'i than he'd been the night before. An eastward drift, however, was likely to send him onto the reef before Upolu. But Willis's native good fortune—"the right thing at the right time"—came to his rescue once again in the form of a stiff easterly breeze that kicked up with the setting sun, and he took advantage by setting all of his sails, including the new wing sails, which gave the *Age Unlimited* a forty-foot spread of canvas from tip to tip. Sailing slightly north of west, Willis was finally driven clear of danger.

While he was pleased with the extra speed his new wing sails provided, Willis was now flying appreciably more canvas and rayon than he could hope to handle with any dispatch. The added velocity would be crucial in helping him maneuver around the various reefs he was almost certain to encounter on this leg of the trip, but even a quartering wind stood the chance of making complete havoc on board by threatening more flapping and backing sails than Willis could possibly manage.

He got a taste of what he was up against his first week out, when the raft swung into a stiff wind as he was attempting to take a sight. The mainsail "began beating against the mast with such force it threatened to reduce it to rags. The whole raft was shaking." As Willis was struggling to lower the main, the sail begin to rip in a "demonic blast" of near-gale-force wind that tore the thing from his hands and sent him lurching off the bow and overboard. "I was in the sea," Willis wrote, "upside down and struggling to get to the surface and grab hold of something while the raft was plunging over me." His salvation proved a length of chain that connected the rudders—he managed to hook a leg over it as it passed and climb back onto the deck. With the same perverse sense of timing that had prompted Willis to strap on his truss only after his attack, he took this occasion, still dripping and shaken, to fasten a fifty-foot float line to the aft mast on the outside chance that a fellow might actually fall into the drink.

*　*　*

Willis had proposed to follow a route that would carry him north of the Fiji Islands and then south to put him well east of New Caledonia, which would make for a clear sail to the southwest directly for Sydney. But after only a week under way, a steady southeasterly wind had driven the *Age Unlimited* much farther north than Willis had planned for, well beyond twelve degrees of latitude, so he was already doubtful that he could recover sufficiently to steer east of New Caledonia.

The fishing proved poor, and Willis had caught nothing by the end of the first week in July. Unhappily, his supply of potatoes had rotted in their mesh sack on the deck, leaving him with onions, lemons, canned goods, and a lingering dose of regret over the produce he'd left on the Apia wharf. A stave in one of Willis's water barrels had cracked, and the contents had drained away, but he was catching enough rainwater to leave him confident of his supply. He took a mug of seawater daily "for medicinal reasons" and continued to suffer from his hernia, his tightly cinched truss notwithstanding. The pain was all but constant, and on July 9 Willis endured his second strangulation attack.

Again he tied a line around his ankles and hoisted himself off the deck. After two hours Willis found relief when the occluded bit of intestine slipped back through the tear in the muscle wall. "This time my cure weakened me considerably," he admitted, "and for quite a while I had to remain lying on deck before I could get up." He had been at sea all of thirteen days and was already suffering from the ordeal. Willis remarked that his waistline was down to twenty-six inches, "the lowest I could remember having had."

On July 14, Willis crossed the international date line, 180 degrees of longitude. He had remained much farther north than he'd expected or wished and was conflicted as to how he should proceed. Waiting for the wind to shift and drive him on his proposed route east of New Caledonia was a bit of a gamble, and if Willis were obliged to pass the New Hebrides to the north, he would be best served by setting the appropriate course while he still had ample sea room to guarantee good maneuvering. As a further complication, steering a course north of the New Hebrides would bring Willis into the Coral Sea on his approach to Australia, which meant he would either have to work his way through the Great Barrier Reef to reach the continent or continue north to New Guinea.

In the end the choice wasn't Willis's to make. The winds and currents made it for him, and he yielded to the inevitable and steered a northerly course that he hoped would bring him safely between the New Hebrides and the volcanic, sparsely populated Banks Islands to their north. By the last week in July, day upon day of murky, squally weather had kept Willis from taking reliable sights, and he was none too sure of his position. His dead reckoning put him perilously close to the northern-most islands of the New Hebrides chain, Pentecost and Maéwo, but Willis knew that his calculations could be miles off, and he was allowed only the odd, tantalizing glimpse of land on the horizon during rare breaks in the gloomy weather.

As a precaution, he attempted to send an SOS. Since he could hardly be sure of his position and wasn't remotely per-suaded that his raft would survive the night without breaking up on one rocky shoreline or another, Willis cranked his transmitter, only to find that the Salvita III was, once again, dead. Dawn found him sailing in clearer weather on a landless sea. Able to take a proper noon sight, he established his posi-tion at fifteen degrees, forty-eight minutes south latitude, which put him on a course certain to carry him safely north of Maéwo by a few miles and might have given Willis cause to relax but for an added caution on the Hydrographic Office chart he relied upon:

The north coast of Maewo
is rep. to lie 6 miles N. W.
of its charted position.

Accordingly, Willis pressed on to the north to be sure of clearing the island of Maéwo, no matter where it might lie, and so brought himself unexpectedly into the vicinity of the southern Banks Islands, particularly Merig and Mere Lava. The drift of the current proved more forceful and northerly than Willis had allowed for, and though he dozed off content that he was clear of the New Hebrides with sea room to spare, he awoke in the moonless midnight to make the mortifying discovery that a "high, black mountain lay close behind me—close enough seemingly to be touched." Blindly, while he was sleeping, Willis had passed within a mile of Mere Lava, and he and the *Age Unlimited* had been spared by sheer dumb luck.

Ahead of him lay Merig Islet, and as the wind died down and the sea flattened out the following morning, the drift of the current carried Willis's becalmed raft to within a mile of land. He scoured the shoreline with his binoculars. He saw no sign of human life but fixated instead on the thick growth of coconut palms lining the shore. The trees were heavy with fruit, and Willis was driven a little batty by the sight of so many coconuts almost within reach. He had been at sea for over a month and had yet to catch a single fish. He'd had to toss his rotten potatoes overboard, and his onions were beginning to spoil. Fresh food in the form of coconut meat and milk impressed Willis as just what he needed. "Those coconuts," he decided, "would give me new life."

Willis had picked up in Apia a ten-foot Samoan canoe that he carried lashed to his cabin roof alongside his kayak. He unstrapped it and settled it into the water beside the becalmed raft. He stowed on board two paddles, "a machete, a hatchet, an ax, some rope, a fishing line, a can for bailing, and some sacks to hold the coconuts, also some matches." The shrine of his altogether curious philosophy notwithstanding, Willis

knew in his bones that the foray he'd determined to make bor-
dered on idiotic:

> I was fully aware of what I was doing, paddling away
> from the raft and leaving it in the open sea, and felt
> guilty of an almost unpardonable offense. But I wanted
> coconuts, fresh food—my very soul cried for them.

But merely knowing he was about to do something almost
unpardonable failed to prevent Willis from doing it, and he cast
off from his raft, leaving it unanchored and floating freely on
the swell.

The canoe was equipped with a lone outrigger, but the vessel
was so short and narrow that it was far tippier than Willis had
anticipated, which prevented him from paddling with the brand
of vigor he would have preferred. Willis skirted the shoreline of
Merig Islet, looking for a clear break in the surrounding reef
through which he might pass and gain the beach. There was no
sign of human life, not so much as a lone hut, just the verdant
temptation of the coconut palms. In clearing a headland, Willis
drifted out of sight of the raft and was indulging in a daydream
about life on the island—"this green paradise full of fruit and
fish, lobsters and clams"—when he noticed that "the sea had
become a bit ruffled and the sky darkened a little." Willis made
his choice in an instant: He pivoted the canoe and plunged his
paddle deep into the water, digging for the *Age Unlimited* as
hard as he dared.

Within a matter of minutes, Willis had brought the raft back
into view. She was floating freely with her sails down in the
freshening wind, and he was closing on her when the stern

lashing of his outrigger parted. The rope was made of coconut fiber, and more than a month out of the water on the cabin roof had caused it to dry and rot. Willis had sufficient fishing line for a repair, but the canoe proved too unstable for him to work from inside, so he slipped into the water and set about reattaching the outrigger. The job was nearly finished when the front lashing broke. Willis was over an hour at the repair before he'd succeeded in finishing the job. The mends were makeshift by necessity, and he had to paddle gingerly, creeping along in what was now gathering dusk. By the time he'd finally reached the raft, it had been dark for an hour.

Upon reflection, Willis embraced the full folly of his coconut expedition. "I could hardly believe that I had been guilty of such stupidity," he acknowledged, "leaving the raft adrift in the open sea and paddling off to an island to get coconuts."

* * *

By early August, Willis had put the New Hebrides to his stern, having passed between the Banks Islands and Cape Cumberland, and he continued on a course slightly south of due west into the Coral Sea. His plan—more a fond hope, actually—was to attempt to dip toward Brisbane and thereby avoid the troublesome complication of having to reach the continent of Australia by passing through (more likely over) the Great Barrier Reef. And early on, with a favorable wind, Willis made a little southern headway before, on August 8, he met with a calamity that cost him his heading and could well have cost him his life.

The night of the eighth was unsettled and stormy, with a brisk southeasterly wind hitting the raft in stiff gusts. Willis was sailing under his jib and mizzen with the main furled when he decided to pull the jib to port in a bid to make truer headway south. The wind, though, had all but pinned the sail in place, and Willis tugged on the sheet to no effect, finally applying both hands to the rope and leaning back with his full weight. He was pulling with everything he had when the block that the sheet passed through broke loose from its mooring and Willis was flung backward against the iron jib boom and knocked to the deck.

"For a few moments," he wrote, "I lay benumbed by the shock but sensing that something terrible had happened to me." He discovered that his legs had gone limp. Willis feared he'd broken his back but could feel no pain—could feel nothing, in fact. He dozed off (passed out, really) on a pile of clothes by the cabin and didn't awaken until morning, when he realized his condition was unimproved. He couldn't stand, could barely move, and certainly was in no state to sail. Willis could see by the sun that he was drifting north now, away from Brisbane and directly toward the Solomon Islands.

Off and on for the next two days, he slept and remained incapable of standing, dragging himself around the raft by his arms. Fortunately, his food was in wooden boxes on the floor of the cabin, so he could get at his beans and his biscuits when appetite took hold. "My flesh, where I had struck," Willis wrote, "had swollen so enormously that it felt as if a pillow were attached to me, and within that smashed flesh, if I touched it right, the pain was extreme." Willis suspected a fracture or some sort of misalignment of his spinal column, so he was pleased and a little surprised when, on the third night after his accident, he began to feel a bit better, or at least "more hopeful."

In fact, his spirits were sufficiently lifted to prompt Willis to compose a sort of commemorative ditty, which he sang to the tune of "The Prisoner's Song," a traditional Australian ballad about transported convicts:

I lay on my raft on the ocean,
The night was black on the sea;
My body was weary and broken,
And I slept and a dream came to me.

I saw my mother come walking
Through the waste, through the foam and the spray;
I heard her gentle voice talking
As I did in the days faraway.

She stood by my side in the tempest,
She kneeled by my side on the sea,
Her hand touched my brow like a blessing;
Then I was all alone on the sea.

I lay on the planks in the tempest,
And the stars stood in glory above;
And I slept like a child in its cradle—
Like a child that has only known love.

Once the composition was complete, Willis allowed that "a peace and happiness almost beyond comprehension" took hold of him and endured through the night.

Another three days had passed before Willis could finally stand, and only then with appreciable effort and by hanging on for support with both hands. His recovery from that point forward, however, was so swift as to border on miraculous. "Strength flooded into my legs from a mysterious source," he declared. "I had made it!" He was soon negotiating the deck with little trouble. In examining himself, Willis found that his buttocks were "a black and purple mass such as I had never seen on a human being." His bruised and swollen posterior made for such a remarkable sight that he "took pictures of it, movies and stills, feeling that I had to make a record of it."

On August 12, Willis plotted his position to find that he'd drifted well north during his incapacitation and was less than two hundred miles from San Cristóbal in the Solomon Islands. While prepared to concede that "Sydney was almost out of the question" due to the contrary winds and prevailing currents of the Coral Sea, Willis remained undaunted and boasted that he would "tackle the Great Reef itself or sail north around it" in order to reach land. His stamina, though improved, remained far from perfect after his mishap, and he allowed that he was "still moving around like a cripple, and occasionally my legs went numb, which frightened me."

Just after midnight on August 19, Willis's seventy-first birthday, he spied the light of a ship dead astern and approaching. The *Age Unlimited*'s heading through the Coral Sea had put Willis in the path of Hong Kong–to–Sydney steamers, so he'd been alert to the peril of increased traffic, and he played a light on his sail to make himself visible to the helmsman. He then flashed an SOS in an attempt to bring the ship alongside and raised by it a blink of response from the bridge.

The steamer closed so hard from astern that Willis feared being run down. She swung off at the last moment and played a blinding searchlight on him as a voice called out demanding to know who he was and what he wanted. Willis replied with his name and that of his craft and then requested his position be reported to his wife in New York. Fat chance, he had to think, given his experience with the SS *Whakatane* on the first leg of his trip. But that very day Teddy received a telegram from the office of the Australian consulate general in Manhattan:

MRS. WILLIAM WILLIS

AUSTRALIAN AUTHORITIES ADVISE MASTER OF BARON JED-
BURGH REPORTS HAVING SIGHTED RAFT AGE UNLIMITED
12:15 AM AUG 19TH POSTION 15° 44′ SOUTH 159° 45′ EAST

Far better than telepathy, or at least more precise, and on her husband's birthday no less.

For some days thereafter, Willis had no sun and was obliged to establish his position by dead reckoning, until at last the sky cleared sufficiently for a useful sight, which put the *Age Unlimited* 40 miles farther north than he had calculated and on a direct course for Marion Reef, a sizable expanse of coral with a mean elevation of seven feet. Willis steered north to put himself well clear of danger and then west toward a more substantial piece of treachery—the Great Barrier Reef, a scant 120 miles away.

* * *

Extending over four thousand miles from end to end, the Great Barrier Reef was far more of an obstacle than Willis could reasonably hope to maneuver around. Though he had entertained the notion of clearing to the northwest for New

Guinea once conditions had put Sydney out of reach, wind and current in the Coral Sea were conspiring to drive him virtually due west regardless of the heading he preferred. As was his habit, Willis embraced the inevitable with some savor and "made ready for the assault."

Unfortunately, he would be sailing blind into the maze of coral outcroppings and navigable channels that make up the Great Barrier Reef. Impossibly thrifty as a matter of course and with an intended destination of Sydney, Willis had purchased no chart with coverage west of the 147th meridian or north of the nineteenth degree of latitude. So in driving around the New Hebrides to the northwest and approaching the Australian continent at close to seventeen degrees of southern latitude, Willis had effectively sailed off his map. He would have no reference for depth and no indication, other than what he could see from his mast, where the most inviting channels might lie once he reached the reef. The chances, then, of the *Age Unlimited*'s snagging on the coral and suffering destruction beneath breaking waves were pretty substantial, which meant Willis could well be left to make his way through the reef, into the inner passage, and across it to shore in either his shabby, broken Samoan canoe or his puny kayak.

Willis, quite naturally, found the challenge bracing, and he made ready by checking his running gear, coiling his lines, and positioning his homemade anchor (an iron box filled with ballast) at the deck edge, where he could shove it into the water at a moment's notice. He then hung his binoculars on a nail by the cabin door, lowered his mainsail, and drove west on jib and mizzen into what even Willis admitted were very uncertain prospects: "I realized that tides and currents and the timing when hitting the reef might have the final say whether I would get through. But was it possible to get through?"

Passing through the Great Barrier Reef—thirty miles wide in places—with a proper chart and a responsive craft would have been challenge enough, but Willis would be obliged to feel and blunder his way on a vessel that, under the best of circumstances, was difficult to manage with even passable precision. To make matters worse, the shallow bottom would call for him to sail with his centerboards raised, so his control over the *Age Unlimited* would be further compromised. Willis seemed to expect the raft to get inextricably hung up on the coral, but even still he was only beginning to chew over a plan for escape as he closed within sight of the reef:

> If the raft struck and remained fast, I had decided to build a catamaran by lashing my kayak and canoe together, put my instruments and valuables in one and, sitting in the other, try to paddle through the reefs to the Inner Passage and so eventually reach Australia.

Of course, if the raft suddenly came apart in the surging surf, an authentic possibility, Willis's having merely "decided" to build a catamaran wouldn't do him terribly much good.

The Great Barrier Reef initially revealed itself to Willis as a "white line on the horizon." With no chart to consult, he couldn't be sure if he were seeing "an isolated shoal or a spur running out from a larger mass." Since the day was waning, Willis veered off and passed the night tacking to await sunrise. With the dawn he steered west all day but failed to spy breakers and was obliged to pass another night tacking to avoid harm. By the following morning, Willis had encountered the reef again and had climbed the mast to search for an opening in the coral. Thinking he had found a channel, he steered the *Age Unlimited* through the gap. "I saw reefs closing in on me from either side," he wrote. "I was already trapped."

Willis had put himself in a boiling confusion of breakers and surging surf:

> The sun was shining on the blue water and glittering on the white crashing walls. Everything was thundering as the cataracts rose and tumbled before me. I looked over the side while skirting the edge of the reef and saw the foul ground beneath, dirty green and yellowish black, like lumps of rags. The roar of the seas had become a soothing melody, for there was little wind, and the tide, I thought, was ebbing.

Willis made way in a channel some fifty yards wide. He'd covered not more than a quarter of a mile when he first struck bottom. The raft bumped on the coral, continued, snagged again twenty yards on, and stuck fast. Willis lowered all sail and climbed the mast for a better taste of his predicament. The tide was, in fact, ebbing, and much of the surrounding reef was draining bare. He descended to the deck, grabbed a bucket, and went over the side onto the exposed reef to gather crabs and shrimp and clams for his dinner. He returned to enjoy a regular feast on the deck—"my first fresh food since leaving Apia."

In the small hours of the morning, the incoming tide jolted Willis awake. Gradually but steadily, the sea washed over the coral, submerging it while boiling up through the decking of the raft with ever-increasing violence. Willis climbed into the rigging, forced to wonder "whether the tide would float us off before the cabin went over the side." He was an hour clinging to the mast before the raft began to pitch from side to side. With only the jib unfurled, the *Age Unlimited* lurched forward in galvanic fits and starts. Willis climbed down to check his rudders and found them free of the reef. The pontoons clattered against the coral spikes and spurs, but the raft drove ahead in the darkness.

Willis could only steer to avoid roiling patches where the froth was apparent to him. He sailed for nearly a mile before hanging up again, this time just briefly, before a following sea had lifted the raft and carried her into deeper water. Willis took a sounding and found bottom at fourteen fathoms. Ignorant of his position, he was tempted to believe he'd already gained the inner passage, but dawn broke to reveal more breakers forward—he saw them too late to maneuver with any effect and ended up ramming the bow directly into a spur of reef. The *Age Unlimited* bumped along briefly before sticking fast. Once again the tide was ebbing, and Willis lowered sail in the dawn light. He climbed the mast with his binoculars and was heartened to see, to the west and northwest, open water to the horizon.

Willis wandered the freshly exposed reef with a bucket, this time collecting sea cucumbers along with his clams before returning to the deck to await the flowing tide. By afternoon the coral was awash, and once more Willis climbed into the rigging to avoid the lapping waves and the spray. Battered for over an hour by increasingly violent seas, the raft finally stirred on its perch.

Willis descended to set his sail, and the *Age Unlimited* surged forward, hung up briefly, and then drove free into open water. "For a while I could still see foul patches beneath me," Willis remarked. "Then they disappeared." He took soundings and once again found bottom at fourteen fathoms. "Was I in the Inner Passage now?" Willis wondered. He had no conceivable way of knowing and couldn't decide if he should sail west for the coast of Australia or steer north throughout the night in hopes of avoiding any coral ahead until daylight.

He eventually chose the latter option, reasoning that a westerly heading, even if he were clear of the reef, put him in danger of "smashing into one of the rocky islands strewn along the Australian coast." Willis proceeded under his jib and mizzen, made himself a meal of dehydrated vegetable soup enlivened with Great Barrier Reef crab and shrimp, and took regular soundings, which found bottom reliably at fourteen to fifteen fathoms. Eventually, he dozed off, only to be awakened by the dull roar of breakers. "A white wall was just ahead, thundering and smashing up high," and Willis made a futile attempt to steer clear before the inevitable collision.

The sea broke with such vehemence that he donned, for the first time in his rafting career, a life jacket. Once more he climbed into the rigging, where he clung to the mast until the raft was rudely shoved clear of the coral. Eventually a cloudy day dawned, and the depth beneath the *Age Unlimited* was down to seven fathoms. By late morning Willis had spied more breakers, boiling sea ahead to his left and to his right. He steered for what looked like a channel between the reefs but soon discovered that what he'd taken for separate spurs joined together before him. With the tide in his favor, Willis kept headway over the reef, bumping and scraping against it but never snagging. "I sailed on and on, hour after hour," he wrote, "always only a few feet above the coral, seeing the same beautiful colors and exquisite shapes laying [*sic*] beneath me." With the coming of nightfall, Willis "sailed over the edge of the reef into deep water and, to judge by the heavy swell, was in the Inner Passage."

Conquering the Great Barrier Reef had a curiously enervating effect upon Willis: "My mind was benumbed—all enthusiasm, all zest and eagerness for living had gone out of it." He felt sure he'd reach the coast of Australia the following day, and the prospect of arrival, of his voyage's soon being over, served to make Willis not just gloomy but inattentive. Unsure of his position and sailing without a chart, he nonetheless spread out his poncho on what was now a shattered deck and dropped off to sleep. Willis suddenly awoke to high seas, rising winds, and the dreadful impression that he'd seen a light off the starboard bow.

He checked his compass heading, unlashed the wheel, and detected the flash of "a tiny light about a point to starboard." He climbed into the rigging for a clearer view, and as his eyes adjusted to the moonless darkness, Willis made out a lighthouse on a promontory ahead with a beacon that flashed four times between eight-second intervals. "If I had had a chart," he noted, "I would have been able to identify it and know my position." But he didn't and couldn't and so wasn't at all certain where the danger might lie. Dead ahead? To the right? The left? Willis didn't believe he could be within sight of the Australian coast and so speculated that the lighthouse occupied an island in the Inner Passage. He strained to see the outlines of the terrain but could make nothing out until a collision was all but guaranteed: "Suddenly during the eight seconds of darkness, I saw the island, sprawling black in the sea beside me—sinister, terrible, and strangely close."

Willis spun the wheel to shift course, but the raft drifted forward until the lighthouse was lost from view. "I realized that I had sailed into the obscure sector," he wrote, "the ultimate warning that rocks were ahead." The raft struck hard, with "shattering force, reeled, and went into what I can only call convulsions, bounding up and down like something demented." The beam of Willis's flashlight revealed

> a large bulging rock on which the raft lay in its throes. Beyond, on the starboard side, were masses of jagged, high rocks standing like tombstones, while ahead was a solid wall of still larger rocks; to the left I could only see breakers.

It was enough to make a fellow long for the forthright, shark-infested peril of the Great Barrier Reef.

The raft seemed to Willis quite hopelessly ensnared, and it was lifted and pounded in turn by onrushing seas. Willis held to the rigging, expecting the *Age Unlimited* to come apart at any moment. "It was, at times," he remarked, "like hanging on to the inner edge of an exploding crater. . . . Never had I experienced such helplessness, such inadequacy of human strength against the aroused elements." The raft listed acutely, threatening to turn over while Willis clung to a nearly vertical deck. She then rocked onto her other pontoon, and somehow the motion served to free her from the boulder she'd been snagged on. Willis stared at the flowing water beneath the deck, hardly believing he was sailing again.

With his jib standing full in gale-force winds, Willis drove away from what proved to be one of the Brooks Islands. Once well clear, he inspected for damage, and, in addition to dents and dings to his pontoons, he discovered that the lower ends of his rudders had been rolled up "like scrolls of tissue paper." So the *Age Unlimited* was growing less responsive, almost by the hour, as September 9, 1964, dawned to reveal Goold Island to Willis's port, Combe Island to his starboard, and in the gap between them a "grayness over the water" that was, finally, the low-lying Queensland coast.

The sky spit rain as Willis approached a "dismal-looking stretch" of Australian shoreline. Though he feared rocks and protecting reefs, the flat bay Willis made for turned out to be unobstructed and inviting. The surf was moderate and broke on a sandy beach lined with eucalyptus trees. Though he saw no houses, he set off a pair of flares as he approached, and shortly before noon he swung the *Age Unlimited* into the wind and dropped his makeshift anchor into waist-deep water.

Willis was seventy-two days and twenty-four hundred miles from Apia. Altogether, from Callao to Queensland, he had been on the water for 204 days and had covered nearly eleven thousand miles.

Carrying his passport and clearance papers, Willis waded ashore and walked the length of the beach in hopes of finding someone—anyone—to whom he might announce himself. He ventured into the adjacent scrub and came across only a steer and a small kangaroo. Cresting a dune, he saw houses beyond a modest bay and a man and woman walking on the shore, their backs to him. When they failed to hear his call, Willis set off a distress flare to gain their notice. He waved them over, and the two climbed into a boat and motored across the bay, though they hung off once they'd gotten full sight of Willis. "They were somewhat taken aback," he confessed, "when they saw a gaunt, old and sea-stained man with a beard down to his chest and rolled-up dungarees."

The man was Hank Penning, a schoolteacher from the town of Tully, just inland; the woman, his wife. The bony, ragged captain of the *Age Unlimited* cordially stuck out his hand as he informed them both, "I'm Willis from New York."

Overcoming their misgivings, Hank Penning and his wife carried Willis across the bay in their boat and then drove him to the Tully police station, where his claims were met with a fair dose of skepticism. "No one up here, it seemed," Willis declared with a hint of disappointment, "had ever heard of me." His papers were thought forgeries, and one man in attendance was all but certain he was a runaway convict from the prison on Norfolk Island, a facility that had closed in 1850. "Do I look that old?" Willis asked as he glanced around for a mirror. Then the telephone rang, a wire-service reporter from Sydney calling for a Mr. William Willis of the *Age Unlimited*. Word, it seemed, was out.

11

Full Stop

TEDDY JOINED WILLIS IN Australia, where he was celebrated as a nautical marvel and applauded for his triumphant crossing of the Pacific from continent to continent. With arrangements made by the future prime minister, Harry Holt, Willis's raft was transported from desolate Queensland to Sydney on the HMAS *Boonaroo*, and then was carried on to New York aboard the SS *Pioneer Gem* in transit to the Mariners' Museum in Newport News, Virginia, where Willis expected the *Age Unlimited* to go on "permanent exhibit."

Willis and Teddy remained behind in Australia for several months, touring the country and enjoying the benefits of Willis's celebrity. He sat for a number of interviews in Sydney, including one with a reporter for the *New York Times* in which he condensed his ordeal into a melodramatic teaser for the book he intended to write:

> "I came in on my last set of nerves," Mr. Willis said. "I was at the point of death many times. The weather was extremely bad and I had many catastrophes."

Willis added that his immediate plans included a return trip to New York, where he would lecture about his adventures at the ongoing World's Fair in Queens.

Willis's written account of the voyage was a year in the making and saw publication initially in England in 1966 under the title *An Angel on Each Shoulder*. (The American edition, *Whom the Sea Has Taken*, wouldn't come out until the following year.) Willis, his book completed, turned his attention to his next adventure, driven by unflagging restlessness and, even at the age of seventy-three, incapable of so much as contemplating retirement. He had two projects under consideration.

The one more favored would see him return to the Pacific, this time on a legitimate boat to take him only so far as the Galápagos Islands. A Guayaquil acquaintance familiar with islands had told Willis of a sheltered bay full of massive sharks, some nearing thirty feet in length, and Willis had long harbored plans to fit a boat with film equipment, travel to the Galápagos, and make a movie of the life of this particular bay. Of course, he had no qualifications as a filmmaker beyond the raw footage he'd returned with from his *Age Unlimited* voyage, and he was certainly no naturalist, but Willis remained keen on the prospect of spending a year among the islands until he'd exhausted his search for backers and resorted instead to Plan B.

"It was then," he wrote, "that I decided on an Atlantic crossing in a small boat." Willis claimed to have mined inspiration from the voyages of W. A. Andrews, who had initially taken to the sea out of a curious brand of necessity. Intent upon visiting the 1878 Exposition Universelle in Paris but lacking the means to buy passage, Andrews and his brother went in together on a bare-bones twenty-foot sailboat, the *Nautilus*, and embarked in early June on an Atlantic crossing from Boston. Neither man had ever been to sea before. They knew precious little of navigation, and when they sailed east out of sight of land, Andrews couldn't help but wonder "whether we should ever see it again."

Though they were hardly capable of establishing their position with any accuracy themselves, the brothers succeeded in hailing thirty-seven ships on their crossing and so were regularly given reliable coordinates and in forty-five days saw themselves safely through to Penzance and then on to Le Havre and Paris. Eleven years later, his brother now dead, William Andrews embarked on another crossing, again bound for Paris. On this occasion his boat was but fifteen feet long, and Andrews departed Boston on June 17, 1889, before a crowd of twenty-eight thousand ticket-holding well-wishers (Andrews got a cut of the gate). He met with persistent headwinds and high seas and after a month on the water was only 150 miles from Boston. Two weeks later he was 100 miles from the city and gave up the attempt.

In 1891, Andrews competed in the first single-handed transatlantic race in a fifteen-foot boat, the *Mermaid*, which he would eventually declare "wrongly constructed" once the craft had capsized seven times. Andrews ultimately gave up the race, hailed a passing steamer, and was taken on board. Undaunted, he made numerous subsequent crossings, a few of them in a collapsible canvas boat, and Willis professed to admire both Andrews's resourcefulness and, unsurprisingly, his thrift. Willis knew all about plying oceans on the cheap, and he was fully prepared to face the Atlantic in a boat as modest as his budget. "What really decided me on a small boat," he wrote, "was that the cost to build it would be comparatively little."

Constructed on his favored City Island, the craft Willis christened *Little One* was only eleven and a half feet long and a mere five feet at the beam. She was free of decking and entirely open but for a canvas cover with which Willis meant to secure himself "like an Eskimo in his kayak." Inspired by a nautical exhibit in New York's Museum of Natural History, Willis had approached his friend and storied City Island sailmaker Gunnar Vallentine to stitch the cover for him. Vallentine's response should have given Willis pause. "I'll fix you something," the sailmaker told him, "but with the canvas we get now shrinking as it does, I don't know whether it will stand up. If it doesn't, you'll be in trouble out there. The North Atlantic is no place for an open boat the size of yours when it blows."

Willis, in typical fashion, remained unfazed by the warning and ordered up the cover, only to have it shrink from the salt and the sun in precipitously short order and leave him, as Vallentine had predicted, unprotected and vulnerable to even moderate seas.

Willis proposed, by way of justifying his crossing, that he intended the voyage to serve as both a "dietary experiment" and an opportunity to observe and measure the physiological strain of the trip on his nearly seventy-three-year-old body. To that end, Willis planned to keep a daily record of his "blood pressure, respiration, pulse, temperature" and perform regular urinalyses, crucial in this instance, since his supplies would include no fresh water. His plan was to drink only seawater and survive otherwise on a diet of whole wheat flour, evaporated milk, and daily spoonfuls of olive oil, honey, and lemon juice. In reality Willis proposed to repeat his *Seven Little Sisters* experience, just in a smaller craft and on a different ocean. He would attempt, in effect, to cross to Plymouth chiefly because he couldn't sit still.

In Willis's account of his preparations for his initial Atlantic foray, Teddy figures nowhere in the narrative. Unlike with the *Seven Little Sisters* and the *Age Unlimited,* when she argued against both trips but was eventually won over by Willis's pluck and determination, Teddy was silent and invisible where *Little One* was concerned. By then she must surely have felt that she'd been called upon to sit at home and wait for Willis quite enough, and the chances seem high that she was inconveniently, probably even adamantly, opposed to the whole venture. Her response to a reporter suggests as much. When asked if she considered it "silly" for a man of Willis's age to attempt a solo crossing of the Atlantic, Teddy snapped back, "What do you think?"

Teddy's disapproval served as no impediment for Willis, however. He embarked under tow from the foot of East Twenty-third Street in Manhattan on June 22, 1966, and dropped his line near sunset several miles beyond the Verrazano Narrows Bridge. "It took a few days," Willis allowed, "to adjust myself to my new existence." *Little One* was so terribly confining that he recognized his leading challenge to be psychological, and he approached the problem with his usual unorthodox flair. Willis had long been practicing rhythmic breathing as a means of slowing his metabolism and relieving anxiety. He would inhale for twelve seconds, hold the breath for four seconds, and then exhale for twelve seconds and go breathless for another four seconds. At sea the practice became what Willis deemed "effortless," and he boasted that he used it "almost automatically." In fact, he proved so willful a rhythmic breather (one hesitates to say "accomplished"), that he could render himself senseless, usually inadvertently.

When awake and alert, Willis found diversion in keeping "a permanent record of a modern man plucked out of the heart of millions of other men, and hurled head over heels into solitude, where no heart beat except his own and that of his Creator." He'd decided to keep no logbook for the trip but instead a "book of confessions," and a number of the entries have more than a whiff of gauzy metaphysics about them—"A few times I had the impression that what I saw around me emanated from me—like rays going out from the sun, meaning that I gave it life"—while other entries are decidedly more earthbound— "My rupture had begun to bother me and today I had quite a struggle with it."

The small boat rode poorly, jarringly so in swells of any significance. Early on, Willis took a spill over the side, and his clothes never dried thereafter. Fogbound calms alternated with squalls, and shipping traffic was sufficiently heavy to serve as a near-constant threat to Willis's survival. His craft was tiny and low in the water and his radar reflector homemade (a square of planking wrapped in foil), which left Willis difficult to detect in the best of conditions, and conditions were generally none too good. To complicate matters further, Willis's ruptures had begun to trouble him before he was well out of sight of land. He was particularly bothered by the more recent one, the tear on his left side from his *Age Unlimited* voyage, and he theorized that his largely idle confinement in the small boat, his "continuous sitting and being cramped when sleeping had weakened the tissues."

By the middle of July, discomfort had driven Willis to attempt the brand of hernia relief that had succeeded for him in the Pacific, hoisting himself upside down by the mizzen halyard in a bid to rearrange his intestines, but what had worked well enough on a five-ton raft was much less effective on a half-ton boat. The craft rolled so with Willis's suspended weight that he feared being dunked and drowned, and he was obliged to lower himself into the cramped hold of *Little One* to find there what relief he could.

Willis was afflicted with doubts and self-recrimination, and he passed many a squally night under the shrinking canvas wondering just what he was up to:

> Why was I here? Why was I making this voyage—crossing the Atlantic in an open boat too small to turn around in and without drinking water? What did my experiments amount to and whom could they possibly benefit? Thoughts came and went while I lay there stiff, wet and miserable. . . . Sometimes I saw Teddy's eyes on me during these questionings and heard her say—"You will never learn."

Plagued by deplorable weather—countless squalls leavened with a hurricane—Willis feared that his crossing to Plymouth might take a hundred days or more, and he was not at all sure his body could bear up under the abuse. His strangulation attacks were growing more common and relief from them increasingly difficult to find. During one particularly acute episode, Willis attempted to call for help over his emergency transmitter, only to discover that, like his Pacific transmitters, it didn't work.

Once the strangulation attacks had begun to be accompanied by prodigious nosebleeds, Willis decided that he was in no condition to continue to Plymouth and resolved to hail the next ship he saw and get taken off the water. To that end, he steered toward the Boston shipping channel and then passed almost three weeks on an empty ocean. "I was," Willis wrote, "a monk in a monastery of the sea." The one ship he did spy failed to detect him even after he'd accidentally set his mainsail on fire with a flare.

Not until August 22 did Willis succeed in hailing a ship, the *Sapphire Gladys* out of New York, and since she was Rotterdam bound, he refused rescue but instead requested that the captain call for a Coast Guard cutter and provide Willis's coordinates. Willis then took in his sails, dropped his sea anchor, and waited. Accompanied by a search plane, the cutter *Ingham* arrived just before midnight, and both Willis and his boat were taken on board for the trip north to Argentia on the western shore of Cape St. Mary's in Newfoundland.

The report of Willis's rescue that ran in the *New York Times* was brief and buried and included news of an eastern-bound sailor, Geoffrey Bowdoin, who was making for St. John's from Falmouth. In the article Teddy is reported to believe that Willis would "return to New York for an operation," but there's no reason to think he actually had one. It's much more likely that he held to his pattern: sought a diagnosis, invited the recommendation of a doctor, and then elected to ignore it in favor of some species of exercise or diet that Willis himself had decided would be just as effective and far less debilitating.

By June 24, 1967, only ten months after his rescue, Willis believed himself fit enough to make a second attempt at an

Atlantic crossing. In the interim he'd had *Little One* equipped with proper decking and a puny deckhouse, and she was now a craft Willis preferred to describe as "a pram with a cabin." Again he was bedeviled by North Atlantic storms, was blown appreciably off course, and was finally taken from the water on September 27 by the crew of the Polish trawler *Belona*. Willis was out of food, and flying from his mast, by way of a distress flag, was a red sweater belonging to Teddy. At the time of his rescue, he was in what he described as a "cataleptic trance," coming to only on the deck of the trawler and making a vigorous, ultimately unsuccessful attempt to persuade the captain to put him back on the water.

* * *

Willis's third and final attempt to cross the Atlantic commenced on May 2, 1968. *Little One* was towed to sea off Montauk Point, where her seventy-four-year-old captain raised sail and set a course for Plymouth. There was no word from or of Willis until September 24, when crewmen on the Latvian trawler *Yantarny* sighted his half-submerged boat nearly four hundred miles west of the Irish coast. Only the bow was fully afloat. *Little One* had lost her mast and her rudder. There was nothing on board beyond Willis's log, his papers and passport, and his ensign from the Adventurers Club. The crew of the *Yantarny* readily recognized Willis's name due to the miraculous Russian success of his first book, *Voyage of the Seven Little Sisters*. Willis had made his final log entry on July 21, setting down merely his latitude of fifty-three degrees and fifty minutes north.

The trawler circled for several hours in vain hopes of finding

Willis before *Little One* was hoisted onto the deck of the *Yan-tarny* and the ship steamed for the Baltic port of Kaliningrad.

Six months later, on March 4, 1969, William Willis's widow, Teddy, visited a Brooklyn dock, where the crate containing *Little One* was opened briefly so that she might get a last look before the boat continued on its way to Newport News, Virginia, and the Mariners' Museum there. News reports had the craft "scheduled to become a permanent exhibit." However, both *Little One* and *Age Unlimited* have long since been "deaccessioned"—arid museumspeak for "chopped up for firewood."

Willis's books have lapsed from print, and his accomplishments in the Pacific have all but evaporated from modern memory, eclipsed by Heyerdahl's *Kon-Tiki* expedition, which lingers as the touchstone of the era. A curiosity in his day, a wholesale obscurity in ours, William Willis once claimed the ocean for his "monastery," only to have it for his mausoleum as well. Though it's impossible to say if Willis went overboard by accident or in response to the same strain of "all-pervading summons" that had shaken him so in the Pacific, it does seem fitting that he was lost while closing the circle, while driving east at the age of seventy-four in a bid to cross the ocean he had first plied on the *Henriette* bearing west as but a boy. We can only be sure that William Willis slipped beneath the swell and so in death, as in life, was committed to the sea.

BIBLIOGRAPHY

"115-Day Raft Hermit Flies in with Script, Says He's Theatrical Writer, Not Seaman." *New York Times*, October 25, 1954: 18.

Alsar, Vital, with Enrique Hank Lopez. *La Balsa to Australia: The Longest Raft Voyage in History*. London: Hodder & Stoughton, 1973.

Baker, DeVere. *The Raft Lehi IV*. Long Beach, Calif.: Whitehorn, 1959.

Baker, Nola. *The Raft Dog: Tangoroa Aboard Lehi IV*. Salt Lake City: Bookcraft, 1960.

Bligh, William. *The Mutiny on Board HMS Bounty*. New York: New American Library, 1962.

Bombard, Dr. Alain. *The Bombard Story*. Translated by Brian Connell. London: Andre Deutsch, 1953.

Capelotti, P. J. *Sea Drift: Rafting Adventures in the Wake of Kon-Tiki*. New Brunswick, N.J.: Rutgers University Press, 2001.

Clarke, D. H. *The Singlehanders: The Evolution of a Lonely Art*. New York: David McKay, 1976.

"Cutter Returning Solo Skipper, 72, for Medical Help." *New York Times*, August 23, 1966: 40.

Danielsson, Bengt. *From Raft to Raft*. Translated by F. H. Lyon. London: George Allen & Unwin, 1960.

De Bisschop, Eric. *Tahiti Nui*. Translated by Edward Young. New York: McDowell, Obolensky, 1959.

Doherty, John Stephen. *The Boats They Sailed In*. New York: W. W. Norton, 1985.

Harris, McDonald. *They Sailed Alone*. Boston: Houghton Mifflin, 1972.

Hesselberg, Erik. *Kon-Tiki and I: A Sketch Book of the Famous Kon-Tiki Expedition by the Navigator of the Voyage*. New York: Rand McNally, 1950.

Heyerdahl, Thor. *Kon Tiki*. Translated by F. H. Lyon. Chicago: Rand McNally, 1950.

McKee, Alexander. *The Wreck of the Medusa: The Tragic Story of the Death Raft*. New York: New American Library, 1975.

Prescott, Orville. "Books of the Times." *New York Times*, October 11, 1955: 37.

"Sailor, 74, Returns in Atlantic Defeat." *New York Times*, October 7, 1967: 23.

Severin, Tim. *The China Voyage: Across the Pacific by Bamboo Raft*. New York: Addison-Wesley, 1994.

Slocum, Joshua. *Sailing Alone Around the World*. London: Adlard Coles, 1948.

"A Soviet Reporter Lauds Courage and Skill of Lost U. S. Mariner." *New York Times*, November 10, 1968: 17.

Trumbull, Robert. *The Raft*. New York: Henry Holt, 1942.

"Willis and Raft Reach Pagopago." *New York Times*, October 16, 1954: 22.

Willis, William. *Damned and Damned Again*. New York: St. Martin's Press, 1959.

———. *The Gods Were Kind*. New York: E. P. Dutton, 1955.

———. *Hell, Hail and Hurricanes: Poems of the Sea*. New York: Berkshire Press, 1953.

———. *The Hundred Lives of an Ancient Mariner*. London: Adventurers Club, 1968.

———. *Whom the Sea Has Taken*. New York: Meredith Press, 1966.

ACKNOWLEDGMENTS

For their comments and advice, I am grateful to David Atwell, Barbara Kreuter, Julie Chadwick, and my ever-sensible wife, Marian Young. I am also indebted to Gregg Cina and Claudia Jew of the Mariners' Museum for their generous assistance. Great thanks to Luke Dempsey of Crown Publishers for his editorial expertise and to Betsy Lerner, my agent, for her enthusiasm and (I am sorry to say) graceful forbearance. Last but hardly least, a shout out to Maureen Sugden, copy editor extraordinaire. There'd be no reaching the back of the book without her.

INDEX

ABOUT THE AUTHOR

T. R. PEARSON is one of the most well-reviewed and bestselling Southern novelists working today, and his writing has been compared to William Faulkner and Mark Twain. He is the author of ten novels, including *Glad News of the Natural World*, *A Short History of a Small Place*, and the *New York Times* Notable Book *Blue Ridge*. This is his first nonfiction book.